THE VOICES OF SERIAL KILLERS

THE VOICES OF SERIAL KILLERS

The World's Most Maniacal Murderers in Their Own Words

Christopher Berry-Dee

Ulysses Press

Published in the United States by
ULYSSES PRESS
P.O. Box 3440
Berkeley, CA 94703
www.ulyssespress.com

ISBN13: 978-1-56975-973-8
Library of Congress Catalog Number: 2011926035

Printed in the United States by Bang Printing

10 9 8 7 6 5 4 3 2 1

Acquisitions: Keith Riegert
Managing Editor: Claire Chun
Editor: Richard Harris
Copyeditor: Barbara Schultz
Proofreader: Lauren Harrison, Abigail Reser
Production: Judith Metzener
Front cover design: what!design @ whatweb.com
Front cover photos: red splatter © nicolecioe/istockphoto.com, paper dolls © timsa/istockphoto.com

Distributed by Publishers Group West

CONTENTS

INTRODUCTION

I HAVE BEEN INTERVIEWING AND CORRESPONDING with serial killers for more than 20 years. This exceedingly strange occupation started with a 12-part series of TV documentaries, for which I was researcher and interviewer. British publisher John Blake persuaded me to develop the televised material into a pair of books, which Ulysses Press in Berkeley, California, later consolidated into *Serial Killers: Up Close and Personal* (2007).

I am pleased to report that these previous books became international bestsellers, translated into many languages, and are still popular today on both sides of the Atlantic. They are now required reading for students at the Behavioral Science Unit of the Federal Bureau of Investigation Academy in Quantico, Virginia.

In all of these books, the concept was to tell stories in the killers' own words as much as possible, for while their vile crimes may be well-known, thanks to lurid reports broadcast throughout the world by the news media, it is only through their own perceptions that we may hope to understand the motives of such monsters in human guise. And so it was through interrogations, court transcripts, personal correspondence, and face-to-face interviews that such notorious fiends as "Killer Clown" John Wayne Gacy, "Monster" Aileen Wuornos, and "Amityville Horror" Ronald Joseph DeFeo Jr. became parts of my life—before they were executed by various state departments of corrections.

Somewhere along the way, I realized that I had interviewed more serial killers than any other journalist on the planet.

Month after month, year in, year out, I receive e-mail from students and professionals interested in criminology. Many of their questions are about serial killers, particularly, "In your opinion, Christopher, what makes them tick?" Honestly, if I knew the empirical answer to that question, I would also be clever enough to be able to get fingerprints from running water. But I don't, and I can't.

Of course, there are legions of psychiatrists and psychologists who do claim to be able to answer this question. Unfortunately, most of these "experts" have never met a serial killer in the flesh, let alone spent years corresponding with such a person. Those who think they know what makes a serial killer tick in reality do not. I do not. And of course, you, dear reader, could never conceive of committing such terrible acts on a fellow human being, so you cannot know either. The only ones who *do* know are the killers themselves—sometimes.

So, throughout this book, in their own words, the killers will tell you, either consciously or subconsciously, exactly what made them what they are. We might be able to conclude that what these monsters think and say today must be more or less the same as what they thought when committing their crimes.

This book stands out from my other works on the subject in that, for only the third time in my career, I advocate for the innocence of a wrongly convicted man: Frederick L. Waterfield. I will allow you to form your own conclusions about Fred, balancing his story and the hard facts presented in his favor against correspondence from his diabolical cousin, the sadistic, self-confessed cannibal aptly named David Alan Gore. In these pages, Gore admits for the first time how he strung up several of his victims "like deer and cut 'em, raped 'em, then gutted them" while they were still alive. Then he framed Fred, who is presently serving life in a California penitentiary.

Another chapter in this book concerns a very unusual predator indeed. Dubbed by the media "The Remorseful Serial Killer," Wayne Adam Ford's life story is, as he would say, as tragic as the suffering he caused to the prostitutes he killed and butchered. Yet he walked into a police station carrying a severed woman's breast in his pocket and gave himself up. For the first time, Wayne confesses all from death row.

The religious, morally salted butter Robert Joe Long eats wouldn't melt in his mouth, or so he would have the world believe. But this book lays bare the sexually perverted mind of Bobby Long today. His shocking correspondence reveals the true nature of a deviant serial murderer who killed eight women—and allowed one kidnapped woman to go free, an action that predictably led to his arrest and current residency on Florida's death row.

Gary Ray Bowles is a hustler and serial killer of six homosexuals. Candid, often smiling impudently, Bowles tells his life story from the cradle to his grim Florida penitentiary cell just a short walk from his place of expected execution.

Serial killers, both men and women (along with a few of confused gender), represent social monstrosities of the most terrifying variety. We may view them as some kind of beastly, homicidal objets d'art, but to those who fall afoul of them in lonely places far from the prying eye, they are human predators, often cannibals in a figurative and even a literal sense, uniquely subversive to society's carefully constructed behavioral tenets.

They frighten us because they are part *us*—part monster, yet humanoid in form. They are without the social conscience that, for many, defines humanity. They are morally dead. But they capture public attention because they terrify the neighborhoods in which they troll and prey on victims. They elicit a sort of through-the-peephole curiosity, their behavior so gruesome that the media and motion picture industries feed off their crimes with the same gluttonous ferocity as vultures feeding from carrion—our beloved dead. These murderers personify the human capacity for evil, for they *are* the stuff of our worst Hannibal Lecter, Norman Bates, Freddy Krueger, Leatherface fears. Stories like theirs put butts on seats in movie theaters around the world.

This book gets up close and personal, *very* close indeed. Nightmares, anyone?

***

CHAPTER 1

GARY RAY BOWLES—GAY AND YOU ARE DEAD!

I had sex with thousands of men for money, probably at least 50 women for money, and I probably had sex with at least 100 women on my own. I had a lot of fun, but I also ended up spending over half of my life in prison.

—Gary Ray Bowles,
in a letter to the author, September 30, 2009

Mere words cannot even begin to depict the brutal murders committed by Gary Bowles. The killer wasn't just cooking on gas; he was cooking on avgas injected with nitro. The crime scenes were blood baths.

—the author, after viewing many of the crime scene photographs

Gary Bowles was born January 25, 1962, in Clifton Gorge Hospital, West Virginia. He was the second son of a miner, William "Bill" Franklin Bowles, whose wife was 16-year-old Frances Carole Price. Bill died of black lung disease on July 22, 1961, while Gary was still in his mother's womb. Gary's older brother, William Franklin Jr., had come into this world on February 2, 1960.

Not one to let the grass grow under her feet, Frances,[1] an alcoholic, quickly moved 50 miles west to the village of Rupert (pop. 940). Here, she fell in with one William "Bill" Otto Fields, who, according to her, "was a fine-looking man, with a good physique–six feet tall and weighing around 210 pounds." The couple then moved to Kankakee, Illinois, where they married and raised the boys. Frances had two more children, Pamela and David. Up until he was the age of six, Gary and his brother believed that Bill Fields was their true father—until they paid a visit to their dying grandmother, who told them, ". . . boys, he ain't!"

Gary Bowles, in a letter to the author, September 16, 2009, wrote:

> After our return home things got bad. My Mom worked nights at the Ford Motor Company, and my Dad worked days. After work he would drink and the kids got no help from him. When I got into trouble he would beat me with a belt, a leather strap, fists, and we had a willow tree and he would use a whip like a branch from that.
>
> When I was about eight years old I played a lot of sports. In the Little League Baseball, I was a catcher, pitcher and shortstop. I was really good, and I wanted to be a baseball player. I was and still am a big Chicago Cubs fan. I also played football with all the kids from my neighborhood.
>
> We lived in a three-bedroom house, and most of the houses in the neighborhood were all the same type, about 450 houses altogether in the same area.
>
> I didn't have a normal family life. We never ate together, and there was no one to help us kids with our homework.

---

1 At the time of this writing, Frances has been married nine times.

> I was not very good at school, the Martin Luther King Jr. High, and my best grade completed was sixth grade. By the age of nine I was drinking and smoking pot.

Although Mrs. Bowles would later claim that her sons had a good upbringing, she testified in court that "Bill often beat [her] boys with his belt or fists. He would even throw them against the wall when the notion took him. The boys had bruises and welts all over them." She added that when she had tried to intervene, Bill took his temper out on her. "Bill seemed to enjoy it [the beatings]," she told the court at Gary's trial for murder. "He only stopped when he got tired." With tears in her eyes, Frances concluded with what was the understatement of the trial: "Bill was a *bit* uncontrollable, I think."

When Gary was about ten, Frances divorced Bill, who split, taking his own kids, Pamela and David, with him.

The nomadic Frances next turned up in Joliet, Illinois, where she met and married Chester "Chet" Hodges in 1974. In doing so, she jumped from the frying pan into the fire.

Gary Bowles in a letter to the author:

> I was not even allowed to go to the wedding. Chet drank a lot and so did my Mom. I was forced to live in the basement, and by 13 years old I was kicked out of the house and was living in the garage. There was no heat, and I had had enough.

By no stretch of the imagination could Chet be considered a model husband or a loving stepfather. This was no neighborly guy, and he didn't do church or Sunday barbecue. During most days he wandered around wearing only white underwear and black socks. His most treasured possession was the TV remote, which lived on the right arm of his beer-stained armchair. To him the vacuum cleaner was an alien object, not to be touched by him—ever!

Chet was an alcoholic, a borderline schizophrenic, a slob, and a bully who was known to fly into violent, alcohol-induced rages. He used his family as punching bags, hospitalizing Frances on three occasions. Gary and his older brother Frank suffered similar brutal treatment from Chet and also needed medical attention. "Chet would drink from sunup until he went to bed," Frances told the court. "Then, if there was the slightest disturbance in the home, he'd get up and beat the shit outta the kids."

To escape this less than desirable situation, Gary started hiding in the family's garage. In fact, Chet forced him to live in the garage throughout an entire winter. The boy began drinking, smoking pot, and sniffing glue. Gary says that he was sexually molested at the age of nine by a man, although there is no other evidence to support this claim. By the time he was 12, he was, by his own admission, uncontrollable.

Despite counseling, Gary's teachers were unable do anything with him, and Gary dropped out of school during the eighth grade. Meanwhile, Chet's violence against mother and sons continued unabated and, it would be correct to say that the lads grew to hate Chet with a passion. The boys were ticking mental time bombs, growing taller and physically stronger as each month passed; their minds were like pressure cookers building up a head of steam. Then Gary's brother Frank left home.

Gary was just 13. One night, Chet, chemically imbalanced as was the norm, started beating on Gary once again. This time, however, Gary retaliated. He caught Chet with his back turned, and pummeled him with a brick:

> I messed him up pretty bad, and I might of even killed him, but my Mom stopped me. The cops came, and he went to the hospital. I told my mom that was it. It was either him or me. I will never forget her words: "Don't make me choose." So I put my stuff in a bag, and I left home with a broken heart. She never reported me missing, and I didn't see her again until I was 19 years old.

According to Gary, this was the breaking point for him, and his first night away from home was spent in the back of U-Haul van. Then he bussed down to Los Angeles, where a former school friend's father found him a job as a handyman.

At 14, despite being two years below the legal age for employment, Gary worked a two-week-on, two-week-off rotation. His first paycheck was just over $700. He proudly sent his mother a copy of the check, but she never replied. However, his stay in California didn't last, and soon the teenager was en route to the Big Easy:

> On my way to New Orleans, I learned about hustling. A guy offered me $20 to suck my dick, and I let him. He also gave me some pot and told me all about the hustling game. I learned right away what I had in my pants could make me a lot of money. I would only let guys suck me off, and I even met women who would pay for sex. It was crazy, but I did that for two years, and then I went to Tampa, Florida.

Baby-faced Gary Bowles was a dark-haired, handsome lad with a good physique. He much preferred to date women, but to survive on the streets he used his looks and streetwise ability to the maximum. He sold his body to homosexuals in return for cash—sticking to oral, never anal, and he's adamant this was the case. Nevertheless, he didn't earn enough to afford digs of his own, so he remained homeless most of the time until early adulthood. Yet, occasionally he did move in with girls, and he did have several heterosexual relationships.

At age 20, in Tampa, Florida, Gary Bowles moved in with a couple of two-star hookers, both sporting more tattoos than a fairground worker. The trio lived together under the same roof for about eight weeks. He says he had three-way sex with them and also screwed married women when their husbands were away. "We partied a lot, did drugs and booze," he says. Then, on Friday, June 4, 1982, it is alleged that he brutally attacked one of the hookers, Lesley Blease, who, according to him, had "a mouth like a five-dollar whore."

According to a verifiable medical report, Lesley suffered severe attempted-strangulation bruising around her throat. One of her breasts was bitten. Her face was battered black and blue, so much so that her eyes were swollen shut for more than a week. At some stage during the assault, she claimed, Bowles rammed an empty beer bottle into her vagina and rectum, causing internal lacerations. To testify to the ferocity of the attack, law enforcement officers found "significant quantities of blood at the residence. The blood spatters on the walls reached as high as five feet above the bed . . . she looked as if she had been dropped off the Sears fuckin' Tower," recalled a cop.

However, there is the account Gary Bowles gave to the author to consider. In a contradictory statement, he said:

> One of the girls [Lesley] got beat up one night. I found her and called the police. Three days later I was charged with the crime. The girl, Lesley Blease, said in court I didn't do it, but I had a 75-year-old Public Defender, and he said I would get 15 years if I didn't take a deal. I would never beat a woman, and I got screwed by the system even though she said I didn't do it.

For this alleged offense, Gary Bowles received a six-year sentence: three in jail and three on parole. "All in all, I served five and one half years for a crime I didn't do, so I am a bit pissed about this," said Gary.

To further confuse matters, the Florida Department of Corrections detainee records show that Bowles was released from prison on Wednesday, December 28, 1983, having served 18 months in all. The same records also show that, for an unspecified offense and violating the terms of his parole, he was back behind bars on November 18, 1987. He was released three years later on April 3, 1990. Then, on Saturday, August 4, 1990, he got himself into another jam by committing grand theft—he stole a car. Still very much at large, on Wednesday, February 17, 1991, he committed unarmed robbery in Volusia County, Florida. This crime was basically a handbag snatch during which our master criminal pushed a woman to the ground. In fact, he had known this woman for several months, and on the night of the robbery they had been drinking together before Gary decided to steal her money.

Time on the run was now running out for Gary. On Friday, June 7, 1991, he got himself so worked up that he committed another grand theft. What he stole is unknown, but it earned Gary five years in prison when he was sentenced on July 18, 1991.

Bouncing in and out of prisons like a rubber ball on elastic string, Bowles was once again released on December 30, 1993. He surfaced, penniless, on the eastern seaboard in Daytona, Florida, in 1994.

John Hardy Roberts

On Tuesday, March 15, 1994, police were summoned to the residence of 59-year-old John Roberts, whose brutally beaten body had been discovered on his living room floor. The cause of death was determined to be strangulation, no doubt facilitated by a rag found stuffed down his windpipe. The victim's head had been severely beaten. With eyes like saucers, Roberts's face wore an inextricably confused and terminal expression, and one of his fingers was almost severed from his hand. Gary Bowles's fingerprints were found at the crime scene, and telephone records showed that Gary, in a brilliant attempt to cover his tracks, had made numerous phone calls to his mother from the dead man's home.

A nationwide manhunt was launched, and the FBI became involved. But although the authorities were able to recover Roberts's car in Nashville, Tennessee, their quarry was nowhere to be found. Yet all was not lost, for Gary's trail led police to Silver Springs, Maryland, where another homicide with a similar modus operandi had taken place.

David Jarman

On the very same day that Roberts was found bereft of life, a maintenance man stumbled across the decomposing remains of 39-year-old David Jarman in the dark basement of Jarman's Wheaton home. Like Roberts, Jarman had been badly beaten about the head before having his mouth stuffed and strangling to death. The victim's car and wallet were missing. Police soon learned that on Tuesday, May 17, the night before his death, Jarman had been seen in a gay bar in Washington, D.C., with a man who matched Gary Bowles's description. The two men were seen arguing; some say they were actually fighting. The police also learned that the victim's credit card had been used by Bowles after the killing. Roberts's car was recovered on April 22 in Baltimore. Gary Bowles then found his name on the FBI's Most Wanted list, yet still he evaded capture. Below is the FBI's VICAP (Violent Criminal Apprehension Program) Alert:

> Your MO is like a trail of shit. Like deer hunters would use to track a deer. If you change your MO all the time, you won't get caught.
>
> —SERIAL KILLER HENRY LEE LUCAS

GARY RAY BOWLES

AKA: Gary Ray Boles, Gary Ray Bowels, Mark Ray Bowles, Gary Bowle, Joey Pearson (also used James, Mike, and Mark as first names)

DOB: 1/25/62 (also used 1/25/63 and 1/25/59)

POB: Clifton Forge, VA

SSAN: 338-58-7859 (also used 338-56-5709, 338-58-5878, 330-58-7859, 448-58-7859)

FBI no.: 561 161 V10

Height: 5'9"

Weight: 150 pounds

Tattoos: Heart and ribbon on left arm, cross/star on left wrist

Scars: Inside of left hand, left side of nose, right wrist, left side of chest

Periods of Incarceration: 6/5/82 to 12/28/83; 10/31/85 to 12/28/85; 10/7/86 to 12/27/86; 7/10/87 to 4/3/90; 8/10/90 to 1/30/91; 2/18/91 to 12/30/93

Occupation: Carpenter, construction worker, and agricultural worker

Education: Grade school dropout but completed GED in 3/83 while incarcerated in a Florida State prison

Other Descriptors: Smokes cigarettes (usually Marlboros or Kools), uses marijuana on a regular basis, admitted in previous probation reports as having an alcohol problem

Milton Bradley

The hunt for Bowles then led to Savannah, Georgia, where the decomposing remains of 72-year-old Milton Bradley were discovered behind a golf cart shed on Thursday, May 5. The reason Bradley and Bowles had found themselves compelled to visit a golf course during the night is open for speculation. Thwacking a little white ball around 18 holes in total darkness is not recommended by any pro. Nonetheless, like the two previous victims, Milton had been beaten around the head, his mouth was stuffed with material, and he had been strangled to death.

This murder shocked the city of Savannah because Bradley had been a well-known World War II veteran. According to Bob Morris of the *Savannah Morning News*: "Milton was a quiet and gentle man who was generous to a fault."

The old soldier had suffered a severe head injury during the war, which later resulted in his receiving a lobotomy. The procedure caused slight mental impairment, which undoubtedly made him vulnerable prey to Gary Bowles. During the crime scene investigation, police officer John Best discovered a palm print matching that of Gary Bowles. Furthermore, Bradley had been seen several times in the company of a man matching Gary's description in the days leading up to the murder.

Albert "Alcie" Morris

On Thursday, May 19, 1994, the body of 37-year-old Albert Morris was found in his trailer-park home, in Hilliard, Nassau County, Florida. He had been beaten around the head with a blunt instrument, shot in the chest, and strangled with a rag stuffed down his throat. The victim's car and wallet were missing.

According to Gary Bowles, he was working on Morris's property, " . . . fixing the house and doing the grass," when both men, drunk, had gotten into a fistfight. Morris picked up a cutlery fork and menacingly poked it in Bowles's direction. For his part in the proceedings, Gary picked up Morris's 12-gauge shotgun and discharged both barrels into his host.

"I shot him in self-defense," claimed Bowles, smiling thinly. "I was protecting myself, and some people say I am antisocial. I think I'm quite a social person."

Bowles would later claim that he had lost his mind for a "temporary period . . . six times over a temporary period."

Alverston Carter

That May there was another murder; 47-year-old Alverston Carter Jr.'s body was discovered in his Atlanta home. It was Gary's MO all over again. In an interview, Bowles said:

> He was a big dude, much bigger than me. We got kinda drunk, and back at his place he got kinda rough with me. He was trying to dominate me. I picked up a big butcher knife and stabbed him to death through the heart. But there was no sex involved.

In July 1994, the popular television program *America's Most Wanted* filmed a segment about the crimes. Following its broadcast, the producers received numerous calls from viewers who claimed to have knowledge of Gary's whereabouts, yet still he evaded capture.

Walter Jamelle "Jay" Hinton

In November 1994, on the Jacksonville Beach, Florida pier, Gary met Jay Hinton. The long, wooden structure (now demolished) was a favorite fishing spot for anglers and gays. The latter enjoyed "companionship" and "playing" among the dunes. Although Gary denies this, there can be no doubt that the two men engaged in some form of homosexual activity at this local spot appropriately named Sandy Head.

After spending a couple of days in each other's company, Jay moved into a trailer home at 13748 Coral Drive,[2] Jacksonville, about four miles west of Neptune Beach and the foaming surf of the Atlantic Ocean. Gary helped Jay move some of his belongings from Georgia into the trailer, and by way of thanks, Jay generously invited Gary to stay with him, though on a very temporary basis.

This suited Gary Bowles fine. All went smoothly for two weeks until Gary made a crude pass at one of his host's female friends who was staying with them at the time. On Saturday, November 12, Sharon Ann, also known as "Jo Ann," complained to Jay about Gary's lewd behavior. An argument ensued, and Gary was ordered to leave, which he did. The next day, Gary was arrested for being drunk in the street, but for some unknown reason, he was released from jail on the following Monday. Had the local cops taken a moment to run a fingerprint check, they would have been ecstatic to learn that they had one of America's most wanted men in their custody. But they didn't, and with the tiff between the two men soon settled, Gary moved back into the trailer.

On Wednesday, November 16, 1994, Gary was partying with Jay and a friend named Nick. When Jay took himself off to work in the afternoon, the two other men carried on drinking beer and smoking pot. When Jay returned later, the threesome continued getting drunk and high.

---

2 The exact location can be found on Google Maps.

Around 8 p.m., Jay drove Nick to the railway station with Gary sitting in the back seat of the car. While they waited for the train, the men drank more beer and smoked even more dope. Nick later testified that at the time of his departure to the station Gary was "heavily inebriated from the alcohol, yet coherent"—a remarkable feat of observation in itself because Nick was so drunk he didn't even know which planet he was living on.

After sending Nick down the tracks, Gary and Jay made their way back to the trailer, where they drank more beer. At some point, Jay went to his bedroom to sleep, leaving Gary in the living area "to finish off six quarts of Magnum beers." When the cans were empty, Gary—using his own terminology—"flipped."

For reasons known only to Bowles, he suddenly decided to venture outside, where he located a 40-pound concrete paving slab. Struggling under its weight, he managed heave it into the trailer home where he placed it down onto a table while he caught his breath. Meanwhile, Jay was asleep, almost dead to the world, and soon to be dead in every physiological sense.

Exactly what went through Jay's mind moments later—apart from the impact of the 40-pound slab of concrete, of course—will always remain a mystery, but one thing is for sure: He woke up somewhat stunned by the blow. As one might expect, a brief struggle ensued, during which the inconsiderate Gary stuffed a rag into Jay's mouth, followed by some toilet tissue, before the poor man was strangled to death. It was estimated by the medical examiner that, "from the time of being struck by the concrete slab to the intervention of death, just under a minute elapsed, maybe a bit more than that, but not much more . . . maybe five at best."

Reasoning correctly that Jay would have no further use for his car or the time of day, Gary drove off in his victim's vehicle, taking the deceased's wristwatch with him, only to return shortly thereafter. Gary stayed in the trailer for two more days and, at one point, picked up a homeless girl named Ginger Moye. She was sick, and he knew her quite well. He brought her to Jay's home, had sex with her, then took her back where he'd found her. The girl was apparently unaware that a dead body was in the bathroom, which doesn't say much for her powers of observation or personal hygiene. Ginger would later testify that every time she had seen Gary Bowles, he was "drinking, drunk, staggering drunk regardless of whether it was 7 a.m. or 2 p.m."—this coming from someone who had been pickling herself in alcohol since the age of eleven.

On Friday, November 18, Jay's sister Belinda was celebrating her birthday with her fiancé, William. Late that afternoon, Bill went to Coral Drive to check up on Jay and ask why he hadn't attended Belinda's party. Although the lights were on and Gary Bowles was there, nobody answered the door, and Jay's Cadillac was nowhere to be seen. Bill left, only to return with Belinda several times over the next two days. They also learned that Jay had not been going to work, so they returned to take an even closer look on the following Sunday. This time they forced their way into the place by breaking a back window. Upon entering, Bill was met by a "foul odor," and the bedroom was a mess. In the bathroom he noticed a "large mound covered by blankets." It was Jay's bludgeoned, decomposing corpse, and blood was splashed wall-to-wall. The couple summoned neighbors who, in turn, called the police.

A thorough search of the premises revealed the victim's wallet and personal papers strewn on the bed. On the floor was a large concrete stepping-stone. It had come from the front yard. Police also discovered miniature liquor bottles and numerous beer cans scattered throughout the home. A receipt in the name of "Timothy Whitfield" was found. Jay's car and watch were missing. Gary Bowles's fingerprints were everywhere.

An autopsy determined that Jay had suffered serious injuries to his head. His forehead and cheekbone had been crushed, but the trauma by itself had not been sufficient to have caused his death. He also had five broken ribs. There were abrasions on his right forearm and one leg. The cause of death was asphyxiation from strangulation, which was further facilitated by the toilet tissue and rag lodged in Jay's windpipe. Time of death was estimated to be between two to four days before the body was discovered.

Determining a suspect for Jay's murder would not prove difficult. Several neighbors and friends of the dead man gave a good description of the victim's house guest, so the police started looking for Gary Bowles, aka "Mr. Timothy Whitfield."

First Jay's Cadillac was found abandoned. Then police learned that a "Mr. Whitfield" had checked in at a Jackson Beach motel on the Friday following the murder. In fact, it took a mere 48 hours for the authorities to find their man, who was arrested at the Ameri-Force labor pool in Jacksonville Beach.

Suffering from the delirium tremors, "Mr. Whitfield" soon admitted his true name as being Gary Ray Bowles. Furthermore, the police discovered that he was wanted by the FBI in connection with a series of other brutal slayings, all of which had been committed along Interstate 95, from Maryland to Florida. Then Bowles admitted killing Roberts and Morris. He claimed that he had moved into Roberts's home, where they had sex. Several weeks into his stay the two men had a dispute over a woman. Gary was asked to leave. Blinded by rage, he said, he attacked Roberts with a vase. In his attempt to escape, Roberts tripped over a glass coffee table and fell to the floor where he was strangled to death.

"I think I lost my mind," he told his interrogators. "That's the only way I can describe it. I lost my mind. I kept beating and beating him. There was blood everywhere. An' it took me several minutes to realize what I had done. Then I knew that my own life was completely over with."

Bowles then explained that he stole Roberts's watch and fled in his victim's car.

On Thursday, December 8, 1994, with the Hon. Jack M. Schemer presiding, Gary Bowles was indicted on two counts—the robbery and first-degree (aggravated) murder of Jay Hinton. In mitigation, Bowles's legal team offered:

Serious substance abuse problem
Physically and emotionally abused by two stepfathers
Lived in an abusive, violent home
Never had a positive male role model in his life
Never finished junior high school
Helped the Tampa sheriff's office obtain a conviction of a person who had committed sexual battery
Confessed to the police and FBI
Pled guilty

All of this carried little weight, and the jury was compelled to recommend the death sentence by a vote of ten to two.

Bowles has since been convicted of three more counts of first-degree murder, and at the time of this writing he continues to petition the state courts, hoping that one day he will be granted a new sentencing hearing that will relieve him of the threat of execution by lethal injection. He is currently imprisoned at the Union Correctional Institute in Raiford, Florida, where he will remain, in all probability, until his death.

In the Jay Hinton slaying, Bowles was convicted of murder in the first degree, which, in the state of Florida, and without jury-acceptable mitigation such as proven insanity, carries a mandatory death sentence. Nonetheless, Gary's appeal against this sentence, particularly the aggravating factor, was argued by his defense attorney. In a nutshell, his attorney's argument can be paraphrased:

> While Bowles had strangled Hinton, and he died from asphyxiation, the murder was not explicitly heinous, atrocious, or cruel. The victim was asleep when Bowles started his attack, and Hinton quickly lost consciousness. His struggling was feeble and for a short time. His death was not especially heinous, atrocious, or cruel.

If the state's case was flawed in any way, however, it was concerning the argument that Gary murdered Jay for financial gain; that it was a premeditated act of murder and deserving of the death sentence for that reason alone. There was also the consideration that Bowles was on probation during the time of the murders. But the defense maintained that there was no evidence that financial gain was Mr. Bowles's motive.

Or was there?

During the commission of the other homicides attributed to Bowles, he most certainly had a set pattern of stealing the victims' motor vehicles, money, and credit cards. He most certainly used Hinton's car after the murder. He most certainly stole a sum of money from Hinton's wallet, and he most certainly disposed of the dead man's watch. In simple terms—and this allegation was used many times throughout the trial and subsequent appeals—Gary Bowles hustled and robbed homosexuals for their money. His own testimony that he was most always smashed out of his mind on booze and drugs, which "made the killing easier for me to do," is worth consideration, too.

Finally, and to be fair to Gary, the prosecution constantly maintained that Bowles killed the men because "they were homosexuals, and the defendant had a deep hatred for homosexuals." It was an emotive argument, one almost guaranteed to win favor from any liberal jury, which this one was. Assistant Public Defender David A. Davis had his work cut out in proving otherwise. In fact, Dr. Elizabeth Mahon, a psychiatrist retained by the defense, claimed that Bowles was "a reservoir of hatred," adding, "he was probably not working with what we would say is an intact brain, and he has a mild dysfunction."

It is this author's belief that Gary did not target homosexuals with murder in mind. He did not seek out, like so many serial killers do, victims to kill with robbery in the forefront of his mind, either. So, I suggest that there was no premeditation for the killings here at all.

What I *do* suggest, however, is that in Gary Bowles we find a homeless, out-of-control alcoholic and drug abuser who, throughout his life, contributed nothing at all to society. He used his streetwise skills to target the weaknesses and predatory nature of certain homosexuals, to suit his own short-term ends—to buy more booze and drugs to satisfy his habit. That he flipped from time-to-time, that he bludgeoned his victims, that he stuffed rags and toilet tissue down their throats, strangled them, and shot one of them before stealing what meager possessions the dead men had, was the result of the hatred he had built up against his stepfathers during his early childhood.

But so what?

Millions of folks have suffered dysfunctional childhoods, but they do not become serial killers in later life. Thousands, even tens of thousands of alcoholic dropouts worldwide are content to drink cheap booze and fall asleep without so much as a snore. Indeed, the facts stare us straight in the face: Mr. Bowles went with gays and exchanged sexual favors for cash or a roof over his head, occasionally murdering them, and stealing whatever his victims had to pawn for money to satisfy his inebriated, chemically imbalanced cravings. The fact that this psychically strong young man could have worked and earned an honest living didn't even enter his mind.

According to Gary Bowles:

> I don't think anyone is born a natural-born killer. But if anyone deserved the death penalty it is me because I have killed so many people. But I gotta say that death row ain't all it's cracked up to be.

When asked if he had any remorse for his killings, Bowles replied:

> Well, ah ya know, like I said I feel bad, but I never sought to kill anybody. I didn't go looking for to kill people. Look, I never wanted to become a so-called serial killer. I feel bad for their families . . . I feel bad for my family. Ya know, I cain't take back what I did!
>
> Well, ah. Ya know I will say sorry to all the families of the people I have killed, and with me being executed, maybe they can find peace. I would tell my mom that I love her, and that would be it.

***

CHAPTER 2

ROBIN GECHT—THE MASTERMIND OF THE CHICAGO RIPPER CREW

THE UNSMILING, UNREMARKABLE face staring into the Illinois Department of Corrections camera is that of Robin Gecht—unremarkable in that his could be the face of any bus driver, postman, store clerk, indeed any face on your street, for there is nothing about his appearance that would ever set him apart in any crowd.

Born in Illinois on November 30, 1953, Gecht has blue eyes and thinning brown hair. At five feet five inches tall and weighing 135 pounds, he certainly doesn't look dangerous; but by god, he certainly was until he was locked up—for a very long time indeed—on February 17, 1984.

But Robin does have something to look forward to—he has a "tentative release date" set for December 13, 2045. He will be 92 years old when he is wheeled out of those prison gates, if he is not thrown through the gates of hell before that.

The Chicago Ripper Crew had four members. Robin Gecht, then 30, assumed the role as mentor and leader. Edward Spreitzer was 21, while the Kokoraleis brothers, Andrew and dim-witted Tommy, were teenagers.

Exclusively published in this book for the first time, here is the Statement of Facts concerning victim Beverly Washington, as issued by the Illinois State Attorney's Office (1982):

> Around 1 or 2 a.m., on October 5, 1982, BW [Beverly Washington], a 19-year-old African American prostitute, asked Defendant [Robin Gecht] if he wanted a date and entered Defendant's red Dodge van. Defendant pointed a gun and a butcher knife at the victim and ordered her to disrobe, which she did. Defendant handcuffed her ankles and wrists, tied a cord around her breasts and forced her to commit a sexual act by inserting his penis in her mouth.
>
> Defendant forced the victim to drink soda and take some pills. Then he placed his penis in her vagina. B.W. testified Defendant did not ejaculate at any point. Eventually B.W. lost consciousness.
>
> A few hours later the victim was discovered lying naked in an alley. Her left breast was removed, her right breast was intact. She was bleeding and in shock.
>
> Expert testimony at trial demonstrated that the victim's disfigurement had been caused by a cutting of a knife. The victim described her assailant's van to police, who, two weeks later arrested Defendant.
>
> While in hospital, B.W. positively identified Defendant in a photographic show-up and a police lineup. Defendant was charged accordingly, thereafter.
>
> On September 29, 1983, the Defendant was found guilty and sentenced as follows:

Sentenced to 120 years in prison for the following offenses:

Attempted Murder. Aggravated Kidnapping. Deviate Sexual Assault and Rape.

To which Robin Gecht, #N40573, Menard Correctional Center, 711 Kaskaskia Street, Menard, Illinois 62259, U.S., responds in a rambling sort of way:

> This is the entire [States Attorney's] case to which I stand accused. I will have and will continue saying that B.W.'s ID is a mistake and DNA testing would prove that [sic], but I am being DENIED such testing by the Courts. So whatever else you've read is hearsay based soley on a book long outdated and of course 2 so-called friends that never meant what truth meant. And look where they are today. [sic]. I do know who attacked B.W. Police told her in the hospital I owned the van . . . a long story we'll get into another time . . .
>
> So there you have it. This is what I was charged with [Attempted Murder. Aggravated Kidnapping. Deviate Sexual Assault, and Rape] . . . and to this day I still claim innocences [sic]. This conviction is also still on APPEAL as we write. In 1997 by means of DNA testing in the murders others were charged with. I was found NOT GUILTY and not involved in those matters and cleared as a suspect as I was from 1982 to 1997 . . . based on what other ALEGED to of said to police as I being part of their crime spree . . . *I was not or did not know anything at that time.* [sic]

According to Mr. Gecht, he is the innocent victim of corrupt law-enforcement agencies, a crooked prosecutor, an inept defense attorney, even a biased judge or two. He has been set up by his two-timing, backstabbing, testimony flip-flopping co-defendants. God! The inconvenience of him having being locked up for decades must be worth a few million dollars to him, at least.

Then there are the internet campaigners who are out of their heads with the tragedy of having "our Robin" being so unjustifiably incarcerated "ruling/ruining" [sic] their own lives, while conveniently forgetting that Gecht and his sadistic cohorts were involved with the brutal deaths of at least 18 women.

I have a huge respect for women in general . . . you will be shocked and understand my continuing fight for justice . . . I'm no angel . . . I will not try to convince you of anything . . . I cry, just as you would . . . and, sure, I do have an obsession about women with big breasts. It is a thing with my entire family going back, as I am told, to GREAT GRANDFATHER & his. Each of us have married large breast women. I as well!! My ex-wife is a 39D & YES she was very satisfying to me.

—Robin Gecht

The city of Chester, Randolph County, Illinois, is one of those "nowhere special" places that seem to have just the one popular claim to fame. Sitting prettily on the eastern bank of the mighty Mississippi River, Chester (pop. 8,400), is the birthplace of the late Elzie Crisler Segar, the creator of cartoon character Popeye the Sailor.

Born December 8, 1894, Crisler died prematurely at age 43 in Santa Monica, California. "El" had a vivid imagination. He invented the character Popeye, who outlived him by a considerable span of years and was, incidentally, based upon local thug Frank "Rocky" Fiegal. Indeed, many unwitting residents of Chester would soon become characters in the Popeye stories, so a visit to Chester would not be complete without visiting the six-foot bronze statue near Chester Bridge that is dedicated to the spinach-eating seaman. I have been there, and I have the T-shirt to prove it.

However, Chester has another claim to fame—a proximity to the Menard Correctional Center.[3] Opened in March 1878, sixteen years before the creator of Popeye was born, it is the second oldest prison in Illinois. Moreover, up until January 11, 2003, it housed the state's death row. Then, the-soon-to-depart Republican governor had a change of heart. George Ryan told the 156 condemned inmates that they no longer faced the death penalty.

"I can't live with executed men on my conscience," Ryan said. This, among other statements made by George Ryan, caused a furor among the hang 'em and whip 'em brigade, and if heinous serial killer John Wayne Gacy had been more fortunate, he would have been a beneficiary of George Ryan's farewell gift, too! Unfortunately for John, he was a tad too late . . . as was one of the utterly despicable characters featured in this chapter. Gecht's co-Chicago Ripper Thomas Kokoraleis was injected with a fatal chemical cocktail as well.

The Menard Correctional Center can be reached by driving through quaint Chester, taking a left turn, and continuing down a narrow road to the banks of the Mississippi River. It is then approximately a two-mile drive to the prison, a towering, bleak stone fortress cut into the hillside. Death row inmates used to be housed in a separate unit, high up on the right as one faces the institution and clearly visible from the road. Today that

3 Chester and the road to the Menard CC were featured in the 1993 movie *The Fugitive*, starring Harrison Ford (Dr. Richard Kimble) and Tommy Lee Jones (U.S. Marshal Samuel Gerard).

unit is used for troublesome inmates. Co-Chicago Ripper Robin Gecht, is housed in general population, and he says he should not be in prison at all.

Linda Sutton

Nineteen miles west of downtown Chicago is the non-home rule municipality of Villa Park. With a population of 22,000, Villa Park was also home to the Ovaltine chocolate beverage factory, situated off South Villa Avenue. The place was closed down in 1985, and the empty building was frequently used by the homeless for shelter.

Satanic rituals in which small to medium-sized animals were sacrificed also took place in the abandoned factory's corridors. People who have been to this location have described voices and cries that came from nowhere, as well as voices that somehow knew their name. Also reported were people who had large piles of debris thrown at them violently with no natural explanation behind it, like heavy poltergeist activity.

In December 1997, the place was finally sold and later revamped into residential apartments. Yet even today, occupants of those apartments will report hearing screams or footsteps running on the roof, seeing flickering lights, and most common, feelings of being watched. To make things even spookier, after all the construction was completed, the basement of the building remained closed and, for unknown reasons, it still is. Perhaps the ghosts that still haunt the place are the souls of workers who had died in the factory, or people who had been struck and killed by the trains on South Villa Avenue, where the street now called Prairie Path was once a railway…

After leaving the former factory, take a short drive up South Villa Avenue, hang a left at the intersection, and at 17724 W. North Avenue, Chicago, you can find, among a bunch of seedy stores, bars, and fast-food outlets, the Brer Rabbit Motel. It was here, on the rainy afternoon of Monday, June 1, 1981, that a maid noticed a terrible stench coming from the trash-strewn field at the back of the building. The motel manager investigated the problem. Maybe it was a dead animal, but it was a smell that couldn't be tolerated, and it had to be gotten rid of.

The source of the problem was the corpse of a young woman, whose remains consisted largely of bones and some clinging flesh. The initial assumption made by the detectives who arrived at the scene was that the body had been there for some time, because they could see her ribs and much of her upper skeletal structure. However, closer examination revealed that maggots were still enthusiastically burrowing away, which indicated that her death had been quite recent.

That the woman had been murdered was not in doubt. Her wrists had been handcuffed, a cloth was stuffed in her mouth, and she still wore a sweater and panties, which were pulled down to her thighs. In one of her socks was tucked a small wad of dollar bills, so robbery was ruled out as a motive.

Back in the '80s, the motel was rumored to be a joint where one could meet someone for quick sex or to find drugs. It was an area frequented by hookers, who plied their trade along W. North Avenue, and the practice of rolling money inside socks was a trick used by prostitutes to prevent them from being robbed.

Deputy Coroner Pete Siekman determined that the woman had been dead for only three days. The advanced state of decomposition was due to two large wounds in her chest—her breasts had been removed, which allowed for an invasion of parasites that had devoured the body. She was identified through fingerprints as 21-year-old Linda Sutton, a prostitute well-known to the police through a string of arrests. She was also the mother of two children, both of whom lived with Linda's mother.

However, the exact location where she had been murdered was something the police had yet to determine. Investigators needed to know whether the motel site was the primary crime scene or the secondary scene where she had been dumped after being killed someplace else.

> As for normal obsession with Womans breasts. WHAT NORMAL MAN OUT THERE HASN'T? Not sure if you're large on top or what. But if so, am sure you've walked down any street & some guy notices you & your tits. Why? WE'RE MEN, but that doesn't mean we cut then & have sex with them, cuz we have an obsession with large breasted women. 65% of men are obsessed with big tits. I'm sure you already know that. I'm not obsessed otherwise or for any other reason than a normal Joe. MEDIA FOR YOU, IT SELLS. [sic]
>
> Well, I gotta go. YARD time & DR. [sic] Said I need exercise. Not getting sex so I must walk. Ha, Ha!
>
> —*Robin Gecht in a letter to author Jennifer Furio*

Edward Spreitzer, one of Gecht's accomplices, later told police that Ms. Sutton was gang-raped and sodomized, and her left breast was cut off while she was alive . . . and that Gecht ran the show.

On February 12, 1982, an unnamed 35-year-old cocktail waitress's car ran out of gas. When her car was found, police noted that the tank was empty, her purse was on the front seat, and the keys were still in the ignition. Her nude body was discovered on an embankment near the road. At autopsy, it was determined she had been raped, tortured, and mutilated, and one of her breasts had been cut off.

Lorraine Borowski

May 1982 was the month that blonde-haired Lorraine Borowski was killed after being abducted as she crossed a parking lot alone. She was gang-raped, and a piano wire was used to sever a breast from her body. She died as the result of hatchet wounds to the head. Lorraine's decomposing remains were discovered at a dump site close to Clarendon Hills Cemetery—a 19-minute drive from where Linda Sutton had been found.

According to Edward Spreitzer, he, Gecht, and another man named Thomas Kokoraleis were driving in a red van and pulled up alongside Lorraine as she walked to work. When she declined the driver's offer of a ride, two of the men jumped out of the van and grabbed her. They took her to a motel room where they gang-raped and beat her. One of the men produced some piano wire, which was wound around one of her breasts and tightened until it was severed from the body and fell to the floor. Spreitzer later told police, "Gecht had sex with Borowski's breast and then finished her off with an ax."

Shui Mak

On Saturday, May 29, just two weeks after Lorraine Borowski was killed, a Chinese woman, Shui Mak, was abducted as she returned home from her family's restaurant in Streamwood, 18 miles northwest of Villa Park. She had been in her brother's car, but after they argued, he dropped her off to wait for a ride from other relatives, whom he believed were following behind. Tragically, the "relatives" turned out to be the Chicago Ripper Crew driving in a red van, and she was never seen alive again.

> Robin once became so furious with his wife that he cut off her nipples.
> —Edward Spreitzer
>
> Only a sick person would ever think of that.
> —Robin Gecht

Shui's body was discovered in late August buried at a construction site. It, too, had been similarly mutilated. Spreitzer testified that they had driven her to an isolated wooded area where they "raped her, cut off her breasts, sliced her body to ribbons, and buried her in a hole."

Angel York

In June 1982, Angel York was dragged into a red van, handcuffed and gang-raped. She was able to escape and told police that the men had even forced her to use a large knife to cut her own breast, which drove one man into a frenzy. "This guy cut me more," she said, "and then he masturbated into the wound before closing it with duct tape and dumping me in the street."

Angel identified the man as Robin Gecht.

Sandra Delaware

In August, Sandra Delaware's body was found floating near the shore of the Chicago River. Her wrists were bound behind her back with a shoelace. Her left breast had been removed, and her bra was knotted around her neck. An autopsy determined that she had been dead for just six hours.

Carol Pappas and Rose Beck

Less than two weeks after the murder of Sandra Delaware, Carol Pappas, age 42, went missing, as did 30-year-old Rose Beck Davis. Rose, a marketing executive, was found stabbed and raped on Wednesday, September 8, 1982, behind a stairway of a North Lake Shore Drive apartment building. A black sock was tied around her neck, and her clothing was in disarray. Her face was crushed, and blood pooled beneath the body. She had been beaten with a hatchet; there were deep cuts to her breasts, and her abdomen had been stabbed. Very small punctures were also present, suggesting that a needle had been another instrument that was used.

Beverly Washington

At the start of this chapter I quoted verbatim the Statement of Facts issued by the Illinois State Attorney's Office (1982), with reference to prostitute Beverly Washington, who was able to provide detectives with several significant characteristics about one of the men who had attacked her:

> The driver of the red van was a slender white man who looked to be around 25, wearing a flannel shirt and square-toed boots. He had greasy brown hair and a mustache. He offered me more money than I asked for and he seemed unaccountably nervous. He ordered me to get into the back seat. He had a gun. He told me to remove my clothes, and I did. Then he placed handcuffs on me. He forced me to perform oral sex on him. He threatened me with violence if I did not swallow a handful of pills he handed to me. As I was passing out, I saw him holding a cord over me. I feared I was going to die.

Beverly was dumped out of the vehicle—one breast severed, the other nearly so—but someone found her and called the police. When questioned, she was able to describe the red van. It was a Dodge with tinted windows. It had a wooden divider between the front seats and the rear. She also told the investigators that there were feathers and a roach clip hanging from the rearview mirror.

Around October 20, 1982 (the exact date is uncertain), police stopped a red Dodge van and questioned the driver. Although he did not fit Beverly Washington's description, the van did. The driver, Eddie Spreitzer, said that the van belonged to his boss, Robin Gecht, and a check through the Bureau of Vehicle Licensing proved this to be correct.

The police then took Spreitzer to Gecht's house, where they asked him to beckon the van's owner outside. When Robin Gecht calmly emerged, he matched the description of the man who had attacked Beverly Washington, even down to his shirt and boots.

Ever anxious to clear his name from being associated with a bunch of lowlife sexual sadists, Mr. Gecht had this to say in a letter. The spelling and grammar are his own:

> Have you looked at the Illinois Department of Corrections Website [INMATE SEARCH]? If so, you will notice what I was charged/convicted of there on that site. NO-WHERE does it state "murder!"

That he was charged and convicted of attempted murder seems to have slipped Gecht's mind; nonetheless, he rails on, and on, and on. Once again, Gecht is quoted verbatim:

> These set of charges and this conviction is 1 conviction/1 case/1 victim and does NOT involve any of the other crimes alleged on internet websites that ALL came out of a book written in 1986. I will soon be sending you an *information packet.*[4] That will help you understand facts surrounding this conviction on based website crap. I am in prison and convicted of an alleged NON-FATAL attack on a northside Chicago prostitute by the name of Beverly Washington. [B.W.] as the State's Attorney's refer her as in legal arguments. B.W. is alive and well last time I heared in 199. This victim [B.W.] i.d's me as her attacker in a suggestive lineup held by police on Oct. 1982 while she was hospitalized just after the attack. [B.W.] i.d was based on 2 elements . . . [1] . . . Police told her "I" owned the van she described to police two weeks before the lineup. [2] . . . She i.d-ed a blue company shirt that anyone that worked for me . . . "owned" at that time. I was wearing the shirt and the jeans at the time of the lineup just an hour after [B.W.] was

4 The second "Information Packet' promised has never arrived.

> shown photos taken of myself in the same clothing. [We call that SUGGESTIVE]. Edward and Andrew both also owned this company shit. This entire conviction was souly based on identification by Ms. Washington. No other evidence presented at trial as to *biological* was presented.

Remarkably, it has now been proven that Robin Gecht used to work for one of America's most notorious homosexual, sadosexual serial killers, former Menard CC inmate John Wayne Gacy, out of Des Plaines, Illinois.

Gacy, as we all know, killed 33 young men, burying the majority of their bodies in the crawlspace under his home or dumping the remains into the Des Plaines River.[5] However, of some interest, perhaps even *mega* interest, is the fact that January 1979—a month after he was arrested and long before the Chicago Ripper murders started—Gacy continually told investigators that Robin Gecht, who Gacy claimed was bisexual, had been involved with killing some of the victims attributed to him!

With all of this being said, it is fair to say that Robin Gecht has denied being involved with any murders, and he persists in his arguments today. It is also true that the only witness testimony against Gecht comes via Beverly Washington, a prostitute, and from Eddie Spreitzer in his statements given to police, numbering some 46 pages in all.

It was Spreitzer who first admitted to driving the red Dodge van as Gecht allegedly committed a drive-by shooting that killed one man and left another man paralyzed. This shooting incident was confirmed by police. Therefore, Spreitzer had first-

5 A chapter on John Wayne Gacy is featured in my book *Talking with Serial Killers II*, published by John Blake, London.

hand knowledge of the incident, because he gave an account that only the participants in the shooting would have known. Gecht denied all knowledge of it.

After this shooting, Spreitzer claims that Gecht told him to slow down to pick up a black prostitute. Gecht, he says, had sex with the woman in the back of the van, then took her into an alleyway and used a knife to remove her left breast, which he placed on the van's floor. Although Spreitzer was less than specific, one may assume that the victim was Linda Sutton, for an alleyway ran alongside the Brer Rabbit Motel and Sutton's corpse was found on vacant land at the rear of the premises.

On another matter, it was Spreitzer who said that the sight of blood sickened him, which is confirmed by Gecht. It was Spreitzer who told police that Gecht had shot a black woman in the head after chaining her up and that Gecht had used bowling balls to weigh her down in the water. This could only have been Sandra Delaware, who was found in shallow water along the bank of the Chicago River.

Spreitzer had much to say about other murders allegedly committed by Robin Gecht. He stated that Gecht had "forced him" to have sexual contact with a dead woman's gaping wounds. But one only has Spreitzer's word for this. Again, Gecht denies everything.

By the time Spreitzer was finished, he had offered firm details regarding seven murders and one case of aggravated battery. His interrogators put the matters to Gecht, who was in an adjoining room, and were amazed that Gecht seemed unfazed. "It was as if he didn't give a damn," recalled one of the officers present. "He acted as if he had nothing to hide."

When Spreitzer learned that his boss, Gecht, was sitting in a room just a few yards away, he suddenly changed his story. As if afraid, he said that Gecht had not murdered anyone. His account became so erratic that his interrogators didn't know what to believe, other than that Spreitzer had been involved with at least seven of the murders from start to finish.

Spreitzer said that his girlfriend's brother, Andrew Kokoraleis, had been the killer. Oddly enough, he could not— or would not—offer any further details.

For his part, Gecht admitted that he knew Andrew, and he even provided police with Kokoraleis's home address. He seemed not to know the gruesome things about Kokoraleis that Spreitzer obviously did.

Kokoraleis was arrested and soon confessed about how the threesome had kidnapped women off the streets, raped them, stabbed them with knives, razors, tin can lids, and can openers. He went on to allege that Gecht had a fetish about women's breasts and had used a needle to puncture them multiple times. He told police that in several cases they had amputated one or both breasts and masturbated into them. Kokoraleis admitted the murders of Rose Beck Davis and Lorraine Borowski, and he inadvertently confessed that he had been involved in the deaths of some 17, maybe 18, women.

In the murder of Sandra Delaware, he said that he had shoved a rock into her mouth to keep her from screaming. That he had forced a wine bottle into her vagina that made her bleed badly. That he had stabbed her with a knife.

And, while autopsy reports confirmed that all of this occurred, Gecht steadfastly continued to deny any involvement whatsoever.

As we already know from Gecht's own correspondence, police themselves soon learned from Robin's friends and acquaintances that he had a breast fetish, asking girls he associated with to let him stab their breasts with pins. It is alleged that Gecht's wife suffered the "pin treatment," although she never turned him in. But when the cops began questioning Andrew Kokoraleis's slow-witted brother Tommy, they were in for a surprise. He, too, had been in the Chicago Ripper Crew, and he would break down, confessing to details that would even make an avid Stephen King fan cringe.

Making no bones about it, in the intelligence department Tommy Kokoraleis never held a full deck of cards, but he most certainly had joined in a fad that was sweeping the country during the early 1980s, especially among teenagers—Satan worship. He has admitted to paying many visits, with his accomplices, to the ruins of the former Ovaltine factory in Villa Park. There, among the damp corridors and dank rooms, Tommy claimed they somehow believed they could contact the "Dark One." He said that Gecht and his associates took the flesh they had removed from their victims, cut it up and consumed it as a form of ancient devilish communion. He said that Gecht had an altar in the attic of his northwest side apartment where they all gathered during the nocturnal hours after Gecht's wife had gone to work. Gecht had painted six red and white and black crosses on the walls, he said, and covered the altar with a red cloth—Old

Nick-influenced scenarios that could have come straight from the pages of Dennis Wheatley's novel *To the Devil a Daughter.*

Rising to his theme, Tommy told police that they would all kneel together around the altar and Gecht would produce the freshly removed breasts. Gecht would read passages from a copy of the *Codex Gigas* (the *Devil's Bible*) as each man masturbated into the fleshy portion of the body. When everyone was finished, Gecht would cut it up and hand around the pieces for them to eat.

The police bought Tommy's story lock, stock, and barrel, more so because Tommy said he had witnessed two of the murders himself and had participated in nearly a dozen rituals. When the detectives asked him why he had committed such macabre illegal activities, he told them in all seriousness that Gecht had the power to make them do whatever he wanted. "You just had to do it," he said with conviction. Apparently, he believed that Gecht had some supernatural connection, and he was afraid of what Gecht might do to him if he didn't do what he was told.

One person warned detectives never to look into Gecht's blue eyes. No matter how sick and disgusting an act might be, he could inspire others to get involved. It has been alleged by author Jennifer Furio, although Gecht denies it, that he started off by molesting his sister. He does admit that during adolescence he developed a keen interest in Satanism and its secret rituals. And in this telling comment, Gecht says: "I have no problem with what John Wayne Gacy did. I just think he went about his killings the wrong way."

As the police interviewed more and more people known to Gecht, they learned that Spreitzer and the Kokoraleis brothers were not alone in their fear of Gecht or their belief in his powers. There seemed to be a Mansonesque quality about the man that drew impressionable people to him like some dark, satanic messiah.

Charles Milles Manson is almost unique among mass murderers. Although there have been many such killers in the United States, there have been only a handful quite like "Our Charlie"—for he murdered by proxy. The power of his personality made others want to do his killing for him. To some extent, we can see echoes of Manson in Robin Gecht, for even if we do believe Gecht when he says that he didn't murder anyone, those under his psychological control most certainly did. But how could this happen?

Interviews with Manson and those who knew or followed him bring out very different pictures. To some, he is a racist, misogynist, ill-educated bigot. To others, he is the most dangerous man alive, or even God or the devil. To himself, he was a small-time pimp and thief, yet something in his personality allowed Manson to dominate and manipulate a very small group of devotees in which he was the alpha male.

> From the world of darkness I did loose demons and devils in the power of scorpions to torment.
>
> —Charles Manson

Any study of Manson and his personality yields two overriding images. One is the chameleon, and the other is the dog. As we see with the serial killers featured in this book, they all can be chameleons and dogs. They are all Dr. Jekylls and Mr. Hydes.

Manson frequently characterized himself as a mirror to humanity, a reflection of the sickness inherent in the hippie-versus-establishment culture of his time. Family members attest that he was a changeling. He could be whatever the other people wanted him to be.

Manson could reflect the views of others, specifically his own family of disciples. To use a more simplistic term, he was a control freak, *exactly* like Robin Gecht—and like John Wayne Gacy, for that matter.

For example, in conversations with prosecuting attorney Vincent Bugliosi, Charlie Manson could be rational and quick-witted, bringing out his prison lawyer skills time and again to try and impress. However, Bugliosi could also see the mesmerizing effect Manson had on Lynette "Squeaky" Fromme and Sandra Good, two members of his murderous family. Bugliosi knew that Manson was a changeling, so he played his cards accordingly.

No luck will come to any family in which there is a changeling because the creature drains away all the good fortune which would normally attend the household. Thus, those who are cursed with it tend to be very poor and struggle desperately to maintain the ravenous monster in their midst.

—IRELANDSEYE.COM

With Robin Gecht we can again draw a parallel with Manson, because Gecht had exactly the same mesmerizing effect on Eddie Spreitzer and the Kokoraleis brothers, members of his own murderous "family." Only when this spell was finally broken, when they were free of his threats and influence, did Gecht's cohorts spill the beans on him.

Many people describe Manson as "the Man with a Thousand Masks," ready to be whatever ingratiated him with companions. For a physically small man (Manson is 5 feet 2 inches tall), who has spent most of his life in prison, the ability to agree with all men is obviously a powerful survival strategy.

The same label might also be affixed to Robin Gecht, for the stone-cold killer uses the same ingratiating methods in denying his guilt today. The five-and-a-half feet tall Gecht weighs in at an impressive 135 pounds. When the mind-control techniques of Scientology or satanism are fueled by paranoid anger at the world, the result is a very powerful persona indeed. Both Manson and Gecht had this power in spades.

Manson regards a dog as his own favorite metaphor for himself. Loyal friend, rejected puppy, coyote pariah are all frequent Manson personas. At the same time, when he came across other dominant males—members of biker gangs, for example—Charlie felt it necessary to establish his position by boasting of the killing he had done. Like an unsocialized dog, Manson fed on others' fear. People who showed fear were punished, assigned to a lowly position in the pack hierarchy.

> Charles Manson changes from second to second. He can be anybody he wants to be. He can put on any face he wants.
>
> —SUSAN ATKINS
> MANSON FAMILY MEMBER

Charles Manson was also capable of articulation and understanding. Yet his attitudes revealed stark contradictions; he respected nature but thought nothing of human life. However, if there is any single redeeming factor concerning the monster who orchestrated the Sharon Tate killings, it is that he admits it all, totally unlike Robin Gecht, who hasn't the balls to admit anything at all.

Despite all of his claims of being as sane as the next man, Gecht wasn't slow in trying to avoid trial by offering an insanity excuse. He was evaluated for competency and found to be mentally fit to stand trial; he was also considered to have been sane at the time the offenses took place. But luck favored him, and he received a mistrial decision based on a legal technicality surrounding submission of evidence. Nonetheless, this problem was overcome, and his second trial began on Tuesday, September 20, 1983, with the prosecutor producing some pretty compelling evidence.

During a search of Gecht's home, police found the "chapel" Tommy Kokoraleis had told them about. They also found a rifle that had been used in the shooting of one of the victims. Rummaging through the place, police located satanic literature and a "trophy box" owned by Gecht, in which Andrew Kokoraleis had claimed to have seen as many as fifteen pieces of human breast.

> I don't only face the injustices, but the nightmares that follow. You have no idea the pain and hurt I face and feel every single day I sit here and loose hope [sic]. I am no angel . . . but I never intentionally hurt anyone unless it was to protect myself or my family. I could never live with killing or knowing I was responsible for taking one's life.
>
> —Robin Gecht
> letter to Jennifer Furio

It was also established to the satisfaction of the jury, through surviving victims' statements and autopsy reports, that the victims had been abducted from the streets and held against their will. They had been tortured with implements such as needles and ice picks. They were gang-raped and then forced to endure having their breasts sliced off with a piano wire garrote so the men could use them for satanic sacrifices. Most of the women died, but they had likely felt the horrendous pain of this mutilation before they finally expired. Yet, two women survived their near-death ordeal to testify against their attackers and to live with the nightmares created by Gecht for the remainder of their lives.

Robin Gecht took the stand to speak in his own carefully planned defense. He recognized that the evidence against him in the Beverly Washington matter was so overwhelming that if he fully admitted the Washington offenses, the jury might believe him when he claimed he had not actually been involved with killing anyone else. Attempted murder was one thing, but conspiracy to commit serial homicide was something else.

> To all or most I'm not even a human or if so "deranged" but the fact is . . . I'm a simple person, and I too have feelings. I to cry and I hurt just as you would. That makes me human and I have a huge respect for women in general regardless whats said [sic].
>
> —Robin Gecht

In an attempt to try to pull the wool over the jurors' eyes, Gecht claimed that he was also innocent of rape and aggravated battery. He protested that during the time when most of the murders had occurred, he was not even acquainted with his codefendants. (This was shown to be a complete lie, and one of his letters proves it.) Sadly, despite sworn statements by women who claimed that it was Gecht who had demanded that their nipples be cut off, the testimony of these witnesses was not admissible. With no physical evidence linking him to the murders, there was nothing to corroborate the witness accounts. Gecht, therefore, could not be prosecuted for any of the killings, and his cohorts were not willing to stand up in court and incriminate him.

Nevertheless, the jury did find Gecht guilty on all counts relating to the attack on Beverly Washington: attempted murder, rape, deviate sexual assault, aggravated battery, and armed violence. He was sentenced to 120 years in prison.

For his part in the proceedings, acting on his attorney's advice, the garrulous, dim-witted Tommy Kokoraleis attempted to block his earlier confessions to police from being admitted into his trial. It was a no-brainer, and he lost. In 1984, Tommy was sentenced to 70 years in prison for his involvement in Lorraine Borowski's murder.

Andrew Kokoraleis was tried in two separate counties. The first trial was for the murder of Rose Beck Davis. In his confession, he admitted that he had abducted Ms. Davis with Gecht, Tommy, and Edward Spreitzer. They had forced her into the red van and beaten her with a hatchet until she was dead. This crime earned Andrew a life sentence.

> The murders weren't planned. I guess they were random attacks. Andrew usually drove Gecht's van and Robin would order him to stop whenever he saw a woman who appealed to him, and he was always on the lookout for one with sizeable breasts. He didn't stop talking about breasts . . . he had a fixation about tits.
>
> —Edward Spreitzer

At his second trial, Andrew Kokoraleis decided to recant everything he had confessed—that is to say, four totally different confessions—and went on to deny that he had killed or raped anyone. He claimed that the police had coerced each of his confessions. They had made false promises of leniency if he implicated his accomplices. He told the court that the cops had "beaten the shit outa me" to make him say what they wanted to hear. But prosecutor Brian Telander had the measure of his man. Telander reviewed the interrogations performed by six different detectives and two prosecutors.

"Are all of these honest police officers and attorneys lying?" asked a heated Telander of the jury. "Is this court being asked to believe that this defendant was told *exactly* what to say by these eight law officers, at different times, in different locations . . . that all of these public safety officers conspired to bring this defendant here . . . perhaps to conspire to have Kokoraleis executed, knowing that if they did so, and were found out, they could also face the death penalty themselves . . . that they would all ruin their careers and their families' lives as the result?"

When Telander put Detective Warren Wilcosz on the stand to describe his interrogation, the veteran cop said that when he had shown Kokoraleis a line of photos, he had picked out Lorraine Borowski and said, "That's the girl Eddie Spreitzer and I killed in the cemetery."

You are aware that Edward Spreitzer and Andrew Kokoraleis at one time lived with my family and I . . . correct. Surely had I known about anyone dying or being killed I would of alerted police before I would risk my own families lives [sic]. I had no idea what so ever until police advised and started accusing me as they beat on me. UNtil [sic] that time I never met Thomas nor did I sense anything was wrong with Edward. Now Andrew Kokoraleis is a different story waiting to be told. One sick pup and hated women in my book. He was not a friend. His Sister babysat for us that's how I came to know him and felt sorry for him at times. So I gave him some work with pay.

—Robin Gecht

It all came down to who was more believable—eight different law officers or the sullen, angry Kokoraleis. The jury deliberated for a few hours before reaching their verdict: guilty of the murder of Lorraine Borowski. At his sentencing hearing, Kokoraleis was condemned to death, and subsequent appeals upheld the sentence.

Andrew Kokoraleis was scheduled to be executed on March 17, 1999. He was given a last-minute stay, which was later reversed. But Kokoraleis was still convinced he wouldn't die. Indeed, right up to the morning of his execution he felt certain that it was not going to happen. He was flown to the Tamms Super-Max facility, where he spent the rest of the day praying and fasting. He spoke to a few select friends on the phone, bidding them farewell. Then, sobbing, he was strapped to the gurney, where he offered the Borowski family a belated apology: "I am truly sorry for your loss. I mean this sincerely." He spluttered quotes from the books of Exodus and Proverbs, ending with "The Kingdom of Heaven is at hand." The drugs took effect in just under four minutes, putting the killer to sleep. He stopped talking and breathing at 12:24 a.m.

Kokoraleis became the first person put to death in Illinois's new execution chamber. Previously, executions had been carried out at the Stateville Correctional Center near Joliet. As a double-whammy, Andrew was to earn the unlucky distinction of becoming the last person to be executed in the Prairie State before the death penalty was abolished there.

By the time of Kokoraleis death, Eddie Spreitzer's punishment had already been determined. On April 2, 1984, he pled guilty to murdering Rose Davis, Sandra Delaware, Shui Mak, and a drug dealer named Rafael Torado. He received life sentences for each murder, as well as prison time for a multitude of charges from rape to deviate sexual assault. Appearing on a bench trial in front of Judge Edward Kowal on February 25, 1986, Spreitzer admitted that he and his accomplices had abducted Linda Sutton as she was walking near Wrigley Field. They took her to a wooded area near a hotel where Spreitzer was staying, and he handcuffed her, raped her, and removed her breasts. She was raped again and left to squirm around and die in agony.

Initially, as one would expect, and indeed pray for, Spreitzer was sentenced to death and he wound up on death row in the Pontiac State Correctional Facility in Joliet. However, in October 2002, Spreitzer, at age 41, was among 140 of Illinois's 159 death row inmates to have their cases heard, all influenced by the moratorium on capital punishment. After further appeals, Governor Ryan pardoned just four of them and offered blanket clemency to the remainder. Spreitzer, despite the outrage expressed by his victims' families, was one of the beneficiaries.

Author Jennifer Furio undertook a project of writing letters to serial killers to see how they would respond, and Robin Gecht and Eric Spreitzer both sent letters that she printed in her book *The Serial Killer Letters*.

Spreitzer told Furio that he felt bad about his involvement in the crimes and had "even passed out at the sight of blood." But he insisted that he had done it because he had been afraid of Gecht and his shotgun. "I never did bad things alone," he claimed.

Jennifer Furio describes Spreitzer as being "weak, vulnerable, directionless, illiterate, and an easy target, thanks to a bad home life and substance abuse." This analysis was matched by

Spreitzer's defense attorney, Gary Pritchard, who argued that his client had suffered brain damage: "His IQ of 76 and his troubled history had been instrumental in making him easy for a person like Robin Gecht to manipulate," Pritchard said.

Gecht had offered Spreitzer a job when he was down on his luck and made some empty promises. According to Spreitzer, Gecht then blackmailed him with obscene photographs that he threatened to send to the police.

> NO, NOT AN OPTION—A FACT!! Never killed anyone nor even considered it. Have you?
>
> —ROBIN GECHT TO JENNIFER FURIO

Jennifer Furio's assessment is that Spreitzer was "sweet and gentle . . . He failed to come across as a murderer . . . all he needed was the love of a good woman."

Personally, this author is bound to question Ms. Furio's sense on this point. "Sweet and gentle"?

"All he needed was the love of a good woman"? Jesus Christ! Mr. Spreitzer's prison rap sheet can be viewed at: www.idoc.state.il.us/subsections/search/inms.asp. Perhaps if Jennifer Furio had been present when the "sweet and gentle," mentally retarded pygmy Spreitzer abducted, raped, tortured, mutilated, and slaughtered his victims, she might have noted that this little man was not all she imagined him to be.

With Robin Gecht denying any involvement in the murders attributed to him, it would be quite proper for us to attempt a little lateral thinking here and delve deeper into his manifesto of proclaimed innocence. Is he telling us the truth or a pack of lies? For my part, I think he is living in a world where lead balls bounce, elephants fly, and fairies reign supreme.

Breast partialism: To begin with, let's consider Gecht's own unsolicited admissions that he does have a fetish for female breasts. In fact, for a man who is desperately trying to convince others that he is not responsible for a series of crimes where carving off the victims' breasts played no small part, he is extremely forthcoming in boasting of his fetish with "breast partialism," a clinically recognized type of sexual fetish that involves a sexual interest and psychological investment among males for female breasts.

In defense of Mr. Gecht, however, in today's more enlightened society, the debate still continues as to whether the modern attraction to breasts among heterosexual males in Western society still constitutes a sexual fetish. In the clinical literature of the 19th century, the focus on breasts was considered a form of paraphilia (see definition below), but in modern times, this interest is viewed as normal *except* when the preference overshadows or dominates the relationship with the female partner—or in the case of Robin Gecht, the victims.

Paraphilia: Paraphilia is a medical term used to describe sexual arousal by objects or situations that are not part of normative stimulation and that can cause distress or serious problems for the people associated with the perpetrator, who often treats his partners (or victims) as non-human objects. In layman's terms, this sexual disorder—referred to in the American Psychiatric Association's *Diagnostic and Statistical Manual of Mental Disorders* (DSM-IV-TR) is characterized by recurrent, intense sexually arousing fantasies, sexual urges or behaviors generally involving acting on these urges, and by sadism in acting on these urges with a non-consenting person. There can be no doubt that the crimes committed by the Chicago Ripper Crew were propelled by the recurrent urge to inflict pain and humiliation, linked with a morbid kind of voyeurism, with an exclusive focus on the female breasts.

Sadistic personality disorder: Sadistic personality disorder is a pervasive pattern of cruel, demeaning, and aggressive behavior as indicated by the repeated occurrence of the following:

Use of physical cruelty, blackmail, intimidation, or violence for the purpose of establishing dominance in a relationship

Humiliation or demeaning of people in the presence of others

Treating or disciplining someone under his/her control unusually harshly

Lying for the purpose of harming or inflicting pain on others

Getting other people to do what he/she wants by frightening them through intimidation or even terror

Fascination with violence, weapons, injury, and torture

Absorption in literature relating to the Antichrist and satanism

Breast partialism, paraphilia, and a sadistic personality disorder all combine to make up the psychopathology of Robin Gecht, whether he admits a part of these conclusions or not. He checks all the boxes.

There can be no doubt that Gecht has an obsessive need to control other people and situations; he's a bully who craves power. And it is proven that this type of person will often accuse others of their own character trait when or if they feel that their powers are in decline or brought into question. This control is an attempt to impose excessive predictability and direction on others or on events.

Perhaps we do not need to hear another word from Gecht, who vehemently proclaims his innocence, for laterally he has, through his own words, actions, and deeds, and via his association with three men—two now serving life sentences, and another who was executed—who pointed accusatory fingers at him, proven that he has an unhealthy breast fetish and is a paraphiliac, a sexual sadist, and fully emerged psychopath.

Yet, there is something else we might wish to investigate a little further, and this is Gecht's past relationship with John Wayne Gacy.

Gacy's period of homicidal activity ran from 1972 through 1978. For a good part of the time when Gacy was most active, Gecht, then about age 23, subcontracted for the Des Plaines serial killer, and this is not in dispute.

Gecht, then a slightly built and quite attractive youth, would have been a typical Gacy mark, and Gacy had a homosexual penchant for employing young lads on a casual basis, if not to target them for rape, torture, and murder. Gacy accused Gecht of being involved in murder most foul when he was interviewed by Des Plaines detectives in 1978.

Control freak Gacy didn't simply pull Robin Gecht's name out of a hat . . . surely not! We can be sure that Gacy's modus operandi involved trawling for vulnerable young lads, on whom he inflicted imprisonment or physical restraint, torture, rape, and then murder. We also know that during the commission of several of his confirmed kills, Gacy did not act alone. This being the case, Gacy would have used someone who was comfortable with such heinous activity, a person who could be trusted to keep his mouth shut. Since his arrest, Gecht has, indeed, kept his mouth shut about Gacy.

> A clown can get away with murder . . . I should never been convicted of anything more serious than running a cemetery without a license.
>
> —John Wayne Gacy

While Gacy's preferred victim type has already been established, perhaps we can now use the same criteria to evaluate control freak Robin Gecht, who targeted women with large breasts.

So forget all this devil worship, satanic ritual stuff, for the truth may be even more horrific. Perhaps, just perhaps, Gacy was Gecht's homicidal mentor. Here are the last words from a man who claims that butter would not melt in his mouth:

> I have no problem with what John Wayne Gacy did. I just think he went about his killings the wrong way.
>
> —*Robin Gecht*

***

CHAPTER 3

WAYNE ADAM FORD—ROOM ZERO

My name is Wayne Adam Ford. I am the serial killer.
In 1997 I was experiencing some real problems. My wife left me and took my son away. I started drinking heavily and I was suffering from the lingering effects of a head injury that put me in a coma years ago.
I began a series of killings in 1997 and 1998. During this time I killed four women. I blacked out during the killings but I knew that I was responsible. I cut up one body, burying some of the remains and putting other body parts in my freezer. I was not in my right mind. The remorse and guilt was crushing me.
The police investigation into all four killings had turned up no leads. When I checked into Room Zero, at the Ocean Grove Lodge,[6] *I thought it was very eerie that there was a Room Zero. I had never seen a Room Zero before. It seemed kind of ominous and foreboding.*
Prior to the day of my arrest, I spent the day working up the courage with alcohol and, eh, self-prodding to work myself up to what had to be done.

---

6 480 Patrick's Point Drive, Trinidad, Humboldt County, California.

On November 3rd, 1998, I walked into the Humboldt County Sheriff's Department after deciding that I was too dangerous to be out in society, even if I was out, living rough in the woods. I had realized at this point that I was losing it for short periods of time. I was afraid this was going to happen on a permanent basis. Then I would be, ah, just a roving monster.
I had with me a severed woman's breast in a baggie in my pocket. This, I thought, would be enough to prevent me from having to say anything to the police and that I could say it through an attorney.

—Wayne Adam Ford

Like Gary Bowles, Wayne Adam Ford's family history is riddled with violence and neglect. Ford was born December 3, 1961, in Petaluma, Sonoma County, California, to Calvin Eugene Ford and his German immigrant wife, Birgette.

"My father was in the military," recalls Wayne. "the Secret Service, and stationed at the time at a base called Turlock, eh, right near San Quentin State Prison, as a matter of fact. And I have a brother that's a year and nine months older than me, named Rodney . . . he tried to kill me when I was a baby with a wooden coat hanger."

> You know, the recipe for making a monster is like this.
> First of all you have to have two parents, who, during your formative years, they neglect you. My mother would save up everything my brother and I did wrong and when my father got home the first thing he did was beat the hell out of us with a belt.

> But my mother never hit me until I was bigger than her, and one day she just kicked the shit outta me. The problem was that she gave me too much attention when I was really young, and then after the divorce she cut it off completely.
>
> My dad? Well, he is just flat emotionally abusive and he used us kids as slave labor. I was swinging a hammer at seven or eight years old. I put a roof on when I was thirteen. We were digging asbestos out of buildings that my dad and his partner were buying. Every weekend when we went with my dad, we spend the whole weekend working the whole time.
>
> —*Wayne Adam Ford*

Following a stormy marriage, Wayne's parents divorced in 1971, with Mrs. Ford traveling the world for some six years while leaving her boys in the care of their father, who was now living in the wine country town of Napa. This was a bad choice, because Wayne didn't see eye-to-eye with his father. Indeed, they didn't get along at all.

Wayne left high school before graduating, marrying a young woman and enlisting in the U.S. Marine Corps, working as a chemical and biologist specialist:

> I turned 17 and joined the Marine Corps, a good place to start my life in the right direction. And it worked out just fine until I had an accident. A girlfriend . . . her and I were driving down the freeway. Uh, I saw an accident and I told her to pull over. While I was helping the people in the accident who were hurt, a drunk ran over me. And when they finally found me, I was the other side of the fence, in a field. I was dead on arrival [at the hospital]. They apparently revived me after three days in a coma.

> Due to the accident and the head trauma that I had, my head was swollen up like a watermelon and, eh, my jaw and one side of my body was pretty much non-functional. I was hit pretty hard by all of this, probably three weeks, maybe an entire month before I was able to, uh, function semi-normally.
>
> I think the damage, which occurred to me at that time had changed my personality abruptly. I became very irritable afterwards, very, very quick-tempered, which I had before but nothing like it became after the accident.
>
> —*Wayne Adam Ford*

Around this time following his accident, Wayne was psychologically evaluated at a mental health clinic. His work performance had suffered, and his attitude toward his superior officers worsened as the result of a sudden split with his wife. The physicians found that apart from depression and alcohol abuse, they also worried that he was a threat to himself because he exhibited suicidal tendencies. Consequently, he was transferred to the U.S. Naval Hospital in Long Beach, where he was confined to a psychiatric ward to undergo counseling and drug abuse rehabilitation. Of course, the doctors hoped that Wayne's mental problems would be short-lived. They reasoned that he would soon get over the divorce and settle down. They would be proven wrong.

> Wayne did indeed suffer a serious head injury. Most neuropsychiatrists will tell you that if you have suffered a very serious head injury it can affect your behavior. Your conscience and acquired behavior can be ripped out. There has been a substantial amount of research into people who have suffered similar trauma. In some cases a person can become mentally ill.
>
> —CARLTON SMITH
> AUTHOR OF *SHADOWS OF EVIL*

Wayne did show a few signs of recovery, so he was discharged from hospital and reassigned to duty. In the summer of 1984, he was posted to Okinawa, Japan. About a month after he arrived in the Far East, his mental problems resurfaced, and this time the symptoms were far worse.

After being reprimanded by his commanding officer for failing an inspection, Wayne flipped out and became confrontational. The upshot was that he was diagnosed with "atypical psychosis due to his psychotic behavior." He was also diagnosed with borderline personality disorder, which is marked by inappropriate bursts of anger, frequent suicidal thoughts, irritability, and depression.

In 1985, 24-year-old Wayne, still living in "Wayne's world," was honorably discharged from the Marine Corps:

> I had actually made Sergeant real quick and some of this can be attributed to the fact that I was hyperactive after the freeway accident, and really, really did well. But what happened was, I was put under stress, and I went overseas to Okinawa and I had an incident where I was found in a fetal position in my room. And they couldn't get any response from me, so they took me to the hospital on the base and tried to see if I was on drugs or something. I wasn't. Well, I became violent and injured a number of people, I guess, in the hospital, and they had to have MPs [military police] take me to the psychiatric ward. It was there that I was strapped down to a bed for a couple of weeks, spread-eagled and given massive doses of Haldol to keep me under control and finally they decided to quote from my medical records: "All attempts to take him off medication failed. He was a

> danger to personnel and equipment." And, so then what they did was, they took me off medication and kicked me out of the Marine Corps. But they never gave me a medical discharge. I was given an honorable discharge because I hadn't done anything wrong. It should have been a medical discharge, and I should have been taken care of medically from that point on with the medical issues until they were straightened out. They never were. So, I was finally released into the civilian world for about six to eight months without being able to do anything. I finally got to where I could do a menial labor-type job and this was probably good for me because it was extremely physical and this led ultimately to driving trucks and being on my own.
>
> —*Wayne Adam Ford*

In January 1986, Garden Grove Police arrested Wayne for beating, raping, and robbing a prostitute. He was never prosecuted because the hooker refused to testify.

Later that year, Wayne was working as a mechanic and starting a relationship with another young woman. Sharing an apartment in San Clemente, California, Wayne and his partner had a turbulent affair, one marked with frequent arguments and breakups. According to one of Rick Halperin's *Death Penalty News—California* articles, shortly after the split Wayne was "arrested for animal cruelty after he shot a dog to death in his backyard." He pled guilty to the offense and received a brief jail sentence, but this punishment did little to deter his violent behavior, and his blatant disregard for life steadily grew more intense.

In 1994, Wayne was living in Orange County. There he shared a place with a man named Dave Hoover, who enjoyed the company of a succession of late-night female visitors whom he chose from his list of "Booty Calls." Without belaboring the point, Hoover had a list of ten women, and if he wanted sex, he would telephone each girl in order of their appeal to him, running through the list until he scored.

At the very bottom of Hoover's list was a somewhat plain and unattractive, though ample-bosomed, 19-year-old named Elizabeth. She frequented a karaoke bar where Wayne sang. There is no record of how many times Elizabeth "entertained" Hoover during the late hours, but it would be fair to say that on occasion he "treated her like shit," which Wayne thought was "kinda funny," but said that he felt "kinda sorry for her, too." For her part, Elizabeth started to wash and iron Wayne's clothes and, in return, he says, "I screwed her out of boredom and because she had big tits."

Elizabeth, who lacked any moral realism whatsoever, told Wayne that she wanted to have kids and be a stay-at-home mother. To his own warped way of thinking, and with his self-esteem at an all-time low because he felt that no one wanted him, Wayne thought that she could be a "good mother, cleaner of his clothes, and keeper of the house." He married Elizabeth in Las Vegas and slipped a bun in the oven almost immediately. Cracks appeared in the relationship shortly thereafter.

Wayne is adamant that he never loved Elizabeth. He allowed her to have sex with other men, as he didn't want her for himself. Indeed, he says that he was "truly sickened by her," and although she would later claim that he demanded to watch her have sex with other men, he argues, "I didn't give a damn about her and who she screwed."

Of course, there are two sides to any story. Elizabeth later explained that from the start of the marriage Wayne had suffered from severe bouts of depression, that he also became extremely controlling and aggressive toward her. This was a pattern that seemed to repeat itself in every one of his relationships, and even though Elizabeth desperately tried to please him, there was little she could do to make him happy, as Ford explains:

> I had gotten into a new relationship . . . the person I had my son, Max, with, and ultimately revisiting of the old wounds and mental problems that, uh, came back.
>
> Max was on his way, my little baby . . . I really wanted a family of my own and so did she. And, I was really, really looking forward to the birth of my first and only child, Max. And, I was overwhelmed when he was born.

During Elizabeth's fifth month of pregnancy, the couple had an argument after she refused him sex, so he raped her, or so she claims. The incident terrified her, she says, and what made it worse was his indifference about what he had done. She packed her bags and moved in with her mother, who lived in Nevada. Eventually, however, the ill-suited couple moved back in together only to split up again. Their on-again, off-again relationship continued throughout the remainder of her pregnancy, even after Max was born in December 1995.

According to Carlton Smith, author of *Shadows of Evil*, Wayne frequently demanded that his wife participate in acting out his sexual fantasies, including sleeping with strange men while he watched and stuck needles into Elizabeth's breasts—the latter a trait also enjoyed by Robin Gecht.

One would expect Wayne to deny this allegation if the question was ever put to him, but his record does prove that he exhibited a less than healthy interest in this part of a female's body. Actually, he did cut two breasts off one of his victims. He cooked them, then buried them in the woods. He kept the rendered fat from the breasts in an empty coffee jar for some undetermined purpose. And he kept another breast in his truck's freezer, boldly handing it over to the police when he turned himself in.

Wayne also demanded that Elizabeth clean the house, cook three times a day for him, and care for the baby while he skipped from job to job between California and Las Vegas. No matter how hard she worked, she says, Wayne criticized her. Again, as might be expected, Wayne Ford denies all this.

It wasn't long before Elizabeth realized that her world would be better—a heck of a lot better and much easier for her—outside of Wayne's world. In the summer of 1996 she moved out with baby Max and commenced divorce proceedings. Wayne temporarily went to live with his grandmother before moving into a trailer home in Arcata, California.

Following the breakup, Elizabeth says that she encouraged him to visit their son, and according to her he made only a few attempts to see the boy. "It seems that he was too busy wallowing in his own self-pity and growing hatred," she said.

As one might expect, Wayne Ford tells a different story. He argues that he wanted to make the relationship work, but only because he wanted to be close to his son—a child he says he adored. He also claims that when he tried to arrange visits,

Elizabeth refused to answer the phone. When she did agree to his request, he would drive long distances to see his son, only to find mother and son away from their home when he arrived. Elizabeth says this is completely untrue.

Wayne then slipped deeper and deeper into psychosis, further facilitated by alcohol abuse, and his ire soon turned deadly.

Broadcaster and documentary filmmaker Victoria Redstall sums it all up, saying:

> According to Wayne, his childhood was cold, callous and loveless. He was emotionally abused by both parents; physically abused by his father and abandoned by his mother. He had suffered a very serious head injury in his late teens and was suffering personality changed and psychotic breaks. But now he had a son to love and the child's mother snatched the child away from him. His disrespect toward women, combined with his mental problems, turned into a rage which he transferred onto prostitutes.

Forensic psychologist Dr. Paul Berg is inclined to agree with Redstall:

> In my mind, the killing of the hookers was clearly related to the rage he felt toward his second wife. The fact that his wife ran away to Las Vegas, that he was powerless to care for his own child, and Wayne, being the injured child himself, would have been a totally out-of-control feeling for him.

Indeed, when Victoria Redstall asked Wayne Ford, "Do you believe that you were killing your wife when you were killing prostitutes?" his answer was:

> I believe that might have been a lot to do with the fugue state[7] . . . that I put myself in Max's shoes . . . a little boy's shoes, and I protect myself and that's what I think was going on.

Dr. Berg believes that Wayne Ford was not aware of what he was doing when he was killing. "He was on automatic pilot," Berg says, "but he certainly became aware after the crimes had been committed." However, this author believes that Mr. Ford knew *exactly* what he was doing when he committed murder.

Sonoma County Jane 194-97 Doe

> My feeling was that it [the body] was some sort of plastic man . . . that's what I wanted to think.
>
> —*Robert Pottberg at Wayne Ford's trial*

On Sunday, October 26, 1997, Robert Pottberg's kayak glided through the peaceful waters of Ryan Slough, near Humboldt

7 A fugue state, formally Dissociative Fugue (previously called Psychogenic Fugue) (DSM-IV Dissociative Disorders 300.13) is a rare psychiatric disorder characterized by reversible amnesia for personal identity, including the memories, personality, and other identifying characteristics of individuality. The state is usually short-lived (hours to days), but can last months or longer. Dissociative fugue usually involves unplanned travel or wandering, and is sometimes accompanied by the establishment of a new identity. After recovery from fugue, previous memories usually return intact; however, there is complete amnesia for the fugue episode. Importantly, an episode is not characterized as a fugue if it can be related to the ingestion of psychotropic substances, to physical trauma, to a general medical condition, or to psychiatric conditions such as delirium or dementia, bipolar disorder, or depression. Fugues are usually precipitated by a stressful episode, and upon recovery there may be amnesia for the original stressor (Dissociative Amnesia).

Bay, shrouded by an overcast sky. Accompanied by two friends and a young lad, Robert blissfully paddled along, taking in his surroundings. They were hunting ducks.

Humboldt Bay and its tidal sloughs are open to fishing year-round. The bay is home to a national wildlife refuge complex for the protection of wetlands and habitat for migratory birds, and on this occasion Ryan Slough was the final resting place of a dead body—well, that is to say, just the torso.

At first, Robert thought he had found a tailor's mannequin on the muddy bank. He paddled closer and stopped about five feet away, "close enough to reach out a paddle and touch the body," he says. Almost at once Robert realized that the object was the butchered remains of a woman. "It was skillfully dismembered," Mr. Pottberg recalls. "There were no legs. There were no arms. There was no head." So, having a cell phone at hand, he did what any self-respecting duck hunter would do under these circumstances—he immediately dialed 911 and was put through to the Humboldt County Police Department.

When investigators arrived at the scene, they saw that the victim's torso had been sliced down the middle and gutted. Moreover, the woman's breasts had been cut off, and they noted approximately 30 stab wounds to the body. But because there were no fingers to fingerprint, no head to photograph, no tattoos or unusual features on the torso, the police were literally up the creek without a paddle in any attempt to identify the woman.

Deputy Coroner Charles Van Buskirk remembers being called out to the slough, an area inaccessible by foot:

> I called for a boat. I hiked over some rough terrain and then laid out old boards and driftwood so I wouldn't sink in the mud surrounding the torso. It was face down on a mud flat, in an area that would be underwater at high tide.

Having determined that the object was indeed a human body—and he says he "recognized it as such before he even stepped off the boat"—Van Buskirk added:

> I turned the torso over and found that it had been cut lengthwise and that both breasts had been removed. The pubic mound had been removed. On the lower back I found 27 small stab wounds, similar to what would have been caused by a penknife, and fingertip bruises on the upper back. I estimated that the body had been in the water only a few hours.

The unidentified body was officially toe-tagged as "Sonoma County Jane 194-97 Doe" and further studied by medical examiner Glen Sipma, who determined that she was likely between the ages of 18 and 25 and had a dark complexion. The woman had been dead for at least three or four days before she was discovered. "I would say that the corpse was in one of the worst states I've seen. The head, arms and legs were gone," recalled Sipma.

Ford later explained to Victoria Redstall how he picked this hooker up:

> It was like midnight. She's sitting there shivering on the side of a building. I don't remember that I had a very long conversation with her . . . I think that it was just that: "It is going to get colder where you're at, and I'll give you a ride wherever you want to go, but sitting around here is probably the worst place to sit."

Sadly, this woman is still known as "Sonoma County Jane 194-97 Doe" today. We have Mr. Ford to thank for that. What the coroner and police didn't know was that Ford had baked the breasts in his oven before burying them in the woods. Perhaps even more revolting was the fact that he'd stored the rendered breast fat in an empty coffee jar. Mr. Ford was a "trophy-taker," in that he took mementos of his crimes away with him so he could relive his murderous fantasies another day. Of course, Wayne is not unique in this respect, as any law enforcement officer or student of criminology will understand. Some killers take away the victim's jewelry, as did Kenneth Alessio Bianchi, aka, "The Hillside Strangler," who somewhat perversely gave the stuff to his common-law wife, Kellie Boyd.

As did Joel Rifkin, the New York slayer of prostitutes; he kept the items to furiously masturbate over until he could barely stand up.

Another example is British serial murderer Dr. Harold Shipman, who is thought to have murdered some 250 elderly patients; he also retained much of his victims' jewelry for purposes known only to him.

And John Reginald Christie, a British serial killer of six women at his home at 10 Rillington Place, London, kept cuttings of his victims' hair as trophies. They were found on premises formerly rented by him. Christie was hanged on July 15, 1953.

So in this respect, Wayne Adam Ford was not exceptional. Like Robin Gecht, he had a fetish for women's breasts, the larger the better as far as he was concerned. Of course, the principal resident of Wayne's world will deny this, but it seems clear that one doesn't hack off a woman's breasts, bag them up, and take them home for any other reason than to use them for some perverse, post-homicide sexual purpose.

More than a year after the torso was found, and after Wayne had confessed this murder, police searched the site in the woods where he lived rough for a short while. Deputy Coroner Van Buskirk found, in a shallow hole at the base of a tree, "two human thighs and portions of white, human flesh, in plastic bags." Perhaps Mr. Ford was burying human flesh to later dig the items up again for some form of sexual gratification.

Tina Renee Gibbs

In June 1998, the body of a white female was found floating in the California Aqueduct near the small, pleasantly named town of Buttonwillow (pop. 1,300), some 27 miles west of Bakersfield. The human remains were taken for examination to the Kern County Coroner's Office, where it was discovered that the woman had most probably died as the result of strangulation. It was also suggested that she'd had sex and then been murdered several days before her corpse was found.

Through a fingerprint match, police learned that the victim was known as Tina Gibbs, age 26, from Tacoma, Washington. She was known to law enforcement and had worked as a Las Vegas street hooker during the months before her death.

Lanette Deyon White

Four months later, on Friday, September 25, a woman's naked body was discovered lying in roadside irrigation ditch off

Interstate 5 near Lodi, California. Several items thought to be connected to the crime were found a little farther along the highway: Women's clothing, a bloodied tarpaulin, hair, a white plastic bag with the logo of the Flying J truck, and some pieces of jewelry were scattered around. Investigators hoped this evidence would provide much-needed clues as to the identity of the victim and how she met her fate.

Due to the advanced state of decomposition, it was determined at autopsy that the woman had been dead for several days. A puncture mark was found on one of the victim's breasts, and there was evidence of suffocation. Investigators believed that the woman was murdered someplace other than where she was found and then thrown from a moving vehicle into the ditch.

Fingerprints identified the victim as an attractive 25-year-old named Lanette Deyon White, from Fontana, California. She had last been seen alive by her cousin on Sunday, September 20, as she prepared to visit a grocery store to buy milk for her baby.

Patricia Anne Tamez

> She kinda hung around the corner at Sixth Street and Highway 18. I saw her regularly near the stop sign on the corner. Sometimes she walked into my office to ask for a cigarette. I don't know what her official title was, but I surmised she was a lady of the evening.
>
> —*Larry Halverson,*
> *conductor for the Burlington Northern Santa Fe Railway*

By now, Wayne Ford had moved out of his trailer home and was camping deep in Humboldt County woodlands. According to him—and this is quite an implausible story—he was living rough because he "didn't want to see anymore prostitutes" for fear of killing them, and he "didn't want to see any more babies." The fact that he saw plenty of both during his job as a long-distance trucker seems to have been conveniently erased from his mind.

Aged 29, from Hesperia, California, Patricia Anne Tamez had lived a turbulent life. When she wasn't roaming the streets for a quick fix or prostituting herself to support her drug habit, she could often be found in a mental institution or state hospital, undergoing drug rehabilitation and psychiatric therapy. She was a far cry from the vivacious college student she had once been. Supporting her drug habit had consumed her life and become her sole ambition.

On Saturday, October 22, 1998, Patricia spent the early part of the afternoon soliciting sex with truck drivers at the intersection of 6th and D Streets in downtown Victorville, California. She was wearing a white T-shirt over her panties, a pair of tennis shoes, and very little else, it seems.

After several hours she got her first response when a man driving a large, shiny black truck pulled up with a proposition. The driver worked for Edeline Trucking. It was Wayne Ford, on his way to pick up a load of concrete in Lucerne Valley when he passed through Victorville and spotted the woman advertising her services:

> She flagged me over. Yeah, I saw her from a distance. I slowed down. I thought someone was trying to cross the street. She looked at me and flagged me down. She lifted up her T-shirt to reveal her panties, a cross between pink and

purple. I circled the block, found a space to stop, and picked her up.

—*Wayne Ford to Detectives Frank Gonzales and Jeff Staggs, November 3, 1998*

Larry Halverson, conductor for the BNSF Railway Company, had his office nearby. He noticed that following a brief conversation the woman climbed into the cab and the vehicle drove off. "That's the last I ever seen of her," recalled Halverson at Ford's trial.

The pair continued east on Highway 18 into Apple Valley, where Ford pulled into a vacant lot near a convenience store. The couple climbed into the sleeper portion of the cab and had sex. Ford later told detectives the unlikely story that he awoke to find Patricia not breathing. He claimed that he tried to revive her with CPR but stopped when he got tired.

Ford couldn't quite remember exactly how Patricia Tamez stopped breathing, but he told the detectives how it had "happened before with other women" and said it "involved a form of asphyxiation I sort of used my hands to cut off the blood flow of the carotid artery during sex."

Many serial killers can only achieve an orgasm when the victim is being strangled[8] and at the point of death. Arthur Shawcross and sado-sexual killer Michael Bruce Ross, whom I have met several times, have admitted this. Before his execution, on May 13, 2005, Ross explained to me during a TV interview at Somers Prison, Connecticut:

8 Extreme asphyxiaphilia: a paraphilia in which sexual arousal and orgasm are dependent on, or facilitated by, the lack of oxygen produced by self-strangulation or from being strangulated or asphyxiated by a sexual partner, up to death. Asphyxiaphilia is a paraphilia of the sacrificial/expiatory type.

> I would strangle them [his female victims] almost till they stopped breathing. Then I'd stop and let them revive. They thrashed around a bit, and I had to massage my fingers before reapplying the pressure, and I'd repeat it all until I came which was at the very moment they died. It left some multiple bruising around their necks. It was sort of fun.
>
> —*Michael Bruce Ross*

Ford then told another unlikely yarn, one which had the detectives blinking at each other in disbelief: "I wanted to take her to a hospital, or a police station, but I didn't know the area," he said pathetically. "So, I continued east on Highway 18 and pulled over in a remote area to attempt CPR a second time. When it didn't work, I cried."

"Why did you cry, Adam, why did you cry?" asked Detective Gonzales, during the interview.

"Cause I didn't want that to happen," Ford said.

"Did you cry because you knew it was wrong, Adam?" the detective asked.

"Yeah, it shouldn't have happened. It shouldn't have happened," Ford replied with something short of honesty, before explaining what happened next.

"I was very, very upset about all of this," Ford explained. "I continued to Lucerne for my pickup. On my return trip west, toward Highway 395, I headed south and dumped her nude body in the California Aqueduct."

The evening after Patricia had climbed into Ford's truck, two security guards at the California Aqueduct were patrolling the area when one of the men noticed something bobbing in the rolling waters near the pump house. To his horror, the guard realized that the object was actually the nude body of a woman. It had caught upon one of the many iron gates that snag debris floating downstream. The guard immediately summoned the police.

When the authorities arrived, they fished the body out of the water, making an immediate note that one of the woman's breasts had been cut off. Now it was obvious that she had been murdered, she hadn't simply slipped and fallen into the water where she drowned.

An autopsy examination revealed that the woman had undergone severe trauma before her death. There was evidence that she had been bound: ligature marks from what was determined as nylon rope were found on the wrists and ankles. She had been raped, claimed the prosecutor at Wayne's trial, and then hit over the head with a blunt instrument. Moreover, her attacker had broken her back before he strangled her. It was determined from fingerprints that the pitiful remains were those of Patricia Anne Tamez, who had gone missing a day earlier.

During a search of the area upstream along the aqueduct, police found items that were possibly linked with the murder: a bloodied towel, blouse, pants, and a .22-caliber air pistol. Police were not able to locate the victim's missing breast, nor did they have a clue as to the identity of her killer.

When Victoria Redstall asked Wayne Ford why he had cut a breast off, he gave this somewhat implausible answer: "The breast was cut off because it was tied to the rope. It was quicker to cut the breast off than anything else."

"Because you were trying to push her into the aqueduct?"

"Absolutely, and I wanted to because of the angle of the aqueduct. I didn't want to go in myself, so what I wanted to do was kind of spin the body down, like a top, you know, and it didn't work. So I needed my rope back, but it wouldn't come back."

Wayne Ford had taken the severed breast back to his truck and placed it in the tractor unit's freezer.

Valerie Rondi—one that got away

> I believe that in order for Wayne to do the things he is accused of there had to be a spirit of evil that entered into him.
>
> —*Pastor James Ray,*
> *Ford's spiritual advisor*

Just a few days before Wayne Ford gave himself up, prostitute Valerie Rondi was soliciting near a bus stop along Broadway Street in Eureka, the county seat of Humboldt County, California. Valerie gave her exclusive account of the events to Victoria Redstall:

> Okay! When I met Wayne Ford I was a prostitute. I was walking on Broadway, an' I was hitchhiking. He pulled over and asked me if I needed a ride. I asked him if he wanted a date, an' he says, "Yeah!"
>
> I climbed into his truck. He told me how mean his wife was, and all the despicable things she was doing to him, like kinda ripping him off, an' stuff. But what set him off was I wouldn't take his money. I felt sorry for him. And he said, "Do you know how it makes me feel to have a hooker who won't take my money to fuck me?"

> Please excuse my language, Victoria. But I said to him, "I don't give a shit," and then he punched me, hard, real hard in the face.
>
> He forced himself on me. I wasn't going to take another beating. He raped me roughly. His eyes narrowed and turned red, and he had a real angry scowl on his face, and that's when I started kickin' his ass, 'cause I realized that there was something seriously wrong with this man. His face turned from night to day. It was totally different.

Wayne Ford, agitated in response to Rondi's claim, said: "I never forced her to do anything. I never hit the girl. None of that stuff. That's not even true. She turned into an asshole on me, is what she he did."

Valerie Rondi: "He promised to get me some heroin. He didn't, so I got sicker and sicker, and by the fourth day I was done."

Victoria Redstall asked Valerie if she had tried to escape. "No! 'Cause I was so sick and weak. He never showed me any kindness or sensitivity."

Ms. Rondi then related a time when she went to the freezer in Ford's truck cab:

> He said: "Never open that. Don't even fuckin' look in there." I thought it was kinda strange. . . . he had something in there he didn't want me to see. I just said, "Okay!" I had no idea there was a severed breast in there. I didn't know if there was anything severed anywhere. . . . Then I knew he was going to kill me. . . . we were not going to Vegas . . . all he'd said was bullshit. So I waited for him to get out of the cab [at a truck stop].
>
> So, I waited for him to get out of the truck, and I opened the door and jumped. And I hit the ground and jumped up

> to another truck, and I opened the door, and said: "Please help me." The guy, Gerry, looked like Santa Claus, and he told me to get in.

Wayne Ford says something different:

> Hey, and I got somebody else to give her a ride from the San Jose area back to Eureka and I had to go over the hill. I didn't really know the guy [the truck driver] very well. I walked up to the step. I said: "Hey! Can you give this girl a ride . . . she's a hooker that I picked up in Eureka, an' she wants to go back." And, he said, "Sure. I'll take her back."

Valerie Rondi explained that she didn't report the matter to the police because "they wouldn't do anything about it." Then she claimed that after she saw Ford's face in a local newspaper, she knew that this was the man who could have murdered her.

Laughing in her interview with Victoria Redstall, Rondi told with some pride about urinating into the pickle jar Wayne kept in his truck: "I went to the truck's bathroom and there was a jar of pickles," she said, "so I peed in them. 'Eat those, you *motherfucker*,' I thought. But I forgive him. God forgives murderers, so why can't I? But now I know how stupid I was. I could be lying there with my head chopped off."

Victoria put all of Rondi's allegations to Wayne Ford. His response was one of anger:

> If I was whatever they say I was, why didn't I kill that bitch [Rondi]? Well, it sounds like maybe I should have if she thinks she's pissing in my pickle jar.
>
> It never happened like she says. You see they've got to make up these wild-ass stories. I could have dumped her out of the truck and picked up another hooker anywhere on

> the route. And it's mighty nice of her to forgive me, 'cause nothing was done to her. That's what pisses me off. Oh! She is such a liar. I never did anything. Oh, gosh, that girl . . . if anybody wanted to be strangled, it was her.

On the evening of Monday, November 2, 1998, after a day of drinking, Wayne Ford went to the pay phone at the Ocean Grove Lodge, 480 Patrick's Point Drive, in Trinidad, California, and called his brother, Rod. Wayne was emotional and had something important to tell him. He asked his brother to pick him up from the lodge as soon as he could.

Rod was a five-hour drive away. Nevertheless, despite the distance, he drove to meet up with his brother, arriving at the lodge in the early hours of Thursday morning. Rod was very tired but certainly willing to hear what Wayne had to say, and Wayne Ford takes up the story from here:

> On my last day of freedom I slept in Room Zero. I hardly slept at all, and I had no way of knowing the actual consequences of turning myself in, but it was a necessary thing for me to do, because I had no right to stay out there and be a danger to other people.
>
> I planned to spend the day with my brother because I knew that it was going to be the last day of freedom and possibly even my last day of life.
>
> I wanted to spend the day at the zoo in Eureka with my brother because we had spent many days with my mother when we were little boys and with other relatives, grandparents, aunts and uncles . . . just spend the day eating cotton candy and looking at the animals and feeding the ducks and whatever. So, that was one place that I spent time with my brother previously.

> What I had to do that day wasn't something that just came willy-nilly, and easy to do. I needed my brother's support. I also needed my brother's love and companionship on that last day. I wanted to spend time doing things I knew I'd never ever get to do again and somewhat reminiscing the good times of my life with my brother when we were little kids.
>
> I think it was all just to ease myself into what I was going to do, and I was really in my mind recording everything as best I could, to keep 'til the day I die which may or may not be very long from the point in time that I turn myself in.

During the conversations with his brother, Wayne appeared to be highly emotional and anxious about something. Yet he refused to tell Rod what exactly was wrong. After several hours of trying to pry at least something out of Wayne, Rod gave in to fatigue and went to bed. Later the same day, Rod tried again. Eventually Wayne confessed with a generous salting of understatement that he had "hurt some people." Who these hurt people were, and to what extent they were hurt, remained unclear to Rod.

Nevertheless, Rod spent the better part of the afternoon fruitlessly trying to wrestle information out of his brother without much success. Rod, who had the patience of a saint, finally decided that *if* Wayne had done something that resulted in people getting "hurt," it was absolutely necessary for him to turn himself into the authorities.

After a meal at a Denny's, Wayne finally made the decision that would change his life completely: "After Denny's I told my brother that we shouldn't take his truck to the sheriff's department . . . we should take the truck to my grandparents' house and walk there." So the two men took a long walk, one that would end in Ford's freedom being lost forever.

During the evening of November 3, wracked with guilt, Wayne went to the Humboldt County Sheriff's Department, 826 Fourth Street, Eureka, where he introduced himself to the desk sergeant. Wayne said that he wanted to confess about "people he had hurt" and promptly produced a Ziploc plastic bag from his jacket pocket. It contained a breast from the late Patricia Tamez, and it was only then that the justifiably concerned Rod learned *exactly* what Wayne had done.

> Anytime one turns himself in to the authorities, although the cops say they're befriending you, or helping you, they're really out to do what's worst for you . . . what's best for society. And I was in agreement on that issue. I brought a severed breast with me, and the meaning of that . . . it was to give it to the police and not have to say a word. That would have been enough to put me in jail and not have to worry about whether someone else was going to be injured. My plan was to talk to an attorney and have the attorney tell the authorities what happened. And I thought that I'd probably be found guilty of murder, then executed within a couple of years' period of time.
>
> I was completely stressed out of my mind. I know that I did what I had to do, and it took a great amount of strength to do what I had to do, knowing that I was probably going to die in a very short time. I believed wholeheartedly that I had a good chance of being strung up in a cell that day. In spite of that, I did what had to be done because right is right, and wrong is wrong, so I had to do what was right no matter the consequences to me.
>
> —*Wayne Ford*

After more than a year of struggling to solve the mysterious death of the woman whose torso had been found in a slough near Eureka, Detective Juan Freeman finally got the break he had frequently prayed for. The duty sergeant telephoned him about a man who had walked in to confess details about people he had hurt. "Hey, Juan, this nutball has got a real one-off. He's got a woman's breast, in his jacket pocket, for Christ's fuckin' sake!" sputtered the sergeant, while holding the offending item at arm's length.

> His demeanor was cooperative, depressed . . . he was kind of down. Sometimes he would look directly at me, mostly he would look down. At times, Ford got emotional, even cried, but his voice often stayed at a low volume, at times too low for the tape recorder to even accurately pick it up.
>
> —Detective Juan Freeman on Wayne Ford's interview

Detective Freeman hightailed it down to the police station, but extracting the truth from Ford would not be easy. While Ford easily coughed up some answers, he flat-out refused to respond to others.

Wayne Ford seemed to be a man with a heavy heart, and at this point in time he had no attorney to look after his legal interests. Apparently, he told Freeman several times that he wanted to help the authorities and provide resolution to the victims' families, and Freeman, Wayne claimed, responded that having an attorney would hinder that.

Convinced that Freeman was a straight cop—and the officer most certainly is just that—Wayne fell into that time-honored trap set by a seasoned investigator doesn't want a smart-assed defense attorney blowing smoke in his yard. Ford was now a surefire bet for the killer who had recently killed at least four—

maybe more—prostitutes, and at that moment in time the law actually had jack shit to prove most of it. If Wayne suddenly zipped up, even a half-wit public defender could have his client back walking the streets within hours.

Detective Freeman knew that even if the judicial train did manage to haul itself into the right station, they would find Ford's scrambled brains had been left behind and, at the very least, it would take a fistful of psychiatrists a decade to agree on his state of mind. Then it would be a merry-go-round of appeals, a trip to the state mental institution for more evaluation, back to jail, back to the nut house, and on and on. With the justice system unraveling at the seams, Freeman knew that by the time of sentencing, civilization would be eating at a Wendy's on Mars. Freeman was dead right, too.

And, Detective Freeman didn't need to be cynical, for he knew that every homicide cop in the country had worked on cases that meant years of red-eyeballing overtime, court time, and domestic stress, just to get some asshole free meals, dental treatment, and a warm bed—even if TV "dicks" solve such cases within an hour, including time for commercials. What Freeman didn't need was a somnolent judge along with a jury composed of twelve citizens of average ignorance who might sentence Mr. Ford to death, only for an appellate court to commute the sentence because of a technical foul-up. Then, for some godforsaken reason, they might release Wayne Ford back into society. Freeman had his man. His gut told him that he was on the money; he knew he had to play it careful, yet he still pushed his luck. Partway down the track, he would prove to be successful. Partway along the rails, he would also come unstuck.

Wayne soon confessed to murdering Patricia Tamez, Tina Gibbs, Lanette White, and the unidentified Jane Doe whose torso had been found on the banks of Ryan Slough. He gave investigators a detailed account of how he murdered each victim, why he did it, and where he put the missing body parts. He revealed the location of some of Jane Doe, saying that he had buried the woman's head and arms near the aptly named Mad River, close to a cement works. The remaining human artifacts, including the victim's thighs, were temporarily kept in his freezer before being buried at a Trinidad campsite.

With District Attorney Investigator Jim Dawson now sitting in on the interviews, Wayne said:

> It's hard. I'm fighting the fact that I deserve probably to die for what I have done, and there is this guy right here [Detective Freeman] who's gonna do the best to put me there. I know that in a courtroom they'll give a death sentence. And I know that I am risking a lot by doing what I am doing without an attorney. A lot of advantage that I might have to weasel out of something, in some way, shape or form . . . I know that. Okay. And I know talking to you is legally a very dangerous thing.

Dawson responded with: "It is the right thing, Wayne. That's what we are talking about here."

"It is the right thing, and I wanna do the right thing." Wayne whined. "I didn't wanna kill anybody. I just feel certain, certain things, ya know. It just makes me freeze up. I just want everything to stop."

"Thank *you*, sir," Dawson replied.

The cops visited the campsite. Then they continued on to the Mad River to investigate Wayne's story. They found nothing at the riverbank, but at the campsite they managed to locate six or seven body parts that were linked to Jane Doe.

Wayne confessed that he had picked up Jane Doe, who was hitchhiking near Eureka. He was initially attracted to her large breasts, something for which Wayne had a fixation. He told police that he took her back to his trailer, they had rough sex, and then he strangled her. It was a process he repeated on three other occasions. However, unlike what he did with the other victims, he dismembered this corpse in his bathtub using a saw and knives. He said he did this because it "made it easier to dispose of her body."

A search of Wayne Ford's trailer revealed even more critical evidence. In a coffee can, of all places, investigators found the rendered fat from Jane Doe's breasts. Moreover, a plastic bag bearing the Flying J logo was also discovered. This find matched the bag discovered earlier near Lanette White's remains. Furthermore, they found the freezer in which Wayne stored other body parts.

All the evidence from the trailer and campsite was taken to a police crime lab to be examined. Wayne had explained that at the time of the murders he had worked as a long-haul truck driver, carrying lumber throughout Oregon, California, Nevada, and Arizona. It was during these road trips that Wayne's killing rampage was sparked by anger at his ex-wife, Elizabeth, whom he claimed withheld their son from him.

Quoting from a 1998 *Daily News* article written by Bhavna Mistrys: "Wayne Ford turned himself in because he was afraid he would kill his ex-wife and he didn't want his son to be an orphan."

Wayne's semi-tractor truck and his personal Jeep were examined. The vehicles were of particular importance because Wayne had explained that he had driven for days on end with the dead Lanette White in the cab. Indeed, at one point he was pulled over by a California Highway Patrol officer while White's decomposing corpse was in the sleeper section of the truck. The trooper's olfactory senses were not aroused by the smell of rotting flesh, so Ford was allowed to drive on.

The police also hoped that remnants of bodies might be found in the vehicles, and they inspected the two vehicles thoroughly. They ripped them apart, looking for anything: human hair, fiber, a bloodstain, anything at all that could be used to strengthen their case. For even though Wayne had presented himself on a silver platter to the authorities, investigators wanted to be 110 percent sure that there was enough supporting evidence. They didn't want to take any chances on a mistrial.

On Friday, November 6, 1998, Wayne Ford was arraigned at the Humboldt County Superior Court, Judge W. Bruce Watson presiding. He was charged with only one count of first-degree murder, that of Jane Doe. The other murders were not committed in the court's jurisdiction, so Wayne could only be tried in the counties where those bodies were found.

During the proceedings, Wayne complained to the judge that he didn't have a lawyer, even though he had repeatedly requested one. The court then appointed attorney Kevin Robinson to defend Wayne. Robinson immediately entered a plea of not guilty on behalf of his new client.

One of the most contentious issues that Robinson wanted to address was the fact that his client was allegedly prevented from having contact with a lawyer from the moment of his arrest to his arraignment. The implication, if true, was that Wayne's confessions might be rendered inadmissible as evidence against him. It would prove to be a difficult obstacle for the prosecution to overcome.

In fact, the bottom line was this: If the court found that Wayne had been denied his legal rights when he was arrested, there was a strong possibility that any physical evidence seized by police, including body parts, would be ruled inadmissible. It seemed that he might walk, despite the odds stacked against him.

Another issue raised by defender Robinson was a new serial killer law. It had been enacted about two months after Wayne's arrest. This law allowed prosecutors the right to combine all of the murders into a single trial *if* they could prove that they were related. Thus, instead of Wayne being tried for each murder separately in different counties, he would have just the one trial for all four murders. Whether the law was constitutionally applicable to Wayne's case was a controversial matter because it was enacted *after* the crimes were actually committed.

Nevertheless, on Tuesday, April 6, 1999, Wayne was indicted by a Humboldt County grand jury on a single count of murder. The jury found more than sufficient evidence to move the case to a full trial, but much to the relief of the local taxpayers, he would not be tried in Humboldt County because that June a final decision was made to have Wayne arrested and charged in San Bernardino County for the murder of all four victims. The citizens of San Bernardino would have to foot the bill.

The defense team had lost their first battle, for they now faced the prospect of Wayne getting the death penalty. That August, he was transferred to West Valley Detention Center in San Bernardino to await his upcoming trial.

With the wheels of justice now grinding painfully slowly, in November 2003 a hearing was held at the San Bernardino County Superior Court to determine whether Wayne's confessions to police were admissible in court. This was a cliff-hanger. The defense, now led by attorney Joseph D. Canty, argued that the confessions were the result of unreasonable police actions in the hours and days after Ford surrendered. However, the prosecution maintained that the confessions were legally obtained—that Ford had initially asked for an attorney but later changed his mind.

Superior Court Judge Michael Smith ruled in January 2005 that most of Wayne's confessions would be admissible at trial, but those made after November 5, 1998, two days after Wayne turned himself in, could not be used by the prosecution because the police should have allowed him legal counsel by then. The judge's ruling meant that Wayne's confessions regarding Lanette White were jeopardized. Nevertheless, the prosecution decided that they would likely include the murder charge concerning White at trial because there was adequate evidence linking Wayne to her death.

Almost six years after Wayne's arrest, the murder trial had still not begun because of delays in the legal system. The trial had been moved up on several occasions and was finally scheduled to commence on Monday, March 1, 2004. However, it was stalled once again in mid-January 2004 because the lead prosecutor handling the case, Deputy District Attorney David Whitney, retired from his position. Deputy DA Dave Mazurek was selected to replace Whitney, and it would take some time for the new kid on the block to become familiar with the case against Wayne Ford.

When the case eventually came to trial, with Wayne Ford admitting that he was a serial killer, all that his defense team could do was try to save their client from execution by presenting mitigation for his crimes.

With Judge Michael A. Smith presiding, prosecutor David Mazurek fired off his broadside, determined to shock the jurors with the gravity of the crimes the self-confessed serial killer was accused of committing.

"Mr. Ford gave himself up with a woman's severed breast in his pocket," explained Mazurek, adding, "and this was just the tip of the iceberg."

For their part, the defense team described Ford as a man who knew he had mental problems and sought help when he surrendered to police. "Mr. Ford has a conscience," Canty said, "and he turned himself in because he decided the killings had to stop."

The jury of six men and six women listened intently as Canty explained the root of Ford's problems, complicated by a failed marriage and dwindling chances to see his son, Max. Canty played every card he had, showing the jury a photograph of a pleasant time being had between father and son when they visited a pumpkin patch in October 1997.

"And in fact, this is the last time that Wayne Ford saw his son, Max," Canty said.

The prosecution responded with photographs—colorful and gory crime scene photos of dead bodies, mutilated bodies, white, rotting flesh, the glutinous fat from a victim's breast contained in a coffee jar found in Wayne Ford's possession. They showed the jury indelible images of Lanette Deyon White, whose nude body with blackened head was found floating in an irrigation canal off Highway 12 near Lodi, in San Joaquin County, on September 25, 1998.

"Mr. Ford had killed her a couple of days before," asserted Mazurek, "and he had driven around with her in his truck for a while. Ms. White's head turned black because, lying against the truck's hot floorboards, it decomposed faster."

Canty said that his client cried. "Mr. Ford felt shame and showed moral courage when he turned himself in to sheriff's deputies and gave up details about the deaths of four victims. At the time," added Canty, "the detectives had not solved the deaths, and Ford was not even a suspect"—which implied that his client was doing everyone a favor.

The defense also spoke of Ford's rough upbringing, with photos and descriptions of his mother as "cold" and his father, Gene Ford, as always away from home and striking fear into young Wayne when he did return.

Despite the mental problems, Canty made it clear that Ford was not seeking an insanity defense because he knew the difference between right and wrong. "He was crippled inside," pleaded the attorney. "He was, and he is, a broken man who turned himself in because he wanted to do the right thing."

However, the prosecutor pointed to the deeply depraved way the four women were killed. "Each was raped. Each was tortured. Each was used solely for the defendant's own sexual gratification. Each of the victims was then coldly discarded with no identification, no way to inform police and loved ones of their deaths. . . . Wayne Ford knows what he has done," Mazurek told the jury. "He knows what he is. Despite what he says, not one of these women died accidentally."

On Tuesday, June 27, 2006, Wayne Ford was found guilty of four counts of first-degree murder. Wearing green coveralls and a white T-shirt, the heavily shackled prisoner was sentenced to death in August of that same year. Judge Smith, passing sentence, said:

> Mr. Ford. It is now the judgment and sentence of this court, hereby ordered by judgment and decree for the first degree murders of Jane Doe, Tina Renee Gibbs, Lanette Deyon White, and Patricia Anne Tamez, you are to be put to death by lethal injection, or by any other means which maybe deemed proper, and for it to occur within the walls of San Quentin State Prison.
>
> You are hereby remanded into the custody and control of the San Bernardino County Sheriff's Office, to be delivered by the sheriff within ten days to the warden of the state prison for the execution of this sentence, which of course will not take place anytime soon, and until you have appealed your sentence according to state law.
>
> Good luck to you Mr. Ford.

Being a condemned man does not seem to faze Wayne Ford at all:

> You know, death row doesn't even bother me. I don't even think about it. If I'm executed, you know it's actually more

> than what's supposed to be given to me. But if they kill me, they'll be doing me a favor. I'm not really concerned about it, you know. I don't know what to really say. I don't know what anybody would say under these circumstances. An apology is almost an insult. It's so useless under these circumstances, and if I were them I'd just want to spit in my face. I wish there was just something I could do, and if my death would make them happy, then fine!

When asked by Victoria Redstall, "If you were out right now . . . a free man, would you kill again?" Wayne Ford sighed and responded, "Well, of course I'm going to tell you *no*, aren't I?"

He was also asked what he had learned in his lifetime. He gave the following, somewhat rambling answer:

> Well, I mean that's kind of a broad and vague question. Um, I think mental health is far more important than we give attention to, and it's a lot easier than I think we think it is . . . to take care of. I don't think that people realize how very, very important it is for a father to have his son with him, and his son to have his father. It's a . . . a lot of guys, who are in jail, are in here for that primary reason . . . that they never had a man in their life, and, eh, I think that the stability of a family and not taking the father-son relationship so much for granted is what really needs to be looked at.
>
> I just couldn't handle my baby, Max, going through the same thing that I went through . . . that is wanting my father desperately as a child when I really needed him, and he wasn't there. Unless we change things in our society the way we are going, we're just going to continue to have to lock up more and more people, and mental illness is going to be more and more prevalent.

When Wayne Ford was asked about his thoughts on the afterlife, he came up with this:

> You mean whether I go to heaven or hell? You know, there are lots of possibilities. I tend to believe that we are more than the sum of our parts. I think, me personally . . . I'm going to be an Energy Being when I am released from this body. If the Bible's accurate, and there is monotheist God who created the earth as it states in the Bible, I think I am going to heaven, and the reason being because according to the Bible, Jesus died for our sins and that means if we ask for forgiveness that gift is given to us, and God forgives, and I have [asked for forgiveness] and that entitles me already to the promise in the Bible that says I will be forgiven.
>
> I believe the essence of a person . . . the soul of a person goes to another place after our physical death, and I think that we're in another dimension . . . I think that we're probably back were we started.

This was perhaps the right moment for him to be asked exactly *why* he killed for the first time. The reply from Ford was an emotional and tearful one, although a little disingenuous. He had the clear intention of snatching Max away from his wife, Elizabeth, as the following reveals:

> I had planned on taking Max the day before [he killed for the first time], actually, and I didn't think that it would be legally kidnapping. And I had planned on taking him and fighting from there for custody of Max. And, what happened was . . . just a minute . . . just a minute . . . [now uncontrollably sobbing]. My ex brought Max and she came and spent the day with us, which kind of ruined Max's and my day together, and also it kind of ruined my plan.

Max and I were crawling through this little maze, and Max started to panic in the middle of the hay bales, and he started yelling: "Mommy, Mommy," and I couldn't comfort him.

Max and I didn't have that kind of relationship at that time that he wouldn't be completely traumatized if I took him away because his mother was the only thing stable he had at that point, no matter how shitty she was, and I couldn't take him.

So, I took off in the morning and didn't get to where I met this first victim until midnight. Everything was so surreal to me. There was something wrong with me at this point, ah! And, anyways, I just of ambled there knowing that I had to go to work the next day. And then I meet up with this girl. I really just meant to give her a ride and get a few hours of sleep and go to work. But that's not what happened . . . I'm so sorry for crying right now.

When asked again if he regretted turning himself in, Ford said:

I absolutely do *not*! It was what had to be done! There's just right and wrong! There's no gray lines there. When you think about it, I do not have the right to put anyone else in danger just for my own sake. I didn't know whether I could maintain . . . I thought what was happening to me might end up happening to me, not just little small amounts, but more and more. I was afraid I would lose all control of, eh, conscious thought of what I was doing. So, eh, what choice did I really have? I mean what kind of person could endanger somebody else's life for their own benefit? It's just completely against all of human nature to me.

I don't regret turning myself in . . . even after the conclusion of the trial. I *do not!*

Coroner Glen Sipma: "Identifying any one of our cases, our clients, has been one of our main objectives because we feel that there has to be a closure. We'd like to be able to go to somebody and say we are going to be able to close this case. Actually, the coroner, because a deceased person has nobody else to act for them, we are absolutely the *only* person required to be the advocate of a deceased person. I am still am very hopeful that someday the head [of Jane Doe] will be found because that will help us tremendously in identifying who the victim was." Deputy Coroner Charles Van Buskirk: "I have admiration that Mr. Ford would turn himself in . . . to stop from continuing doing such heinous things and that he would want to subject himself to the legal system. I am sure that it was a very difficult thing to do, and it is wonderful that he did that to stop himself from killing again, even perhaps again and again."

Pastor James Ray: "Wayne Ford asked me a question: 'Do you think God would forgive me?' And, I asked him, 'Do you feel any remorse?' He said: 'All the time, all the time,' and I said, 'Forgiveness is possible.' You know, the scriptures say, 'Who the Lord makes free, is free,' and even if you are in prison you don't have to be bound. You know there are people outside who are bound more than many in prison. To really know that Christ is a forgiving God, you will know that some of the greatest men in the Bible were murderers. I wouldn't recommend it. I would not advocate that to anyone, but, eh, Moses was a murderer. David was a murderer. Paul was a murderer . . . he was on his way to

Damascus with papers to kill Christians, yet he still wrote over two-thirds of the New Testament."

Dr. Paul Berg: "If he were to be released, I am sure that he would kill again."

Bill White, father of 25-year-old victim Lanette Deyon White: "Wayne Ford? I would like to see the bastard hang. Let him see how it feels like not breathing air."

We find, in Wayne Adam Ford, a rather unusual, if not unique serial killer. He is a man who metamorphosed from an innocent child to serve, though for a very short period, as a United States Marine; a man who suffered a traumatic head injury—an accident that undoubtedly changed his mental faculties and personality for the worse—and an individual who ultimately destroyed the lives of four women, leaving a trail of irreversible heartbreak in his wake.

For my part, I have no sympathy for Wayne Adam Ford at all. Without being presumptuous, I would hazard a guess that not too many readers of this chapter would have any sympathy, either. We have seen the mitigation cards, so often played by these predators who deal them out time and time again before sentencing. It just doesn't wash.

That Wayne committed his first murder because he felt that his son should not be brought up like he allegedly had, and that he had been deprived of access to his son, does not pass muster. Perhaps, if Wayne had truly wanted his son to be with him someday, he should have pulled his socks up and started acting like a responsible father. Abducting, raping, torturing, and killing four women was not, at least in my mind, the way to go about it.

To her credit, we have not heard a word from the former Mrs. Elizabeth Ford. Maybe she simply does not want her boy to learn of the atrocities carried out by his dad. However, Elizabeth *is* on record with Social Services as showing a great interest in having Max relate and visit with his father. According to the documents, Wayne Ford was "not that interested . . . he was a non-existent father." That Elizabeth wanted to be in attendance on visitations, she argues, was perfectly acceptable, considering the violence and control heaped upon her by her estranged husband. But with her track record, are we able to believe *anything* this woman says?

According to Wayne Ford, he idolized his son. According to him, he desperately wanted to see his boy as much as possible. "I loved that boy with all my heart," says Ford, "and that *woman—cunt* took the one thing I loved from me, *my son*!"

However, what we *can* determine, with 100 percent accuracy, is that Wayne Ford targeted hookers. Killing is one thing, hacking up their bodies is another. But to take parts of their bodies away with him . . . in two instances, a breast or two, is something else entirely. And we would be right to ask, "Why?"

Conveniently for Wayne Ford, he gives us no explanation; for he has no explanation that would satisfy even the most empathetic psychologist, psychiatrist, or any interested party, aside from the likes of the late Jeffrey Dahmer and his ilk. No one has ever asked him: "Why did you store the rendered fat from two breasts in a coffee jar?"

Pastor James Ray has a few thoughts of his own:

> Why do they [serial killers] choose prostitutes to be their victims? In my mind they see these women as probably

someone that has belittled motherhood and the marriage relationship and possibly they are a little angry because of that.

Of course, not all serial killers "get a *little* angry" and target prostitutes, as the yellowing pages of criminal history will testify. Some kill little boys, others little girls, or boys and girls. Some target the elderly, some murder young men, while others, like Ted Bundy, set their sights on dark-haired, coed look-alikes. Many serial killers wipe out complete families in their homes.

Female hitchhikers and street prostitutes, by the very nature of their work, simply make convenient and easy pickings for a subgroup of killers; Michael Bruce Ross, Arthur Shawcross, Gary Leon Ridgway, Joel Rifkin, and Peter Sutcliffe, like Wayne Ford, are in this group. Yet while these men may have a common target type, their motives for killing are often vastly different, and not all of them zero in on hookers or lonely hitchhikers because they harbor an underlying hatred for their mother or because they enjoyed a less than perfect marriage. Indeed, I will go a step further by referring to the serial murderer Keith Hunter Jesperson, who says, without any frills or shiny bells, "I killed eight women simply because they were disposable and they pissed me off." No bullshit from Keith. No namby-pamby excuses at all. Not a hint of remorse from Keith, who adds, "And I don't give a flying fuck."

Common among serial killers, however, is a psychopathic denial of guilt. On the face of it, Wayne becomes the exception because he turned himself in and confessed all. He *seems* remorseful. He comes across as feeling sorry for what he has done. How perversely contrite! Yet, in the same breath, he transfers all the blame for his antisocial behavior onto his upbringing—his parents, his road accident, his relationships with women, and finally Elizabeth, the mother of his only son. Wayne actually believes that everyone else is at fault, and being the "martyr to moral values" that he now professes to be from behind grim prison walls, he gave himself up because he didn't want to "hurt" anyone else again.

"Hurt"? This man Ford took young, defenseless women off the streets, used them, abused them, terrified them, and subjected them to a ride of terror that not even Stephen King could invent. He raped them and beat them. He strangled them to death, after which he methodically cut their bodies into pieces, selecting the choicest cuts to take away with him. Two of the breasts he cooked . . . another he placed in his freezer, probably to masturbate over later. And God only knows what he kept the rendered breast fat for . . .

What human artifacts Wayne did keep he buried in damp holes in the ground or dumped in slow-moving water like so much trash, to float away—the result being to scare the living daylights out of a couple of duck hunters and a security guard whose main job had simply been to stroll along a peaceful river bank.

Mr. Ford *really* does have a lot more explaining to do, and perhaps his second wife does, too! But what are the chances that Wayne Adam Ford will be executed?

A 2008 report by the 22-member California Commission on the Fair Administration of Justice said that the state's death row population of 670 inmates—the largest in the nation—will continue to swell unless the state nearly doubles what it now spends on attorneys for inmates. The system is "dysfunctional and close to collapse," the report argued. "It is plagued by delays of nearly twice the national average from sentencing to execution, and drowning under a backlog of cases."

While the commission did not advocate abolishing the death penalty, it did note that California could save $100 million a year if the state replaced the punishment with sentences of life without the possibility of parole. "Death row prisoners cost more to confine, are granted more resources for appeals, have more expensive trials, and usually die in prison," the report claimed.

Thirty inmates have been on California's death row more than 25 years, 119 for more than 20 years, and 240 for more than 15 years; therefore, Wayne Adam Ford has a long wait before he meets his maker. Indeed, the California Supreme Court has such a backlog of appeals that only *one* appeal from a conviction after 1997 has been resolved. In point of fact, it takes an average of 12 years to obtain a state high court ruling on their first trials.

Death sentence appeals in California are mandatory, and Mr. Ford is appealing his sentence; upon what grounds is unknown at the present time. However, 14 people convicted in the state between 1989 through 2003 were later exonerated. Six death row inmates who won new trials were acquitted or had their charges dismissed for lack of evidence.

Since 1978, only 13 individuals have been executed in California—averaging around two a year. The most recent occurred at 12:38 a.m., Tuesday, January 17, 2006 (under former Governor Arnold Schwarzenegger's watch), when Clarence Ray Allen was put to death for the murders of Byron Schletewitz, Josephine Rocha, and Douglas White. Allen spent a staggering 28 years behind bars before he received a lethal injection, while running up a tab for the taxpayer of millions of dollars in appeals and upkeep.

And, for the benefit of my death row train spotters, Mr. Allen was 76 years old when he was executed, earning him the meritorious distinction of becoming the second-oldest inmate to be put to death in the U.S. since 2005. First prize goes to hired hit man John B. Nixon from Tennessee, who shot to death Virginia Tucker on January 2, 1985. Nixon spent 19 years on death row. Gray-haired, he was strapped to the gurney at age 77.

Since the reinstatement of the death penalty in California, at the time of writing 38 condemned inmates have died of natural causes. Not surprisingly, 14 have committed suicide. Ninety-eight have left death row because their convictions or sentences were overturned. So even if some miracle did occur, Wayne Ford is going to have to wait at least 16 years for a reprieve, or commutation of sentence, while using up a hefty million of the taxpayers' hard-earned dollars. Furthermore, this vast sum does not include the cost of keeping Ford incarcerated—a tidy $35,587 per annum. But at least the California citizens who do support the death penalty will be relieved to learn that it costs a mere $87 for the drugs that might one day kill him. Chances are, he will probably outlive most of us.

***

CHAPTER 4

ROBERT "BOBBY" JOE LONG—THE BABY-FACED KILLER

Once I've done a crime, I just forget it. I go from crime to crime.

—HENRY LEE LUCAS

IF ANYONE IS A TEXTBOOK SEXUAL PSYCHOPATH, it has to be Bobby Joe Long. Indeed, it is as if serial killing is in his blood, for he is a distant cousin of the notorious serial killer, the late Henry Lee Lucas,[9] who confessed and then recanted, to committing hundreds of murders. And just like Lucas, Bobby Joe had also suffered numerous blows to the head: a fall from a swing; a fall from his bicycle; a fall from a pony; and he only barely survived a serious motorcycle crash.

In addition, Bobby was gene-damaged. He was found to have an extra X chromosome that had produced abnormal amounts of estrogen—which enlarged his breasts—during puberty. To make matters worse, he had slept in his mother's bed until he was 13, and when he finally married, his wife nagged and dominated him, which, as one might appreciate, caused him to suffer blinding headaches and earaches. All of

9 Henry Lee Lucas died of heart failure on March 13, 2001.

this was topped by a driving obsession for kinky sex, as well as the ability to have sex repeatedly with any woman he came across. He was, and still is, priapic.

At age 19, Bobby Joe Long sported a mop of brown hair; today, gray-haired at 55, he remains strikingly hazel-eyed. Six feet tall in his socks, he tips the scales at 202 pounds. He still wears an easy, open smile. He has mischievous twinkle in his eye. Indeed, at first glance he looks the epitome of the all-American boy, the guy living next door to you. Yet he is a "dead man walking," just waiting to meet his executioner. Until that day comes, his earthly address is inmate # 494041, Death Row, Union Correctional Institute, 7819 N.W. 228th Street, Raiford, FL 32026-4000.

Long is always wondering what you are thinking about him and trying, with varying degrees of subtlety but almost unerring effectiveness, to nudge your thoughts in other particular, self-serving directions. If you are a guy asking him a question, he will usually tell you to "Fuck off!" But if you happen to be female, things can go two ways. To some women, Bobby quickly steers his subject matter toward perverted sado-sex, as this chapter proves through his correspondence with small-town Kentuckian murder groupie Annabel Leigh.[10] However, with British-born-and-bred Victoria Redstall he kept things on an even keel—a gentleman, no less—all of which leaves us with a puzzle to solve with this Dr. Jekyll and Mr. Hyde character. Which side of Mr. Long is the real person—the sexual pervert or the charming gent?

So, to help us decide, we now put this killer under the glass, perhaps to analyze him with the fascination of a botanist studying a blowfly preserved in amber.

---

10 Name changed to protect her identity.

Nineteen-year-old self-proclaimed murder groupie Annabel Leigh wrote to Bobby Joe, and from the outset she was deluged with some of the worst filth and perverted writing imaginable. Of course, she encouraged the man, there is no doubt about that, and a sample of the shockingly disturbing letters sent to her by this killer are published in this book.

But as mentioned previously, Bobby Joe Long has also corresponded with true crime writer Victoria Redstall, and his letters to her show a completely different Bobby Long.

On the face of it, Annabel Leigh seems to fit this psychopath's victim type. With a hard-on most of the time, he constantly trolled for "dates" with hookers (although there is no suggestion whatsoever that Annabel Leigh is or has ever been a prostitute), and he frequented strip clubs. In addition to beating them, strangling them, mutilating, and killing them, he also treated these women like dirt. He would use them and abuse them as he wished. There was never any respect. To him they were street trash, enabling him, in his own mind, to justifiably satisfy his darkest fantasies, and this is proven in his correspondence with Annabel Leigh.

The flip side of the coin, the other side of Bobby Joe Long, manifests itself in his dealings with the completely respectable Victoria Redstall. To Bobby Joe Long, here was a woman whom he *could* respect. He recognized "class" in Victoria while perceiving Annabel Leigh as "trash." Harsh labels, indeed, but if we are to try to understand what makes serial killers tick, we need to get inside their heads and find out exactly what's going on there.

But there is another dimension to consider as well, for late one night Bobby Joe Long also abducted a thoroughly decent young woman cycling home from work. He kept Lisa McVey prisoner in his home for several days. He raped her, subjected her to a terrifying ordeal, told her he loved her, then he set her free, probably knowing that doing so would end his killing spree. It seems that he brutally murdered prostitutes, but the one non-hooker he snatched from the streets, he released to live another day. Yet that's not even it, because there were two non-hookers, the second being Elizabeth Loudenback, whom he killed.

So, here is the enigma. Did Annabel Leigh bring out the *real* sicko in Bobby Joe Long? In considering this man's history, I believe she accomplished it in spades.

Did Victoria expose the false mask Bobby Joe Long wears—the facade of "apparent normalcy" that allowed him to convince hookers that he was no threat; that it was safe for them to get into his car? Did this mask allow him, under the pretense of buying furniture, to enter housewives' homes when they were vulnerable and alone?

It seems to me that, in their own different ways, both Annabel and Victoria, from completely opposite walks of life, whatever their motives, contributed something unique to the study of criminology.

Victoria Redstall makes this quite chilling observation:

> Annabel and I each got a different side of this guy. Each of us found the Bobby Joe Long we would have met outside of prison walls. Maybe he would not have killed me, but I would hazard a guess that Annabel might have met a different fate.

Of course, not all of Long's victims were pole dancers, prostitutes, or murder groupies, far from it, for this is a man who would scan newspaper want ads looking for perfectly decent women, alone at home, whom he could brutally rape and abuse. So, without wishing to take issue with Victoria on her observation, what might have happened to her had she placed an ad for furniture in a local newspaper and Long had knocked on her door?

Whatever the case, Victoria and Annabel found the same Dr. Jekyll and Mr. Hyde entity living in the head of another serial killer, Keith Hunter Jesperson. Victoria, who is researching the life and crimes of Jesperson for a TV series pilot, found the "decent" Keith, while Annabel, who wrote sleazy stuff to him while flaunting her kinky sex and photographs of her scantily dressed body, brought out the perverted side of this man. The question is, however, which of these entities is the real Keith Jesperson, or is he a mix of the two? But more of Keith later.

So, we have good reason to wonder about Bobby Joe Long. Dubbed by the media as the Classified Ad Rapist, Bobby Joe has good reason to wonder about himself, too. Wonder, perhaps, about the long road he traveled, which will result in him hitting a stop sign in the form of his execution by lethal injection. Long's twisted character is rife with the kind of paradoxes that can frustrate introspection. Here is a man who had chosen a life that required the discipline of a professional serial killer. He was a human predator, and like a heat-seeking missile, he zeroed in on his targets with pinpoint accuracy, raining down death and destruction again and again.

So who was Bobby Joe Long, and where did he come from?

By all accounts, the founding fathers who named the settlement of Kenova, West Virginia in 1869, were an imaginative bunch, for owing to their unique position between Kentucky, Ohio, and West Virginia, they doodled a little, supped some more moonshine, shouted "Eureka!" and, with an ink-dipped quill, penned "Kenova!"

Born October 14, 1953, in Kenova City, Wayne County, in the Mountain State, to an abusive prostitute mother, Bobby Joe went on to commit some 50 rapes and 10 murders in the Tampa Bay area of Florida. All of the women were killed during an eight-month period in 1984. Nevertheless, we begin Bobby Joe's story in 1966.

> I'd look after you, babe, probably in ways you've never really imagined being *taken care* of sweetheart!
>
> —Bobby Joe Long
> letter to Annabel Leigh

Bobby Joe Long and a girl known to us only as Cathy were just 13 years old when they first met. Drawn to each other because they'd both come from broken homes, they became inseparable. For the first time in his life, Long writes in correspondence, he "felt wanted." He says that he had met someone with whom he could share the shameful stories of his flimsily dressed barmaid mother bringing home men, and of the rage he felt toward her. Bobby and Cathy dated for six years before marrying in January 1974.

Long told this author that at age 15 he started work as an "electrician's helper, working in the Miami summer heat, basically at slave labor, ditch-digger, pipe-bender-threader, wire-puller, and gofer." By the time he was 17, he says, he was running his own electrical service truck and employing a helper.

At age 21, we find Bobby Joe stationed at the Homestead Air Force Base, Miami, Florida. There, he says, he was in "fire control for 90 MIM-14 Nike-Hercules surface-to-air missiles in the Air Defense Artillery." Then a motorcycle accident changed his life forever. His machine was struck by a car, and he sustained severe injuries, including a serious blow to his head. And, this was not his first head injury; he had already suffered multiple traumas caused by his abusive mother during his childhood and adolescence. To make matters worse, the motorcycle accident threatened him with the loss of a leg, a fate he narrowly missed. Nevertheless, the entire episode transformed Bobby Joe in a way that would wreck not only his world but the lives of others. His victims, their families, indeed an entire community would suffer at the hands of Bobby Joe Long.

Discharged from the army, unemployed Long found himself plagued by an increased and insatiable sex drive. He would masturbate five or six times a day. The thought of sex consumed him, and it was then that he devised the idea of using classified newspaper ads to locate women, turn up on their doorsteps, and rape them. It is claimed by those who have researched Long's case that he went on to commit about 50 rapes in total. Although the true number of rapes may never be known, his MO was soon tried, tested, and well established.

Long started making a large number of telephone calls to people who had placed classified ads. In particular, he was pretending to seek bedroom furniture, which Long later explained was because one would have to try it out before purchase. He also targeted properties that bore "For Sale" signs, often forcing his way in when the door was shut in his face and committing rape. A few times, he attacked girls as young as 12 and 13.

After he found an advertisement that suited his purpose, Long would telephone and arrange to look at the piece of furniture during the day, at a time when husbands or boyfriends would most likely be at work. If a man was at home, he could always decline to buy the item and walk away. More often than not, women on their own answered the door, and they often let him in because he came across as a clean-cut, well-dressed, respectable young guy.

Bobby Joe fine-tuned his MO in neighborhoods surrounding Ocala, Miami, and Fort Lauderdale. When a woman opened the door and appeared to be alone, Bobby Joe would pull his knife and bind and rape his victim, often robbing her before he fled.

Years later, Long said, "A few of them got into it, and they even asked me if I minded if they enjoy it [the rape]." He went on to add that while he raped them, he made them talk to him. Most did not resist, he claimed, but those who did received a punch in the stomach that showed that he meant business. "Give a bitch a choice between getting dicked and getting hurt," he said, "you know what she's gonna pick."

In his warped opinion, Bobby Joe said that he was, "doing them a favor because they lived such miserable sex lives with their husbands." The fact that he had had no previous contact or knowledge of his victims' social and domestic lives before he saw their newspaper advertisements had not crossed his mind, or so he would have us believe. Indeed, after his arrest Long claimed that had he not started to kill, he could have kept up his rapist activity indefinitely. To him, it seemed a foolproof MO, and he got a kick out of reading newspaper accounts that labeled the mysterious man as the "Classified Ad Rapist" or the "Adman Rapist."

In a letter to Victoria Redstall (the grammatical errors are all his), he says:

> Of course there's been women in my life I've "respected," and, even *liked*!! Don't know where people got the quote where I'm *supposed* to have said that, "All American women are whores/sluts" . . . because I *don't* think that. *Never* have. Just been my bad luck, I've run into *more* than my share. And *crazy* to boot!
>
> I done some bad things in my life. Hurt a lot of people. I admit it. I have no reason to lie. Can I tell you, early on, I've had 3 crazy cunts try *to set me up* for rape? That's just how my "luck" with females has gone. So, because they got a little more than they bargained for . . . "WAAAH! He raped me!!" Well, 2 of 'em did that to me. The 3red was just a crazy bitch, mad because when I was stupid enough to move in with her, I took off after 3 weeks! That one tried to set me up, *good!* Miserable cunt! Too bad I got locked up. Always meant to track her down, years later, and explain how I really felt about that.

Although he was still married to Cathy, priapic Bobby Joe started sharing a house with a woman named Sharon Richards. Of her we know literally nothing except to suggest that this seems to have been a mutually agreeable, volatile, booze-fueled relationship—one, as any sensible person might envisage, destined to end in failure.

In October 1981, Sharon accused Bobby Joe of rape. The police, however, did not have enough evidence to press charges. Two weeks passed, and then she alleged that he hit her during another drunken argument. The police were called again. This time 28-year-old Long was arrested. He bonded out to stay with his parents in Kenova, a city on a spit at the confluence of the Ohio and Big Sandy Rivers.

In June 1983, Bobby Joe returned to Florida, where he took up work as an X-ray technician at the Humana Women's Hospital in Tampa. Around that time, he also claims to have "got a Degree in Diagnostic Radiologic Technology . . . got Certified as an Air/Mixed Gas, Bell/Saturation Commercial Diver, etc. . . . then got a P.A.D.I. Certification, and a job as a dive instructor on a cruise ship," which he says was his "best job ever."

Bobby Joe Long refers to Baja, Mexico, as being "pretty damn nice commercial diving," adding, "I was diving along the Pacific Coast off Southern California and Baja, Mexico." He says that it was, "basically, hard, manual labor underwater, very deep at 1,600 ft maximum, breathing a Heliox gas, wearing a hard helmet, diving bells, etc."

After hearing all this from Bobby Long, one might be forgiven for thinking that he is telling fairy tales, but it seems that he is telling some truth, for this author spoke to one of the UK's top divers, who says that, apart from the depth of 1,600 feet, Long could not have invented his diving experience.

A friend of the late John Bennett, who still holds the world record at 308 meters (about 1,010 feet), my source confirmed that perhaps Long's exaggerated depth as a PADI-certified (Professional Association of Diving Instructors) diver is 100 meters (328 feet) too deep, and he could never have survived.[11] In fact, 1,600 feet can only be reached by full-saturation divers, and Bobby Joe Long makes no mention of being certified in this profession at all, where the world record is held at 1,752 feet.

---

11 John Bennett went missing off the coast of Korea in 2004. His body has never been found.

Bobby Joe relocated to Florida, were he met a woman named Emma. They started courting. Emma, a religious Bible-thumper, encouraged him to attend church. For his part she seemed ideal, and he was soon showering her with the jewelry he had stolen from his rape victims. Of course, Emma knew nothing of her lover's criminal activity, so it must have come as a devastating blow to her when he revealed that he had to attend court on sexual assault charges stemming from the 1981 incident involving Sharon Richards. He was found guilty and given a suspended sentence.

Bobby Joe was furious at the guilty verdict. He reasoned that it took two to tango and that at least half the blame for the assault on Sharon Richards lay with her. And to give him his due, it has to be said that Sharon was indeed a feisty character, with or without drink inside her. Further, it was also commonly known that she packed a pretty solid punch, as testified by many a local man whom she had displaced from the vertical position to the horizontal in the blink of an eye.

So we find Mr. Long seething with rage and writing lengthy letters to the judge demanding a new trial. But Bobby Joe came unstuck again when, in November 1983, he was charged with sending an obscene letter and equally obscene photographs to a 12-year-old girl in Tampa. Officials had also traced phone calls Long had made to the girl, and he received a sentence of two days in jail with six months' probation.[12]

---

12 As a footnote to the 1981 saga, Bobby Joe eventually earned a retrial. In 1984 he was acquitted of the assault charge against Ms. Richards, despite the testimony of a number of witnesses against him, the majority of whom were her immediate, somewhat inbred and equally drink-dependant family.

On Tuesday, March 6, 1984, Bobby Joe broke into a woman's home and raped her at gunpoint. For these offenses he would, on June 17, 1985, receive four 99-year sentences. However, during the interim period on bail, Sunday, March 11, 1984, he was found again attempting to kidnap a woman in her Jaguar car at the point of a pistol. Valiantly, she outsmarted him by deliberately crashing her vehicle.

After being arrested and scheduled to face charges in July, he made bail yet again, and it was at this point that Bobby Joe decided any future victims would *not* be allowed to live long enough to level accusations against him.

Artis Wick

Tuesday, March 27, 1984 was the day Bobby Joe Long made a transformation. It was the date from which he could never turn back, for it was the day he picked up 20-year-old Artis Wick in Tampa. After raping her, he found himself "strangely unsatisfied." Rather than let her go free, as he had his other victims, he strangled her to death.

Artis Wick's skeletonized remains were found in a rural area on Thursday, November 22, 1984. Long was never charged, much less convicted, of this crime.

Ngeun Thi Long

Bobby Joe now believed that he had discovered the perfect method to guarantee he would not get caught for his crimes. On Thursday, May 10, 1984, while working as an electrician, he spotted a petite young woman with dark, shoulder-length hair, wearing shorts and a tank top, as she strolled along North Nebraska Avenue in Tampa.

Ngeun Thi Long, aka "Lana Long," was a 20-year-old Laotian who worked as an exotic dancer at the Sly Fox Lounge nearby. She normally worked the evening shift and was a known alcohol and drug user. It is believed that Bobby Joe had visited the club that evening and spoken to her. She was desperate to earn money to return to California, and it is believed that she approached Bobby Joe asking for cash. Whatever the case, he stopped his car and offered her a lift. She accepted, and only moments later, her ride turned into a trip to hell.

Driving to a wooded area off North 22nd Street, Bobby Joe pulled over, ordered Lana to strip naked and forced her to lie face down on the front seat. Then he tied her hands behind her back. With the woman unable to move and too terrified to cry out, he drove 25 miles along Route 301 to Symmes Road, then onto East Bay Road, where at the end of a track he turned into a field and raped her. After a desperate but futile fight for her life, she died with a rope knotted around her neck. He dumped the body where she had expired and fled the scene.

Late in the afternoon of Mother's Day, Sunday, May 12, Hillsborough County Sheriff's officers Captain Garry Terry and Detective Lee Baker responded to a report of a body being found. Two boys had discovered the deceased female lying face down and infested with maggots. A white silk cloth was found under her face, apparently used as a gag. Her hands had been loosely tied with rope, about eight inches apart, behind her back, and a different type of rope, approximately 14 inches in length, had been wrapped three times, leash-fashion, around her neck. The victim's legs were spread five feet apart—wider than she was tall. Her killer had cruelly broken them at the hips to allow them to be pulled out at right angles to the body. There was also a large gash in her head. The only other physical clues were tire impressions—three of which were different tread patterns—and some red Triobal Bright fibers, probably from the seat of a vehicle.

At autopsy, Medical Examiner Charles Digg determined that she had died as the result of strangulation. She had also been raped.

Michelle Denise Simms

Two weeks later, at approximately 11:30 a.m., on Sunday, May 27, 1984, the naked body of a young, attractive, dark-haired, white female was discovered by a construction worker in East Park Circle—a lovers' lane some six miles from where she had been picked up by Bobby Joe Long. Apart from a green T-shirt, which had been pulled up in front and back, the remainder of her clothing (a bloodstained white jumper and white panty hose) was found hanging in a tree near the body. She lay on her back with her hands loosely bound at the waist. There was a hangman's noose, again leash-fashion, around the neck. Her cheeks had been slashed. Her throat had been cut in a massive wound almost 12 inches long. She had sustained multiple trauma injuries to the head.

At the crime scene, detectives found a single red Triobal Bright fiber near her left breast. There were several strands of hair on her stomach and under her right hand. Other evidence was a bare footprint in the soil, and tire tracks—one of which was a Vogue, an expensive tire made exclusively for Cadillac. The right rear tire was determined to be a Goodyear Viva with the whitewall facing inward. These matched exactly the tire impressions found at the first murder scene. Therefore, combined with the rest of the evidence, it was enough to suggest to police that the same man had murdered both Ngeun "Lana" Thi Long and this unidentified victim. Moreover, officials now had a Caucasian hair and semen stains showing the presence of both H and B blood substances. They were not hairs from the victim.

At autopsy, it was estimated that this woman, who was probably in her late teens, stood 5 feet 5 inches tall and weighed 119 pounds. She had been dead for about 12 hours. Having suffered five brutal blows to the head, she had been raped, stabbed, slashed across the cheeks, then strangled.

As the victim was unidentified, a composite drawing of her face was released to the media. She was identified as 22-year-old Michelle Denise Simms, a former California beauty pageant contestant who had turned to prostitution to support her $1,000-a-week cocaine habit. Ironically, Simms had only been in Tampa a couple days. She had last been seen alive about 24 hours earlier, talking with two white males near Kennedy Boulevard, a known hangout for hookers, seven miles due south from where Ngeun Thi Long had been abducted.

Bobby Long would later tell police that he'd hit Michelle over the head after an unsuccessful attempt at strangling her because he didn't want her to "suffer when I stabbed her."

To maximize efforts to catch the killer, all of the evidential information was shared with other law enforcement agencies. The Hillsborough County Sheriff's Office sent a detailed description of the crimes to the FBI Behavioral Science Services

Unit in Quantico, Virginia, for an analysis of the murders, and they requested a detailed profile of the killer.

As former FBI Agent Robert Ressler states in his excellent book, *Whoever Fights Monsters*, "Profilers don't catch killers, cops on the beat do," but it is also true that offender profiles are investigative tools that can narrow the search for a killer.

During the early course of the Bobby Joe Long homicide investigation, several FBI agents worked up a profile of the unknown killer's probable background and personality traits. I have selected FBI Special Agent Flowers's profile, shown below, and based on the known facts:

> The victims had to depend on others for transportation.
>
> The victims were essentially nude when found.
>
> The victims had been similarly bound, while one (Ngeun Thi Long) was posed.
>
> They had been picked up in Tampa.
>
> They had been left near interstate highways in rural areas.
>
> There were similar tire impressions at the first two crime scenes.
>
> They were found at quite a distance from where they had last been seen alive.
>
> Red carpet fiber confirmed the relationship of the crimes.

It may seem obvious, but from these suppositions, one is able to determine that the killer used a specific vehicle. Whether he owned the car or it was one that he had borrowed or rented was unknown; nevertheless, it was unlikely to be a rental because the vehicle was fitted with three different tire tread patterns. We know it was a car, not a truck, because the Vogue tire was exclusively made for Cadillacs.

The leash-like hangman's-noose-type rope ligatures around the victims' necks and the brutal beatings that exceeded what was required to kill them were overkill. This showed an enhanced type of sexual deviance. Furthermore, it seemed highly likely that the victims had been randomly selected because they were easy prey, rather than women known to the killer. Unfortunately, of course, history tells us that prostitutes fall easy prey to serial murderers.

Agent Flowers went on to say:

> He [the killer] was deemed to be a white male, in his mid-20s, gregarious, extroverted, and manipulative. In general, he seemed to be what they classify as "organized." He would operate normally in society, but he would be argumentative, self-centered, and exhibit little or no emotion—all common traits of the psychopath/sociopath. Being narcissistic, he would want to be the center of attention. He would also be impulsive, albeit not sufficiently so to risk being caught. It was likely that he lied easily and had a macho self-image. He might even have tattoos to that effect, and carry a weapon as a statement of his manhood.

The Florida Department of Corrections' file on Bobby Joe Long does not indicate whether or not Mr. Long has tattoos, but in every other respect Agent Flowers is almost on the button:

> At best, he'd have a high school education. If he'd even tried college, it was likely that he'd had trouble adjusting to

> the discipline and would have dropped out. He would be intelligent but have issues with authority. He may have been a truant and disruptive. In keeping with his self-image, he would probably take masculine jobs where his manipulative skills would be useful. He probably had trouble holding down a job and would have had multiple short-term employments.
>
> As a child, he probably was delinquent and difficult to control, and exhibited resentment toward efforts to impose discipline. He may have a history of bedwetting, arson, and animal cruelty.
>
> If he had served in the military, he would have joined a masculine unit, such as the Marine Corps. Even here, his issues with authority would have gotten him into confrontations.

However, there is no confirmed history of Bobby Joe Long being a child delinquent or difficult to control. There is no history of enuresis, or truancy.

Agent Flowers:

> On the issue of relationships, and in the tradition of organized killers, he probably would have a woman in his life. He would date regularly, but not have long-term commitments. He would brag about his sexual exploits, and probably date younger women. If married, he would be unfaithful, and his chosen type of woman would be dependent and easily controlled.
>
> His car of choice would be flashy, like a sports car.
>
> It was also likely that he would have a prison record, or some record of problems with the law. Prior to these murders, he may have committed neighborhood crimes,

> such as voyeurism or burglary. Yet if he was ever in jail, he would have been a model albeit manipulative prisoner.
>
> In these crimes, he was sadistic: he probably used some scheme to lure the women into his car, and then proceed to torture them mentally and physically, keeping them alive for some period of time. He would leave little or no evidence behind. In all likelihood, he would kill again.

As far as offender profiles go, Agent Flowers had more or less hit the nail on the head. Unfortunately, before the FBI could find the man who fit Flowers's description, the murderer killed again.

Elizabeth B. Loudenback

Aged 18, shy, bespectacled, dark-haired Elizabeth was employed as an assembly-line worker. Liz had last been seen alive on Thursday, June 7, 1984, when she left the trailer park home that she shared with her mother, stepfather, sister, and brother, in the Village Mobile Home Park.

Although known to wander around the red light district of Nebraska Avenue and Skipper Road, Elizabeth had no criminal history. Indeed, the Florida Department of Law Enforcement has confirmed to the author that she was most certainly not a prostitute. She had never been brought to the attention of police. She was not a drug addict, a hitchhiker, or an erotic dancer.

On Sunday, June 24, a body was found in an orange grove in Brandon, southeastern Hillsborough County. The corpse was fully clothed and in an advanced state of decomposition—the total body weight, including her clothes, was only 25 pounds.

There were no ligatures present and, in this instance, the victim was not found near an interstate highway as the first two victims had been.

Initially, Elizabeth's boyfriend became the prime suspect. He failed a lie detector test. And, because the location of the crime scene and the state of the victim differed from the victimology of the first two murders, no attempt was made to submit the evidence to the FBI for comparison purposes until much later. Then, and only then, were red fibers recovered from the victim's clothing and found to match those found on both Ngeun Thi Long and Simms.

Bobby Joe Long later admitted that he had offered Elizabeth a ride along Nebraska Avenue. He said that he had pulled out a knife, then ordered her to remove her pants. He tied her up, forced her face down on the reclined front seat of his car and raped her. Then he drove to the orange grove, where he savagely raped her from behind. When he had finished, he did something quite different: he untied her, told her to get dressed, and returned with her to his car.

Bobby Joe claimed that he had not intended to kill her, but that her incessant crying forced him to change his mind. His patience snapped. He dragged her, screaming for mercy, from the car, and then he strangled her with a rope before heaving the body into shrubs.

Again he deviated from his usual MO. As he drove away, he searched through her purse, finding an ATM card with the four-digit pin number in an envelope. Over the next few hours, Bobby Joe Long used the card to withdraw cash from several banks before throwing it away.

Vicky Elliott

On Thursday, September 6, 1984, the manager of a Tampa Ramada Inn coffee shop became concerned when one of his staff, the habitually punctual 21-year-old Vicky Elliott, failed to turn up for her 11 p.m. shift.

Two days later, police searched Vicky's apartment. Here they found an airline ticket indicating that the vivacious young woman had intended to return home to her parents in Muskegon, Michigan, in two weeks. This, of course, suggested to police that her disappearance was not intentional—that something was truly amiss.

It would be two months before her parents' prayers that their daughter would return to them safe and well were shattered completely. Vicky's remains were found floating in a river on Sunday, September 23, 1984.

Bobby Joe Long would later direct police to the location where he had dumped Vicky's body. He stated that he had killed her after she had tried to fight him off with a pair of scissors.

The autopsy revealed that Vicky had suffered a broken hyoid bone. The scissors were still inserted in her vaginal cavity. Police also found red carpet fibers, which, once again, linked her to Bobby Joe Long and the previous murders.

Chanel Devon Williams

Eighteen-year-old black prostitute Chanel Devon Williams was known to frequent a gay bar on Kennedy Boulevard in Tampa. She had last been seen alive on the night of Sunday, September

30, 1984, by another hooker with whom she had been working. The pair had been soliciting in the area of Nebraska Avenue when Chanel's companion was picked up by a john. They were two-tenths of a mile from the motel where they conducted business, so Williams's colleague rode back to the motel in her client's car, while Chanel walked slowly back to the premises to check on her friend's welfare. She never arrived.

The Florida Department of Law Enforcement confirms:

> On Sunday, October 14, 1984, Chanel Williams's naked body was discovered, by a stockman, near the Pasco/Hillsborough County line. The remains had been pushed under a barbed wire fence and [were] lying close to the dirt entrance of a cattle ranch. Her bra, which had been tied in a knot, was found hanging from a gate, her panties were draped on a five-strand wire fence. The head was infested with maggot activity and in an advanced state of decomposition—much more so than the remainder of the body. Her wrists and her legs had been tied with a long, thick boot lace.

Although it was evident that she had been beaten around the head, an autopsy revealed that a gunshot wound to the neck was the cause of death. Chanel had also been raped and strangled.

FBI lab technicians found two different types of red Triobal carpet fibers on her clothing, a brown Caucasian public hair on her sweater, and semen stains that contained both A and H blood group substances.

Identifying the body proved a relatively easy task. Chanel had just been released from jail for soliciting, and her fingerprints were on record. She had only just moved to Tampa to escape the mundane life of her nearby town of Bartow, just 56 miles to the west, and with no qualifications to speak of, she saw prostitution as the only means to generate enough money to provide her with the life she had always wanted.

Bobby Joe Long later told police that he had picked up Chanel. Then he savagely beat her and forced her to lie down on the reclined front seat. He forced her to undress and tied her hands behind her back. He beat her again. As Chanel lay terrified in the car, Long drove ten miles toward Morris Bridge Road, where he stopped and raped Chanel from behind while she was in the front seat. He then attempted to pull her out of the car and strangle her, but she struggled. An athletic girl, she refused to surrender quietly, and Long quickly grew impatient with her spirited fight for survival. Taking out his gun, he shot her in the back of the neck and then pushed her lifeless body under a wire fence.

Karen Beth Drinsfriend

During the early hours of the very same day that Chanel Williams's corpse was found, 28-year-old cokehead and prostitute Karen Beth Drinsfriend was seen soliciting in the area of Nebraska and Hillsborough Avenues in Tampa. Attractive as hookers go and semi-streetwise, Karen was known to police as having a long criminal record for larceny, prostitution, and drug-related offenses.

The body of the semi-naked white female was discovered in an orange grove, about 30 feet from a dirt road, in a remote area in northeastern Hillsborough County. Crime scene officers believed that she had, in fact, been dragged along the road, the body's state being consistent with drag marks in the dirt.

The victim's yellow T-shirt was pulled up to her neck, exposing a bruised and bloodied torso. The rest of her clothing was scattered nearby. Karen had been wrapped in a gold-colored beach blanket, and a blue jogging suit was tied around it. The blanket had been tied at both ends with ordinary white string. The victim's hands were bound in front with a red and white handkerchief. Her right wrist and legs were also bound. The ankles were tied with a drawstring arrangement.

Once again, police found brown Caucasian pubic hairs and red fibers on her clothes. There was also semen indicating A and H blood.

At autopsy it was determined that she had been struck on the head. Cause of death was attributed to strangulation.

Kimberly Kyle Hoops

On Tuesday, October 30, 1984, the nude, mummified remains of yet another white female were discovered by a 71-year-old man who was clearing a ditch near Highway 301 in northern Hillsborough County, just south of the Pasco County line.

No clothing, ligatures, or any other type of physical evidence was found at the scene.

Due to the amount of time the body had been exposed to the elements and the fact that the victim was naked, no foreign hairs, fibers, semen, or any other type of evidence was recovered. This victim would not be identified until the arrest of Bobby Joe Long, who referred to her by her street name, "Sugar." He had strangled her with the black choker she wore around her neck, then rolled her body down an embankment.

Shortly thereafter the woman was identified as Kimberly Kyle Hoops. The 22-year-old hooker had last been seen alive getting into a 1977 or '78 maroon-colored Chrysler Cordoba. Hoops would eventually be forensically associated with her killer through a comparison of her head hairs and some found in Long's car.

By now, every available police officer in the Tampa area was assigned to the case, with officers patrolling the major streets and highways in an attempt to capture the serial killer. Tension and frustration mounted as officials worked too hard and too long with no results. But on Saturday, November 3, 1984, their efforts would finally be richly rewarded, as Bobby Joe Long got careless. He made a mistake that led the police right to his front door.

Lisa McVey

At 2:30 a.m. on November 3, Bobby Joe Long was trolling for his next victim when he spotted 17-year-old Lisa McVey on Waters Avenue, Tampa. She was riding her bicycle home from a donut store where she worked along the two-way highway. The stretch of road was usually packed with traffic during the day but would have been pretty much empty at such an early hour. As he passed her going in the opposite direction, Bobby Joe knew he had found another victim. He spun his car around at the next intersection, followed her slowly and, as he passed her, studied the young woman in his rearview mirror.

Lisa was slender and athletic with shoulder-length, dark auburn hair. With his uncontrollable sexual urges now overpowering him, Long pulled into the Real Life Church parking lot, 6818 West Waters Avenue, where waited for Lisa to pass. As she did, he grabbed her by the hair and pulled her off her bike.

Holding a gun to her throat, Long responded to Lisa's terrified screams by assuring her that he would kill her if she made another sound. He forced her back to his car and ordered her to undress. Long unzipped his pants and forced the young woman to perform oral sex on him as he drove. Before he ejaculated, he ordered her to sit up, at once warning her to keep her eyes closed the entire time.

Lisa McVey was terrified but equally determined to survive this ordeal. She complied with Long's every order, knowing that refusal to do so could provoke him, and she had no idea what horrors this man was capable of.

Long cruised the streets for some time before taking Lisa back to his apartment on East Fowler Avenue, some ten miles east of where he had abducted her. He ordered her to put her clothes on and tied a blindfold around her eyes before they got out of the car. She did not see the red carpeting covering the two flights of stairs Long forced her to climb, nor would she have known the significance: Fibers from the same carpet had been found on several of the murdered women and their clothes.

Long took Lisa to his bathroom and forced her to undress again. Ordering her to bend over, he attempted to sodomize her, stopping when she cried out in pain. Instead, he took her to his bedroom and raped her. When he finished, he took young Lisa, still blindfolded, into the shower with him. He then dried her hair and brushed it gently, telling her how beautiful it was.

Long returned Lisa McVey to his bedroom, ordering her to lie down on his water bed. He tied her legs tightly, turned off the light and removed her blindfold. To ensure she continued to comply with his demands, he let her feel the cold steel of his gun barrel against her skin before placing it on a shelf above the bed. They spent the rest of the night and most of the next day in his bed, where he touched her body and made her do the same to him. He asked her to massage his back and shoulders to relieve the pain caused by some heavy lifting he had done at work. He raped her repeatedly, forced her to perform oral sex on him several times and sodomized her at least once.

Throughout the entire ordeal, Long spoke to McVey as if they were new lovers spending their first night together. He asked her about her family and work. He called her "Babe" and said that he didn't know why he had done this. As evening approached, Long realized that she must be hungry and prepared a ham sandwich for her. While she ate, he went into the living room and watched television until the news announced Lisa McVey's disappearance. He turned the set off and returned to the bedroom.

Climbing into bed with his victim, Long turned off the light. He removed Lisa's blindfold again but allowed her to stay dressed. As they lay together in the dark, he nibbled at her ear and neck, telling her how much he liked her and that he wished they had met under different circumstances. Then he made her remove her shirt and caressed and licked her breasts before ordering her to get some sleep.

At 3:30 a.m., the alarm clock sounded. Long told Lisa to prepare to leave, blindfolding her before the walk to his car. As she climbed in, her head hit the door frame, and he apologized. He leaned down to put her shoes and socks on her feet, and then he kissed her before starting the engine. After a few moments of driving, Long stopped at an ATM to withdraw cash. Alone in the car, McVey dared to adjust her blindfold slightly. Through a tiny opening, she was able to note that the bank was a white building and that the car was red or maroon with a white interior. On the dashboard was a brown strip with the word *Magnum* in silver letters and a digital clock with green numerals. Long returned to the car, but McVey's blindfold remained positioned to allow a small line of vision. They drove around a corner to a gas station, after which a ten-minute drive took them to the interstate, where she noted signs for a Howard Johnsons Motel and a Quality Inn.

Long stopped his car in a parking lot at the corner of North Rome Avenue and Hillsborough Avenue. He told her that he didn't want to let her go, but then he helped her to gather her things and get out of the car. Instructing her to wait a few minutes before removing her blindfold, Long hugged and kissed his victim one last time. She complied exactly with his order, standing stock still until she heard the sound of his engine fade into the distance. Several long minutes passed before she removed the blindfold. Then she fell to her knees and wept uncontrollably before she could compose herself enough to walk home.

It was 4:30 a.m. when she arrived home and woke her father, who immediately phoned the police. Lisa McVey had been a captive of Bobby Joe Long for 26 hours, and she had, by the grace of God, survived.

When detectives arrived at her home. Lisa gave the officers a description of her abductor: white male, approximately 30 years old, medium build, slightly pudgy, with conservatively cut brown hair and a moustache.

The police immediately sent out a "BOLO" (Be on the Lookout) for a man answering this description. He might be driving a red 1978 Dodge Magnum with a white interior. On the glove box door was a digital clock, and on the dash was the legend *Magnum.*

Virginia Lee Johnson

On Tuesday, November 6, two days after Lisa McVey told police her sordid and degrading account of abduction and rape, law enforcement from neighboring Pascoe County became involved in another homicide. A woman riding her horse on her ranch discovered the animal-gnawed skeletal remains of 18-year-old Virginia Lee Johnson scattered throughout the field.

Officers found a skull and upper torso dressed in a tank top. A shoelace was twisted twice over a piece of fabric wrapped around her neck. Another shoelace was wrapped around one of the victim's hands. Upon closer inspection, police noticed a heart-shaped pendant around her neck. It was later identified by friends of the dead woman as belonging to her.

At autopsy, it was determined that Virginia had been strangled to death.

By the time that Virginia Lee Johnson's remains were discovered, there were approximately 30 officers assigned to the task force, and they immediately flooded the north Tampa area searching for the man, the apartment, and the vehicle described by Lisa McVey.

Only a 1978 Dodge Magnum had the word *Magnum* on the dash, so a task force member was flown to the state capital, and he returned with a list of every Dodge Magnum registered in Hillsborough County. An examination of the printout of these registrations revealed Robert Joe Long's name as a registered owner of such a car.

Each team of detectives was assigned certain areas to search, and on Thursday, November 15, as Detectives Wolf and Helms were driving to their beat, they noticed a red Dodge Magnum driving down Nebraska Avenue. The vehicle was stopped. The officers told the driver that they were looking for a robbery suspect. The driver identified himself as Robert Joe Long of East Fowler Street, Tampa. He was photographed. A field interrogation report was written up before he was allowed to proceed on his way, very much relieved. But Long only had a short breathing space of freedom remaining.

The detectives who had spoken to Long alerted the task force officers, who were working frantically to obtain enough evidence to link Bobby Joe to the murders. Bank records revealed that Long had made a withdrawal from a Florida National Bank ATM at 58th Street and Fowler Avenue at 3:39 a.m. on November 4—the morning that Lisa McVey was set free.

From the Parole and Probation Office in north Tampa, the task force learned that Long was on probation for his attempted abduction of Mary Hicks earlier in the year and that he had also been charged with rape in Dade County in 1974. So within hours of Long's encounter with Detectives Wolf and Helms, ground and air surveillance teams were monitoring his every move.

Officers watched as he left his apartment late in the afternoon and drove to the post office on 5th Street in Temple Terrace. They saw him return home briefly before going to a Laundromat at 56th and Whiteway. Next, they followed him to the outdoor tennis and handball courts at the back of the University of South Florida and watched as he sat in his car reading a newspaper for some time before moving to a bench in the racquetball area. Long was completely oblivious to an undercover cop who passed within three feet of him, providing the task force with a detailed description of Long's blue and white jogging shoes, blue jeans, and gray T-shirt.

At 5:45 p.m., Bobby Joe returned to his apartment for the night. When his ex-wife Cathy called to arrange an upcoming visit with his children, he asked her if she knew about the murders in Tampa. He warned her that it was a dangerous world and she ought to be really careful.

Outside, cops watched and waited, but he had killed again.

Kim Marie Swann

On Wednesday, November 12, the day before he was stopped in his car by detectives, Bobby Joe Long had spotted 21-year-old Kim Marie Swann, who was intoxicated and driving erratically. He pulled alongside and told her to stop. In her drunken state, she accepted Long's invitation to join him for a drink. Shortly after getting into his car, she suspected something was awry and began to fight with him. He punched her several times before binding and strangling her. Swann had fought so hard that Long didn't even bother to rape her; instead, he simply dumped her under an overpass.

Kim's body was found by a sign painter on November 14. A leash-like noose was tied around her neck, and the body bore rope-burn trauma. Her face had been badly beaten. Her legs had been forced open for a shocking display reminiscent of the Ngeun Thi Long murder. Her clothing had been discarded nearby, and fecal matter was on her shirt.

Red carpet hairs and brown Caucasian pubic hairs were discovered on her denim jeans, and in one of the pockets was a driver's license for a Kim Marie Swann. Like Ngeun Thi Long, Swann had worked at the Sly Fox Lounge in Tampa.

At autopsy, Dr. Miller estimated that Swann had been dead for two or three days. The cause of death was strangulation.

By the time that Swann's body was found, Lisa McVey had identified Long from the photos taken by the detectives and from his mug shots. Based on the combined evidence, the ATM withdrawal and the photo-ID, an arrest warrant and search warrants were drawn up and approved by a circuit court judge, while the task force surveillance team continued to monitor Long's movements. Between

> When I saw them [his victims] walking down the street, it was like A, B, C, D. I pull over, they get in, I drive a little ways, stop, pull a knife, a gun, whatever, tie them up, take them out. And that would be it. And they all went the same way until McVey came along.
>
> —BOBBY JOE LONG
> IN A POLICE INTERVIEW

noon and 1:30 p.m. they watched as he cleaned out his apartment and threw the refuse into a nearby dumpster. As soon as Long drove off, a detective retrieved the discarded trash from the bin, and further possible evidence was collected after he vacuumed his car at a gas station on 56th Street. From there Long went to see a movie at the Main Street Cinema. Munching popcorn, he watched Chuck Norris as Colonel James Braddock, waging his battles on the big screen in *Missing in Action*—a film that had only just been released.

At 4:00 p.m. on Friday, November 16, 1984, Bobby Joe Long was arrested as he walked out of the Main Street Cinema. Forensic technicians searched his car and sent a sample of the floor carpet to the FBI for analysis and comparison with the red fibers found at so many of the crime scenes. Indeed, they literally took the vehicle apart, bagging any fibers that may have come from the victims' clothing, as well as rope and hair. They also searched for fingerprints, blood, and any other potential trace evidence.

Upon entering Bobby Joe Long's apartment, the detectives noted that it was just as Lisa McVey had described it. An officer found Lisa's barrette, while other cops found a hoard of photographs of naked women, including many that Long had obviously taken. There was also some women's clothing.

Back at the precinct house, Long signed a Miranda waiver form and gave up his right to have a lawyer present. During the course of the interrogation led by Detectives Latimer and Price, he quickly admitted to kidnapping Lisa McVey and to having sex with her many times. However, in a weak attempt to mitigate his actions, he claimed that at one point she told him that she didn't want to leave. He also explained that he had unloaded his gun and put the bullets in a trash can so he wouldn't be tempted to shoot her. When asked about the blindfold she wore, Long said that he had fashioned it himself two days before the abduction—just in case he found another victim.

With the McVey admission in the bag, the detectives drew Long's attention to the various pieces of evidence that had been collected. They produced a photo array of his victims. Asked if he knew any of them, he replied, "No!" and asked to use the washroom.

Upon returning, Long sat down and his interrogators immediately returned to the subject of physical evidence. They asked him about the left-rear Vogue tire on his car. They said that it matched a similar tread pattern found at two of the crime scenes. The officers then referred to the other tires on his car, specifically the mismatch of patterns and the Viva brand tire, to which Long responded, "I think I might need an attorney."

Rather than end the questioning at this point, as required by law, Detective Sergeant Latimer urged Bobby Joe to be honest and get everything off his chest. "Besides," Latimer explained, "we have enough evidence against you already."

Bobby Joe Long smiled. "Well, I guess you got me good," he said, adding, "Yes, I killed them . . . all the ones in the newspaper. I did them all."

Long went on to describe in some detail each case from the abduction to the murder of the victim. He acknowledged that setting Lisa McVey free was a grave error of judgment. Author Joel Norris quoted Long as saying, "I knew when I let her go that it would only be a matter of time. I didn't even tell her not to talk to the police or anything . . . I just didn't care anymore, and I wanted to stop. I was sick inside."

Bobby Joe Long was charged with eight counts of murder and sexual battery, and nine counts of kidnapping, with one count of murder pending for Virginia Johnson. He was also charged with the minor offense of violating his probation for aggravated assault. He was refused bail.

Bobby Joe Long went on to face a lengthy series of trials in Florida. His supporters argue that each trial was deeply flawed, while others say his intent was to drag out the legal process as long as he could.

Long admitted that he was aware of what he was doing and that it was wrong. He claimed that he had basically turned himself in by allowing Lisa McVey to go free. But here is a man who also suggested that his raping of women was good for them. More recently, Long has argued that if he had known his problems were medical, he would have sought treatment.

Many different attorneys came into his cases and just as quickly exited, including celebrity defense attorney Ellis Rubin.[13] Two of Long's death penalty convictions were later overturned by the Florida Supreme Court because, among other problems, the panel of justices deemed that the police had gone over the limit in their interrogations. For example, the justices specifically noted that only four hours of testimony had been presented on the murder for which Long was charged, while three entire days

13 More on Ellis Rubin can be found at: en.wikipedia.org/wiki/Ellis_Rubin.

had been spent admitting highly prejudicial evidence of other murders with which he had *not* been charged.

Perhaps Long's guilt was never really an issue, but whether he should be executed or granted life in prison was the next primary consideration.

As in so many high-profile serial homicide cases, a veritable parade of mental health experts was brought into the case to prove or disprove that Long's genetic abnormalities and head injuries accounted for his antisocial behavior. Even his parents were blamed, along with his being subjected to pornographic material during his formative years.

The notable Dr. Helen Morrison, who had interviewed Bobby Joe for 23 hours, diagnosed him with "atypical psychosis." He had a distorted perception of reality and was unable to make moral decisions. "His mind was fragmented and noncohesive," she concluded, "and had been so since he was a very young child. He eventually lost the ability to maintain control. Thus, he could not comprehend the criminality of his actions."

A broad definition of *psychosis* is: a symptom or feature of mental illness typically characterized by radical changes in personality, impaired functioning, and a distorted or nonexistent sense of objective reality.

Patients suffering from psychosis have impaired reality testing. That is, they are unable to distinguish personal, subjective experience from the reality of the external world. They experience hallucinations or delusions that they believe are real, and may behave and communicate in an inappropriate and incoherent fashion. Psychosis may appear as a symptom of a number of mental disorders, including mood and personality disorders. It is also the defining feature of schizophrenia, schizophreniform disorder, schizoaffective disorder, delusional disorder, and the psychotic disorders (e.g., brief psychotic disorder, shared psychotic disorder, psychotic disorder due to a general medical condition, and substance-induced psychotic disorder).

Those readers who have read my book *Talking with Serial Killers* and its sequel, *Talking with Serial Killers II,* specifically the chapter on Kenneth Alessio Bianchi in the latter, will realize that once again we find a distinguished forensic psychiatrist speaking gobbledygook.

Of course, Dr. Morrison must have realized that Bobby Joe Long comprehended the criminality of his actions. Of course he had the ability to maintain control, and he was no schizophrenic, drug addict, or heavy drinker. In fact, the bottom line is that Bobby Joe Long raped, tortured, and murdered, time and time again, because he enjoyed inflicting dreadful suffering on his helpless and vulnerable victims.

No doubt, if Dr. Morrison had her way, we might excuse the likes of Ian Brady, Myra Hindley, Fred and Rose West, Ted Bundy, Harvey Louis Carignan, Kenny Bianchi and Angelo Buono, Arthur Shawcross, Michael Ross, Kenneth Allen McDuff, Peter Sutcliffe, Dennis Nilsen, and just about every other serial killer who has infested our society over the decades, to mitigate their sins for having suffered some form of psychosis; lock them up for a spell, hit them with a few therapy groups, and release them with apologies for having detained them for so long.

However, perhaps I am being a little unfair by singling out Dr. Morrison, when even Dr. John Money—renowned for his work in confused gender identity—came into the case. A psychologist and sex therapist, he took the stand and pontificated about the effects of the extra female chromosome, exacerbated by the head injuries Bobby Joe suffered, on a fragile ego. "This combination," he stated, "had created in Long a Jekyll-and-Hyde syndrome." Money ignored that quite famous quote by Jekyll to Gabriel John Utterson, a lawyer and friend: "The moment I choose, I can be rid of Mr. Hyde." Unfortunately, Dr. Money later was exposed as a bit of a charlatan; it was revealed that his most famous case was the result of fraudulent reporting.

The subject of the doctor's fraud was his involvement in the sex reassignment of one David Reimer, in what later became known as the "John/Joan" case. Money reported that he successfully reassigned Reimer as female after a botched infant circumcision in 1966.

In 1997, Milton Diamond, professor of anatomy and reproductive biology at the University of Hawaii, reported that the reassignment had failed, that Reimer had never identified as being female or behaved in a typically feminine manner.

At age 14, Reimer, who had fought against being forced to see Dr. Money since the age of seven (and for very good reason) refused to see Money again, threatening suicide if he were made to go. Reimer's parents then decided to tell their son the truth about his past and biological sex. Reimer immediately ended the hormone treatments he had been forced to undergo to stimulate female sex traits and began hormones to bring about the male puberty prevented by the removal of his testes by Dr. Money. He ceased using the name Brenda—which his parents had chosen for him after he began treatment with Dr. Money—and chose a new name, David, for himself.

At 15, with a different medical team, he sought a mastectomy, testosterone therapy, and a phalloplasty (artificial surgical modification of the penis). Later he married a woman, who luckily had children from a previous marriage, and Brenda/David lived as an intractably confused person until, at age 38, the reoccurring thoughts of successful suicide finally overwhelmed him.

For his part, at the ripe old age of 85, Dr. Money passed away in his sleep on July 7, 2006.

But I have digressed. The flip side of Bobby Joe's state of mind was presented by psychiatrists called by the State of Florida. Almost in unison they announced, "Mr. Long does have an antisocial personality disorder. This is *not* deemed a mental illness. He is a pathological liar, and he knew that what he was doing when he raped and murdered was wrong, and he knew the stiff penalties that awaited him should he be caught."

In the end, no jury accepted any of the defense's psychiatric testimony. By the time Florida was done with Bobby Joe, he had received two death sentences (one was later commuted) and a staggering 34 life sentences, plus an additional 693 years imprisonment.

After his first death sentence had been handed down, Bobby Joe left the court whistling a tune. He had decided that since he was, "no killer like other guys on death row," his sentence had been "political." But if one were to imagine this was the last one would hear about Mr. Long's trials and tribulations, one would be mistaken.

During 1997, the FBI lab came under the eagle-eye scrutiny of the Department of Justice, which issued a blistering 500-page report about the efficiency of the crime lab's technicians. In the firing line, specifically, was the work of renowned fiber expert Special Agent Michael Malone, many of whose previous findings suddenly proved contrary to the career that he had been trained for when his work provided grounds for successful appeals against convictions.

In a nutshell, Malone had allowed his once methodical expertise to slip. In fact, a 1992 assault conviction was overturned in 2003 based on Malone's neglect to do proper testing of fiber evidence, and defense attorneys, quick to jump on the bandwagon, demanded that their cases also be re-examined. The publicity was too much for the FBI, and Malone's once sterling reputation came into question. He was allowed to retire in 1999.

Long's attorneys seized on the criticism leveled at the FBI's crime lab, but their client had confessed to the murders, and there was Lisa McVey's evidence and hair samples to boot; the appeal merely delayed the legal process, costing the taxpayer millions more dollars while the lawyers were well-paid in the bargain.

At the time of this writing, Bobby Joe Long is on death row, awaiting his appointment with his executioner. If this stone-cold killer had learned anything after fessing up to his heinous crimes, he should know when to keep his lips firmly zipped up.

He hasn't, for what follows is correspondence written by Bobby Joe to murder groupie Annabel Leigh. It is published verbatim here for the first time. It truly shows the sick workings

of this serial killer's mind, perhaps illustrating *exactly* why Bobby Joe Long was sentenced to death.[14]
In 2007, Annabel Leigh (not her real name) began writing to Bobby Joe Long. Long answered and asked for a photograph of Annabel, and when it arrived in his prison cell he immediately started putting pen to paper—lots and lots of paper, filled with writing on both sides.

He began by detailing his preferred reading material, which included *Bizarre Magazine, Redemption, Centurion* and *Rose Comics*—the last containing a good deal of blood and violence meant for readers aged 18 and up. He also advised that she familiarize herself with this material, providing the publishers' addresses for her convenience. "Be sure to sign an age statement," he wrote, "and I think they'll all send you some catalogs you'll find . . . interesting☺. Who knows, maybe even some stuff you've *never seen before!*"

Then, without blinking, he asked:

> Have you ever watched a hard-core XXX rated, graphic "Fuck-Video"??? If so, what did you see that *most interested* you? If not, would you like to??? I also have some catalog addresses for very *good* videos of this type. What sexual subjects do you like? And would you *like* to see? Ever seen two guys suck each other's dicks? Then Butt-Fuck each other? Tell me baby, *what* would interest you, to *see?* So much about you I don't know—and want to!!:)

Quite what Annabel Leigh made of those first few lines from our man-about-death row is unknown. Hopefully, her

14 Bobby Joe Long's current prison sentence history can be found at www.dc.state.fl.us/ActiveInmates/Detail.asp?Bookmark=1&From=list&SessionID=698669499.

deeply religious parents, born and raised in the Hopkins County town of Dawson Springs, Kentucky, didn't get sight of the letter, either. Had they done so, I can testify, as I have visited this redneck place, that the news would have traveled fast. Everyone from the boss of Thrifty's Drug Store to the local branch of the Imperial Klan of America would have been juiced up on the local "shine," curtain-twitching would have been rife, and it would certainly have made the headlines of the local newspaper in a heartbeat. That Henry Dodson, aged 98, had died while carp fishing at Old Mill Dam, leaving his teenage wife and six kids, would have missed print altogether.

Nonetheless, not one to be fazed by a man who certainly had no claim to the label "shrinking violet," Annabel wrote back and asked Bobby Joe about his music preferences. To which he responded like a greyhound out of a gate, and ignoring her request, wrote:

> Here is where you tell me about shaving your puss, *completely* . . . year around. Now this is the kind of stuff I like you to tell me about ☺. Have you ever thought about letting just a little strip of your fur grow in above your clit? Just a little strip of that "FIRE!!" is all keeping the rest shaved? How long ago—how old were you—did you first start shaving your little "monkey'?
>
> How would you feel about doing a nipple print for me, on a page of a letter? Do you know what I mean?

By now you will be getting the drift of Bobby Joe Long's letters to Annabel—page after page of drivel and filth. However, he soon returned to his memories of commercial diving, explaining to Annabel that he had quickly learned the importance of keeping warm "out there on the rigs" and that "fortunately in commercial diving, we used hot-water wet suits, and at around 1000 ft, believe me it gets *cold* down there . . . Hey! You'd like it out on a Miami beach on a blue day . . . wearing a little nothing of a bikini . . . don't ya think? ☺."

Eventually, Bobby Joe Long did go into some detail about his musical preferences, but I won't bother you with more pages of his mind-debilitating rubbish.

The final question we must ask ourselves is this: Who is the *real* Bobby Joe Long?

Perhaps the most chilling aspect of Bobby Joe Long's persona is his physical mask, the one he has worn since the day he was born. He simply does not look like a serial killer, or how we might imagine a serial killer to look.

If we were to peel away his physical mask, as one might peel an apple, we would find in parts that he is rotten to the core, with the brown mush eating away at what fresh fruit remains.

"'Oh God!" I screamed, and "Oh God!" again and again; for there before my eyes . . . pale and shaken, and half fainting, and groping before him with his hands, like a man restored from death . . . stood Henry Jekyll!"

—Robert Louis Stevenson: *Dr. Jekyll and Mr. Hyde*

In Bobby Joe Long, we do not find a simplified Dr. Jekyll and Mr. Hyde character. We find a multifaceted personality, a complex role that any actor would be proud to portray successfully.

Every man and woman has dimensions and facets to their true character, all of which are parts of the "real" them. Bobby Joe Long is no exception.

Within this moral duality rests the true nature of Bobby Joe Long.

***

CHAPTER 5

DAVID ALAN GORE AND FREDERICK L. WATERFIELD JR.—FLORIDA REDNECKS

Man's destructive hand spares nothing that lives; he kills to feed himself, he kills to clothe himself, he kills to adorn himself, he kills to attack, he kills to defend himself, he kills to instruct himself, he kills to amuse himself, and he kills for the sake of killing.

—Joseph de Maistre

Once in a blue moon a serial killer's criminal history comes to us not quite as clear-cut as the authorities would have us believe. The trial and conviction of Fred Waterfield is a prime example.

The following account features:

A detective suppressing vital evidence and planting false evidence to obtain two rape convictions against Waterfield;
Two false allegations of rape made against Waterfield;
A court official "losing" vital appeal documents;

A state prosecutor bribing witnesses and withholding crucial evidence that would have proven Waterfield to be innocent;

David Gore's sworn affidavits, which categorically state that Fred Waterfield was *never* involved in any of the rapes and subsequent murders committed by Gore; and

Made public for the first time, the shocking full and frank confessions of how David Gore, a self-admitted cannibal, entrapped his victims, raped, tortured, and murdered them, and ate their flesh.

Indeed, this chapter clearly exposes a gross miscarriage of justice in respect to Mr. Waterfield. But I will allow my readers to work it out for themselves and form their own opinions.[15]

Born in Indian River County, Florida, on Monday, September 29, 1952, inmate #0956510 Frederick Levin Waterfield has brown hair and brown eyes; he is six feet tall and weighs 222 pounds. He is currently serving a life sentence for offenses he did not commit at the Florida Department of Corrections Okeechobee Correctional Institution, Okeechobee County, Florida.

Born in Indian River County, Florida, on Friday, August, 21, 1953, inmate #081008 David Alan Gore can be described as brown-haired and blue-eyed; at six feet tall, he weighs 206 pounds. He is one of only a few former cops under sentence of

---

15 This chapter has been compiled from hundreds of court documents and letters sent exclusively by Frederick Waterfield to the author.

death for crimes he *did* commit and is a resident in the Florida Department of Corrections Union Institution, Raiford, Florida.

David Gore has always had the look of a stereotypical "'Gator Everglades" redneck. A firearms fan, he studied gunsmithing in his free time. He also studied women, but in a different fashion . . . He was a sexual pervert who would screw any piece of skirt he came across. Indeed, he lost one of his jobs as a gas station attendant after the owner found a peephole Gore had drilled between the men's and women's restrooms.

Apart from this snippet of information, little else is known about the aptly named Gore. He would have us believe that he was physically abused as a child by his father, but there is no evidence to support this. In fact, Gore's brother-in-law, William Bowling, says that "Gore's father, Alva, was a good, genuine man." Alva Gore would later testify that although his family was impoverished, his son never went hungry or without medical attention when he needed it, adding: "My wife stayed home and took care of the children growing up."

Details concerning Fred Waterfield's formative years are even less clear than his cousin's. Waterfield refuses to discuss this at all. But we do know his mother is named Mildred, that he has a sister named Constance, and that he was a high school football star. Some argue, quite erroneously, that he had a violent temper and a liking for sex, "which made him and David Gore seem like brothers." However, after Fred reached the age of nine, he says, he had little to no contact with Gore for many years:

> I was considered a workaholic by family and friends. Two of my ex-wives and none of my children could tell you what

> Gore looked like. I worked 10 to 14 hours a day and raced all kinds of vehicles on weekends. In 1975 I moved from Vero Beach to Clairmont and eventually Orlando, where I opened my own automotive business from 1977 to 1983. To expand my business I found a 9.9-acre tractor trailer shop in Vero Beach and moved back there in May, 1983.
>
> —*Frederick Waterfield in a letter to the author, October 21, 2008*

Lynn Elliott and Regan Martin

Just before 4 p.m. on Tuesday, July 26, 1983, the Vero Beach Police Department received a 911 telephone call from a Michael Rock. The young cyclist had furiously peddled home to report a naked man firing shots at an equally naked girl on a residential street. The police turned up a few minutes later and found nothing of note.

At 4:23 p.m. a second emergency call came into the police station. Another male caller said that he had just heard screams coming from a nearby orange grove and that a man was chasing an injured woman. Then the phone went dead. Police soon determined from which address the second call had come, so officers knocked on the front door. It was opened by Gore, who told them that the property was owned by his parents, who were away on vacation.

In the driveway, officers found a car with fresh blood dripping from its trunk. Inside was the naked body of 17-year-old Lynn Elliott. She had been fatally shot in the head. Gore was immediately arrested, after which he directed officers to the attic, where they discovered 14-year-old Regan Martin, who was also naked and tied spread-eagle fashion to the rafters.

Back at the police station, the sobbing Regan Martin explained that she and Lynn had been hitchhiking when Gore and another man (later identified as Fred Waterfield) picked them up. Gore had flashed a pistol at them and also threatened his companion before driving them to the house. Here, Regan said, the two men had a heated conversation, and Waterfield left immediately. Thereafter, the young women were stripped, tied up, and raped repeatedly by Gore in separate rooms.

Lynn, it seems, had managed to free herself and escape on foot with Gore in pursuit. She had not been fast enough. He knocked her down, dragged her back to the house, put her in the trunk of his car and fired single bullet into her head.

In her police statement, Regan Martin was adamant that the as yet unidentified man (Waterfield) had not threatened either girl in any way. Indeed, in her initial statements to police she said that Gore had also threatened Waterfield with the gun when Waterfield said that he wanted nothing to do with the unplanned abduction.

Regan also said that Waterfield had not sexually assaulted the girls in any way, and she asserted Waterfield's innocence for ten months before suddenly, and without warning, she changed her mind at his trial. After the trial, she retracted her court testimony, saying that the police had pressured her to testify that Waterfield was involved.

Detective Daniel Nippes stated in his evidence that he had found that Gore's jeans had saliva and sperm traces in the crotch and fly area. "The forensic evidence is consistent with Lynn Elliott being forced to perform oral sex," he concluded.

The Medical Examiner stated that: "Elliott's injuries were very painful . . . the abrasions to her hip, shoulder, and knees were consistent with being dragged, and all of the injuries occurred before death."

Gore had soon cracked under questioning. He explained to Detective Phil Redstone that he had made his telephone call to police in an effort to lead them away from the house after seeing police cars responding to the first 911 call—that made by Michael Rock. And despite Regan Martin's insistence that the other man was completely innocent, Gore implicated his cousin Fred Waterfield as being as responsible as he was in the double abduction, rapes, and the murder of Lynn Elliott.

With this confession under his belt, Detective Redstone contacted Assistant District Attorney Robert Stone, and an arrest warrant was issued for Waterfield.

Frederick Waterfield was picked up later the same day and, in Case No. 83-361.B, a grand jury issued a true bill of indictment on August 10, 1983, charging him with one count of first-degree felony murder (Lynn Elliott), and two counts of kidnapping (Lynn Elliott and Regan Martin).

To be fair to the grand jury, however, they had been kept in the dark, for State Attorney Robert Stone had suppressed the statements made by Regan Martin that would have proven that Waterfield was innocent.

DA Stone also suppressed the evidence given by Michael Rock, who, in a lineup, had identified the naked Gore as being the man chasing the equally naked Lynn Elliott down the street. For their part, police were still falsely insisting that the naked man had been Fred Waterfield.

Waterfield's attorney, Michael Bloom, then got wind of Regan Martin and Michael Rock's testimony favoring his client, so he applied for disclosure of the statements the two witnesses had given to the police. On October 10, 1983, Judge G. Kendall Sharp ordered that the state's attorney's office make the statements of Rock and Martin available to the defense.

State Attorney Robert Stone flipped, for he now realized that the already flimsy case he had against Waterfield would collapse completely if Martin and Rock's statements fell into the defense attorney's hands, for it would become obvious to the judge that Stone had unlawfully misled the grand jury to secure a true bill of indictment, the first step toward a full trial.

Now desperate, in order to extricate himself from this extremely dangerous situation, Robert Stone made a formal and scurrilous complaint to the state supreme court requesting an order that would remove Judge Sharp from conducting any further proceedings in the case.

Later, under examination in court, Stone admitted that his complaint against Judge Sharp was "without merit," and, that it was a tactical move on his behalf to prevent Waterfield from presenting Regan Martin and Michael Rock's testimony and evidence in the defense's favor.

Nevertheless, Judge Sharp now found himself between a rock and hard place. An honest and decent man, nonetheless he made the decision–on a technicality that is still obscure today–to deny the defense's request for disclosure, the result being that the testimony of Regan Martin and Michael Rock would go unheard.

DA Stone then returned to David Gore and started to make phony promises of a plea bargain agreement, which, he said, could save him from the very real possibility of execution. Gore started to sing like the proverbial canary, and between the DA and Gore they concocted a series of crimes that the cousins had committed "together," way back in 1976.

Diane Smalley

The first incident allegedly concerned the two men following a woman driver near Yeehaw Junction, a major stopping point for tourists on the Florida Turnpike. Gore claimed that Fred had fired several rifle shots into the vehicle's tires, the car had skidded off the road, and the intended victim had escaped on foot.

Detective Redstone located the case file, and soon afterward Diane Smalley identified one of the two men as David Gore. She also positively identified the man who had fired the shots at her car as one Eugene Franklin, *not* Waterfield. When Redstone showed her a photo of Fred Waterfield, Smalley said that she absolutely had never seen Waterfield before. Notwithstanding this, acting on DA Stone's instructions, Redstone used correction fluid to remove Franklin's name from the file and inserted Waterfield's.

Diane Smalley maintained that Waterfield was not involved in her attempted abduction right up to Fred Waterfield's trial, when suddenly, without warning, and just like Regan Martin, she flip-flopped and identified Waterfield as Gore's accomplice.

Clearly, Diane Smalley had been "gotten to" by the prosecution. Nonetheless, the case was dismissed against Waterfield because fingerprints showed that in no way could he have been involved. Franklin's prints would confirm it, and this is one of a number of reasons why DA Stone was later fired from his job.

Anjelica Hommell

The second incident had far greater consequences for Waterfield. Gore, District Attorney Stone, and Detective Redstone concocted the Hommell case in an attempt to prove that Waterfield was capable of rape and attempted murder.

The matter concerned a woman named Anjelica Hommell, who reported her rape some seven years previously by two men, whom she identified as Gore and Waterfield, near Vero Beach, Florida.

This sudden pretrial Waterfield revelation was investigated by Captain Joe Sardella, Detective Bill Brumley, and Detective Redstone. Both Sardella and Brumley, in their comprehensive 13-page supplemental report, ruled Waterfield out of the allegation entirely, and in fact, proved that Hommell's accusation against Waterfield was pure fabrication.

The reason why Hommell had lied would remain a mystery for some time. Nevertheless, Detective Redstone and DA Stone proceeded against Waterfield as if the Sardella/Brumley findings had never existed. If there was ever a frame-up, no better example can be found than this blatant attempt to pervert the course of justice in a capital case.

The Lings

Gore then claimed that Fred had offered him $1,000 for every pretty girl he could find. Gore went on to say that this was an offer he couldn't refuse, for in February 1981, while working a nightshift as an auxiliary sheriff, wearing a badge, and packing a sidearm, Gore was well-placed to abduct women from the streets when on patrol; during the days, he held down a menial job looking after his father's fruit orchard. The problem was that Waterfield had never made such an offer, but more on this later.

In February 1981, Gore picked up 17-year-old Ying Hua Ling as she stepped down from a school bus. He tricked her into his car with a flash of his police badge. Driving her home, he "arrested" the girl's mother and handcuffed his two victims together before allegedly phoning Waterfield, who was in Orlando.

Gore said that he then drove out to his father's orchard, where he waited for Fred to turn up. Gore admitted that he raped both of his victims but added that Fred was more selective—rejecting Mrs. Ling as being "too old." Gore claimed that he then tied Mrs. Ling up in such a fashion that she choked to death while struggling against her bonds, while Fred raped and murdered the pretty teenager. Gore said that his cousin had given him a check for $400 before leaving him to get rid of the bodies in another orchard a mile from the Lings' residence.

Waterfield vehemently denied these murderous allegations, and it would soon be proven that he was right.

Judith Daley

Five months later, on July 15, 1981, Gore claimed that he had driven out to Round Island Park to look for a blonde to fulfill Fred's latest order. Spotting a likely candidate in 35-year-old Judith Daley, Gore says that he disabled her car then played Good Samaritan by offering her a ride to the nearest telephone, where she could summon assistance.

This time, Gore claimed, "Fred was happier with this delivery" and wrote Gore a check for $1,500 after both men had finished with the terrified woman. Gore told DA Stone that he had fed Judith's body to alligators in a swamp ten miles west of Interstate 95.

Fred Waterfield vehemently denies any involvement in this murder, and, once again, it is perfectly true to say that we only have Gore's testimony against his cousin to say otherwise—testimony that Gore would later retract as a "buncha lies given 'cuz the cops promised to get me off the hook."

However, what we do know to be fact is this: During the middle of July 1981, Gore had fallen under suspicion when a local man reported that a deputy had stopped his teenage daughter on a rural highway and attempted to hold her for "questioning." The deputy, soon identified as David Alan Gore, was arrested on Tuesday, July 21, when officers found him crouched in the back of another woman's car outside a Vero Beach clinic. He was armed with a pistol, police-issued handcuffs, and a police radio scanner. Convicted of "trespass property armed," Gore was sentenced to five years' imprisonment before being paroled in 1983.

> In May 1983, I was in the process of buying the Vero Beach property and building a new central shop, and Gore was in the process of being released from prison. His mother, Velma, asked me to give him a job and he could not be released from prison until he found employment. I told Gore's parole officer, Don Coleman, Gore now could work for me and he was released. He worked for me for about two weeks before he stopped showing up.
>
> —*Frederick Waterfield in a letter to the author*

Gore then told Detective Redstone and DA Stone that after his release from prison he and Waterfield took up again where they had left off—with raping and killing.

Angelica LaVallae and Barbara Byer

On Monday, May 20, 1983, Gore claimed that he and Waterfield had tried to abduct an Orlando prostitute at gunpoint, but she slipped away. The following day, he alleged that they picked up two 14-year-old hitchhikers, Angelica LaVallae and Barbara Byer, whom they raped before Gore shot them to death. Byer's body, Gore said, was dismembered and buried in a shallow grave, while LaVallae's corpse was dumped in a nearby canal. Of course, Gore had committed the murders, because the decomposing bodies were discovered exactly where he said he'd dumped them. But apart from Gore's claims that Waterfield had been his accomplice in the double murders, there was no other evidence to support Fred's involvement in the crimes.

Gore would later retract his testimony implicating his cousin, and there would surface another witness who testified in Waterfield's favor—none other than David Gore's father, Alva.

On March 16, 1984, David Gore was convicted of one count of first-degree murder, two counts of kidnapping, and three counts of sexual battery. In February 1985, he received five life sentences and was sentenced to death for the first-degree murder of Lynn Elliott.

Meanwhile, at one of Waterfield's pretrial hearings on February 14 and 17, 1984, the defense's continual requests for the release of Regan Martin's initial police statements had born fruit.

To begin with, DA Robert Stone made the mistake of calling Detective Phil Redstone to testify about his evidence gathering, and the cop falsely testified that he was the *only* investigator involved with the alleged Hommell rape.

On cross-examination by defense attorney Michael Bloom, Redstone was asked if he could identify any other investigators, or had seen investigative reports from Captain Joe Sardella or Detective Bill Brumley in the Hommell case file. Robert Stone butted in, claiming that Redstone's report was the only report in the file, which wasn't true.[16]

Michael Bloom now had the bit between his teeth. He called defense witness Debbie Jenkins—the former wife of DA Stone—to the stand. Under oath, Debbie said that she had taken Mrs. Hommell to Waterfield's home on no less than two occasions

16 The reports made by Captain Joe Sardella and Detective Bill Brumley, which completely exonerated Waterfield and proved that Detective Redstone had conspired with DA Robert Stone to have Waterfield convicted of the rape of Anjelica Hommell, finally came to light in 1992.

and they had spoken to Mrs. Waterfield. Debbie Jenkins confirmed that DA Robert Stone had forced her to make a false complaint about Fred to the police.

Upon hearing this shocking testimony, Judge Vocelle ordered the state to turn over all of David Gore's statements and other investigative documents to Waterfield's defense.

Upon careful study of the newly released papers, Michael Bloom found that the state attorney had withheld even more evidence in the form of a witness statement that would have cleared Fred Waterfield of any involvement in the May 21, 1983 Byer-LaVallae homicides. Alva Gore, the father of David Gore, said prosecutors told him several times that, in effect, his testimony—which was in favor of Waterfield—was no longer required because Waterfield's "properly scheduled depositions were canceled."

Alva Gore had told police that he had spoken to Fred Waterfield on the phone on the morning of Saturday, May 21, 1983. This was a crucial date, as it was the day that David Gore alleged that he, with Fred Waterfield, raped and killed Angelica LaVallae and Barbara Byer.

Alva Gore had given a statement to investigators in which he said that on that Saturday morning, he had agreed to loan Waterfield a tractor to clear ground in preparation for lime rock. David Gore was to have delivered the tractor but inexplicably he didn't show up as agreed. When David Gore failed to appear, Alva picked up Fred Waterfield and drove him to a barn on his fruit orchard, and Fred drove away on the tractor. "It was my son, David, who brought the tractor back to the barn some time Sunday, May 22," Alva said.

Another witness had seen Waterfield using the tractor around the same time the two girls were abducted and murdered; clearly, he could not have been in two places at the same time. Yet despite these three rock-solid alibi witnesses in Waterfield's favor, the state prosecutor had tried to hide Alva's evidence, which would have cleared Fred of any involvement in the murders of Byer and LaVallae.

By now Judge Vocelle was losing his patience with the prosecutor, who, in trying to suppress evidence, had stalled Waterfield's trial date for months. The judge opined that the state was still interfering with defense discovery and preparations for the trial, so he set another date for May 1984.

After jury selection on May 17, 1984, in Charlotte County, DA Robert Stone rose to his feet to address the jury. Omitting the fact that he had suppressed "actual innocence evidence" from disclosure to a grand jury and from Waterfield's defense team, that he had paid witnesses for false testimony, fabricated inculpatory evidence, and made false disclosures sensationalizing the alleged criminal events to the media, Stone laid into Waterfield big-time.

"The evidence," he said, while pointing to Waterfield, "will show Gore and Waterfield have a long history of crime dating back from 1976 to July 29, 1983."

Of course there was no evidence other than the false accusations made by Gore (which he later retracted) and the evidence given by others, which DA Robert Stone had paid money for, to substantiate any of this. Yet, undeterred, Stone went on:

"You'll hear evidence Waterfield participated in the July 26, 1983, crime by tying up Lynn Elliott so tight the rope cut all the way to the bone. The very same rope found by investigators in his vehicle," he said, still glaring at the defendant. Almost at once, Stone contradicted himself by adding, "Gore tied Lynn Elliott's hands behind her tightly, and then he had her kneel down and he tied her feet together." In his closing speech to the jury, DA Robert Stone didn't even acknowledge that Waterfield was, indeed, present, participated, or in any way aided Gore in this crime, and he reasserted that it had been Gore alone who had tied up Lynn Elliott.

But what of the rope that had been found by investigators in Waterfield's truck? Once again, the prosecutor shot himself in the foot when he called evidence technician Gerry Fitzgerald. Fitzgerald testified that he had found a mechanic's rag, marijuana, and a length of rope in Waterfield's vehicle and had photographed the items close to the locations where he found them.

Judge Vocelle stopped Fitzgerald in his tracks, asking him to clarify a matter regarding the rag, marijuana, and rope. "You *actually* found those items in the defendant's truck?" the judge asked, sensing that something was wrong.

Hastily backtracking, Fitzgerald admitted that he did not *actually* find the items in Waterfield's vehicle; he had received them from Detective Redstone and had taken them to the crime lab where Waterfield's truck was impounded and placed them inside.

This was a clear case of planting evidence, and Detective Redstone's name was all over it. In fact, Redstone had found the three items in Gore's vehicle, not Waterfield's. Fred vehemently denied ever seeing the rope, rag, or marijuana before.

Notwithstanding the fact that the police and state were obviously trying to set Fred Waterfield up for rapes and murders he had not committed, the prosecution recalled Detective Redstone, who testified that he had been the lead investigator in the Hommell case and that Waterfield was the perpetrator of that crime, too, despite the fact that Mrs. Hommell had told police that Waterfield had certainly not been involved.

Almost immediately under cross-examination, Redstone admitted that he had knowingly given perjured testimony to Judge Sharp to secure a search warrant for Waterfield's vehicle. But in the Elliott case he said that he had had no contact and had received no items from the truck. "It must have been someone else," he added limply. "I gave no evidence to Crime Technician Fitzgerald at all."

However, this claim under oath by Redstone totally contradicted his August 2, 1983, notarized sworn affidavit, in which he specifically stated that he had personally seized the mechanic's rag, rope, and marijuana and handed it to Fitzgerald.

Undeterred, the state then called Regan Martin, who suddenly changed her tune by stating that Waterfield *was* present "and aided by David Gore" in the commission of the crime by tying up Lynn Elliott and herself.

Michael Bloom seized on her sudden change of tack. "Have you not previously stated, under oath, and to police that Fred did not do any act that made you believe that he had planned the things that had happened . . . with reference to the house and the gun and everything . . . that Fred planned this with David Gore . . . that he was helping David Gore to carry it out, or that he was in any way involved in completing the events that happened?"

Robert Stone shot to his feet. "*Objection! . . . Objection!*" he shouted. The trial judge stopped the questioning, and the defense was refused an answer.

The state rested its case without calling David Gore as anticipated. When counsel questioned why Gore was not called, Robert Stone had the gall to tell the court that he could not vouch for the credibility of Gore at all. What Stone did not tell the jury was that Gore had since given sworn statements that completely exonerated Waterfield of all culpability, and that Fred *was* an innocent man.

On January 21, 1985, Fred Waterfield was convicted in the Byer–LeVallae murders. He received two consecutive life terms for his part in the crimes. Shortly, thereafter, Governor Bob Graham requested Robert Stone's resignation in an agreement to prevent the FBI and Drug Enforcement Administration (DEA) from prosecuting Stone for attempting to pervert the course of justice.

> Christopher. I really do not care to know about Gore's crimes. Nothing he says would surprise me. It will be extremely difficult to determine who won "The Liar's Contest," when comparing everything Gore and the prosecutors said and testified to with eyewitness suppressed documentary evidence and unrefutable [sic] victim testimony.
>
> —*Frederick Waterfield in a letter to the author*

One of the first problems we encounter when we examine the so-called true statements given to police by David Gore is the claim that Waterfield paid Gore for his "women-abducting services" with two checks: one for $400, and the second for $1,400.

Prosecutors had frozen all of Waterfield's bank accounts shortly after he was arrested, and the defense had requested numerous hearings seeking disclosure of why the bank accounts were frozen and requesting the court to order the accounts released. Finally, in December 1983, the state's attorney claimed that Gore had given sworn testimony indicating that Waterfield had written him the two checks for the Ling and Daley murders sometime in 1980, or 1981, both from Waterfield's 4x4 Inc. bank account.

However, in January 1984, Waterfield was able to prove that his 4x4 Inc. bank account was not opened until April 1983—two years *after* the checks had been written out—and, in any event, that the two payments were for Gore's employment with him shortly after he was released from prison.

The state attorney would later reluctantly admit in court that, ". . . all of Mr. Gore's three initial statements (which included the matter of the two checks) are not only inconsistent, but lies." Nevertheless, the untruthful allegation that Fred Waterfield paid his cousin to abduct women for his sexual perversions is still peddled as the truth on the internet today.

But you can take it from me that—having read all of Mr. Waterfield's appeal papers, which include four weighty volumes of motions, briefs, and quotes of testimony, all independently authenticated by sworn certificates and affidavits—the shocking fact is this: David Gore had admitted to prosecutors, prior to Waterfield's trial in 1984, that Waterfield had *not* been involved with any of the murders, yet the defense was never informed. After Waterfield was found guilty and sentenced, and when he learned of this obvious miscarriage of justice, he sought discovery of the statements made by Gore that would have exonerated him. All of Waterfield's motions for discovery were denied, the records were removed from the court files, and as a result no appellate hearing was held.

Was this the end of Waterfield's troubles? No way!

The reader will recall the ten-month period during which Regan Martin insisted that Fred Waterfield had been threatened by Gore at gunpoint when they were picked up while hitchhiking, that Waterfield had not touched or threatened the girls at all, and that after a heated exchange he had left Gore's residence within moments of arriving. We will also recall that Regan suddenly changed her mind and gave testimony against Waterfield at his 1984 trial.

It is now a matter of the court record that in November 1992 she recanted her testimony given at Waterfield's trial, reverting back to her original insistence that Waterfield had nothing to do with the abduction, subsequent rapes, and murder after all.

Prior to Waterfield's trial, a defense investigator discovered that Gore had written an article that had been published in Chaplin Ray's *Prison Ministries* periodical. In it, Gore claimed that he had become a police deputy so that he could learn how to "get away" with committing serial murder. When Waterfield's defense attorney tried to bring this article into evidence, the prosecutor put up a smokescreen. While Chaplin Ray would testify that the article had been written by Gore—he had the original letter and envelope to prove it—both Gore and the prosecution maintained that the article had been written by someone else, so the judge ruled it inadmissible as evidence.

It is an established fact that in the U.S. hundreds of serial crimes are committed by police patrol officers who use their position of authority to kidnap, rape, torture, and murder. Literally thousands of police officers commit offenses every year, and the majority of these crimes are not reported or disclosed to the media for the obvious reasons. For instance:

In 2005, the Duvall County Sheriff's Department asked for the resignation of 26 officers for sexual battery on people in police custody. But David Gore is one of the very few former police officers to receive the death penalty, and this penalty was handed down for just *one* of his murders.

In three of Gore's crimes, surviving victims testified that Gore was alone, and posing as an undercover cop. In another case he was driving an unmarked sheriff's department car when he made an abduction attempt. Therefore, it is correct to say that Gore had a well-established MO when trolling for his victims. And, even when two victims reported that Gore had made these abduction attempts, the only action taken by the sheriff was to ask for his resignation, despite the fact that he was already the prime suspect in two missing persons cases. These three women wanted to testify on Waterfield's behalf at his trial; however, Judge Vocelle denied their requests, saying that their evidence was, "not material to the state's case." Indeed, everyone who has stepped up with eyewitness accounts of Gore's criminal conduct has been prohibited from testifying before a jury, and their sworn affidavits were suppressed from disclosure to the media.

To make matters even worse, it is fact that state prosecutors have eyewitnesses to the conduct of David Gore during and around the time of each one of his admitted crimes. Once again, these witnesses' identities have been suppressed from disclosure because their accounts conclusively confirm that Waterfield could never have been involved.

As an example: In the Lings' murders, Gore's psychiatrist, a Dr. Tingle, provided the state prosecutor with the name of a witness who had watched Gore bury both women. It was not Waterfield, and this information has previously been denied media scrutiny.

Prompted by the testimony given by Regan Martin, a detective asked Gore during one of his interrogations, "Why didn't you shoot Waterfield during the commission of the Elliott/Martin crime?" To which Gore responded: "It is hard for me to kill someone I know. Fred is my cousin. Anyway, how can I shoot someone who ain't even there?"

> About a year and a half ago, Jean Elliot, Lynn Elliott's mother, recognized my sister at a yard sale. She introduced herself and told my sister and niece that she did not blame or hold me responsible for the murder of her daughter. You would not believe the relief I felt to know she knew I never meant any harm to Lynn. This turned me into an emotional wreck for weeks.
>
> Gore has admitted all of his statements implicating me are lies, and he has completely exonerated me of all of the murders no less than six times.
>
> —*Frederick Waterfield in a letter to the author*

Of course, if we only had Fred's word that Gore had admitted committing all of the murders alone, we would be right to be suspicious of Mr. Waterfield. However, Gore signed an affidavit to this effect before Constance L. Maher, a notary public for the state of Florida. It is published here for the first time:

AFFIDAVIT OF DAVID ALAN GORE

STATE OF FLORIDA
COUNTY OF UNION

BEFORE ME the undersigned authority personally appeared David Alan Gore, Inmate/DOC # 081008, who being duly sworn deposes and says:

I am an inmate at the Union Correctional Institution, P.O. Box 221, Raiford, FL 32083.

I was a co-defendant of Frederick Waterfield in two cases that originated in Indian River County, Florida.

I entered into plea negotiations with the State of Florida in which I agreed to testify against Frederick Waterfield.

The case the State of Florida presented against Mr. Waterfield was not accurate or factually correct. The Assistant State Attorney, detectives, and investigators involved in the cases knew or should have known that the testimony presented against Mr. Waterfield was neither accurate nor factually correct.

Mr. Waterfield had nothing to do with the murders of Lynn Elliott, Barbara Ann Beyer, or Angelica LeVallae. Mr. Waterfield is serving time under a conviction for offenses he did not commit.

FURTHER AFFIANT SAYETH NOT.
Dated this 1st day of December, 1997

Signed
Sealed

In 2001, David Gore filed another affidavit, this time in the Supreme Court of Florida. It is published here for the first time:

IN THE SUPREME COURT OF FLORIDA
(Before a Referee)

THE FLORIDA BAR, CASE NO. SC00-2406
Complainant, TFB NO. 199-10,769(13D)

v.
LOREN DAVID RHOTON
Respondent

AFFIDAVIT OF DAVID A. GORE

STATE OF FLORIDA
COUNTY OF UNION

BEFORE ME, the undersigned authority personally appeared Affiant, DAVID A. GORE, who being first duly sworn, deposes and says that:

I am over eighteen (18) years of age and have personal knowledge as to the facts and information set forth therein.

I am currently incarcerated at Union Correctional Institution and am serving sentences for the murders of Barbara Byer and Angelica LaVallae.

My cousin, Frederick Waterfield, is also incarcerated at Union Correctional Institution.

I testified in my cousin's trials in the Barbara Byer and Angelica LaVallae criminal cases as a condition of plea negotiations with the State of Florida.

My cousin was convicted of first degree murder in both of those cases and was sentenced to consecutive life sentences.

I did not appeal my convictions and sentences in the Byer and LaVallae cases, and I did not have any attorney representation for the Byer and LaVallae cases after I was sentenced in those cases.

After the Byer and LaVallae trials, I began corresponding through letters with my other cousin, Constance Maher, who is Frederick Waterfield's sister. True and correct copies of some letters that I wrote to Constance are attached to this Affidavit (Composite Exhibit A).

Constance contacted Frederick's attorney to arrange a meeting with the attorney, so that I could talk with the attorney personally about my previous testimony in the Byer and LaVallae trials.

Before the meeting, I received from Frederick's attorney, Loren Rhoton, an affidavit restating what I had previously written and said about my trial testimony.

I read the affidavit before I met with Mr. Rhoton, and I made no changes to it.

When I later personally met with Mr. Rhoton and Constance, I executed the affidavit (A true and correct copy of the affidavit is attached hereto as Exhibit B).

I executed the affidavit voluntarily and of my own free will and with no threats or coercion.

Mr. Rhoton did not make any promises or guarantees to me regarding the affidavit before or after I signed it.

I knew at all times that Mr. Rhoton would be using the affidavit in his representation of Frederick in Frederick's appeals in the Byer and LeVallae cases, and that Mr. Rhoton would be filing that affidavit with the court.

I gave Mr. Rhoton permission to file the affidavit in my cousin's appeals.

Mr. Rhoton did not tell me that he would be sending the affidavit to my attorneys who were representing me in the Lynn Elliott case and I did not ask him to do so.

Mr. Rhoton did not tell me or suggest to me that he would be getting the permission of my attorneys in that other case before he filed my affidavit in my cousin's appeals.

Mr. Rhoton told me that, if he needed a more detailed affidavit from me later on, he would then have my attorneys review any other affidavit that he would have to prepare.

Mr. Rhoton used my affidavit exactly in the way and for the purpose that I had authorized him and exactly as he said he would.

FURTHER AFFIANT SAYETH NOT.

Signed: DAVID A. GORE

The foregoing Affidavit was acknowledged before me this *28th* day of March, 2001, by DAVID A. GORE, ~~who is personally known to me or~~ who provided for identification the following: *Prison ID*

Betty Ann Lewis-Alvarez

Signature of Person Taking Acknowledgment

Betty Ann Lewis-Alvarez

Name of Acknowledger Typed, Printed or Stamped

(NOTARY SEAL)

Notorial Serial Number # CC884482.

RHOTON & HAYMAN, P.A.

412 East Madison Street

Suite 1111
TAMPA, FLORIDA 33602.

On Monday, June 12, 2000, David Alan Gore sat down in his squalid death row cell and started writing. What follows provides a verbatim and sickening insight into the mind of a psychopathic killer—a true Hannibal Lecter if there ever was one.[17] This material has never been published before, and, for the obvious reasons, the names of his victims have been deleted.

> You should hear some of the names I was called by people in my home town when I abducted my victims. But I did manage to thin-out the population a little! ☺.
>
> You have no idea how thrilling it was to me to have a victim in my secluded place when *NO* one could find us, and just be able to concentrate on ENJOYING my prey. Most serial killers they get someone and their so concerned with being seen that they really can't enjoy their victim completely. But I could. I could take my time with them & enjoy them.
>
> There were times when I'd enjoy a victim for *DAYS*. I'd do so much to her, that she would be close to death at the end, and I'd just finish her off, or butcher her for dining. ☺.
>
> I had a 14-year-old girl one time that I raped at least 30 times. Her name was *********. I kept her tied to a bed for two days, and when I didn't rape her, I had this 18" dildo I used to rape her with both in the pussy & asshole. She would pass out a couple of times.

---

17 The content and grammar is exactly as Gore has penned in his quite neat hand. Copies of Gore's letters have been forwarded to Fred Waterfield and his legal advisors, as a matter of course.

Toward the end she was asking me to go ahead & kill her. I told her, OK, and I gave her a choice as to how I would kill her, & I ended up dragging her ass out on the ground, laying her down face down, then I straddled her back, grabbed her hair, pulled her hair back & cut her throat. When she was dead, I hung her up by her ankles from rafters in my barn & butchered her. I probably cooked & ate 80% of her meat. She was especially tender.

Before I get into one of my victims, let me share something with you that I didn't share with others. All of my victims were females. This wasn't because I hated women, it was because of a couple of reasons. See, one of my primary purposes for abducting females was to engage in cannibalism with their meat. I discovered that the meat from the youngest females was SUPER in taste & quality. So when I wanted to stock my freezer with meat, I would get 13- to 16-year-old girls because their meat was the tenderess.

When I abducted an older woman in her 30 or 40's it was simple to ENJOY the thrill of the rape & kill.

Another thing that no one knows is I collected trophies off my victims. Sometimes it would be HAIR, sometimes it would be an ear, or their lips. Or sometimes it would be a breast, or I'd shave their pubic hair off & save it.

And when I abducted a woman I was pretty brutal in what I did to her. Like I said earlier, I had them in a place [a barn on his father's fruit orchard] where I could take my time with them and really enjoy doing things to them. I literally tortured them unmercifully.

I mean, while they were tied spread eagle on the bed, I'd cut off their NIPPLES one at a time. And then I'd cut out their CLIT, while they were alive & kicking. Sometime I'd stuff their severed clit into their mouth & make them swallow it☺.

Now the victim I want to share with you was a 16-year-old girl. Her name was ********! I saw her get off a school bus one afternoon and the minute I saw her, I *WANTED* her. She lived way out in the country & and she got off the school bus and would walk about a half mile down this lonely dirt road to her house.

So for a few days I would secretly watch her get off the bus, to make sure of her *routine*. So I laid out a plan to abduct her. What I did was impersonate a police officer, with FULL uniform & all. I even rented a car that looked like an official police car.[18]

On the day I planned to abduct her, I waited down the road until she got off the bus & had started walking home. I then drove down the road & pulled up beside her & when she looked & saw a "COP," she stopped & smiled. I told her that there was an escaped convict somewhere in the vicinity & that she shouldn't be walking down the road. She acted scared & and I told her that I would be happy to give her a ride to her house ☺.

She practically jumped in my car ☺.

As I started down the road, I pulled my gun on her & stuck the barrel into her ribs & told her that if she tried anything I would shoot & kill her. She was stunned. She didn't know what was happening. All she said, "Oh my God . . . please don't."

---

18 At the time of this offence, Gore was a deputy police officer, and he did use a rental car circa this period.

I kept driving until I came to a secluded citrus grove & I pulled down into the trees. I had to get her tied up & secure so I could drive on out to my trailer.

I got some handcuffs out, & I pulled her hands behind her back & cuffed her. I also put a pair of cuffs on her ankles. I then told her we were going to take a little drive and if she tried *ANYTHING* I would kill her. I told her to sit there & look straight ahead.

Now she went to one of these private schools for *RICH* kids. And she had on her little uniform they wear, with a white blouse, and a little plaid skirt. As we were driving, she kept asking me what I was going to do to her☺. I just told her to shut up bitch, do as I say, & you'll live. Ha! ☺.

She started to cry & I told her to stop or I would kill her.

We finally got to my secluded trailer, & I pulled up to the door, got her out of the car. I held her arm & led her into the trailer, walked her back to the bedroom, & when she saw the bed, & ropes attached to each corner she said, "Oh, God, please NO!" She knew what was going to be done. She went to begging me *NOT* to. She told me she was a *VIRGIN*, and to *PLEASE* don't. I grabbed a handful of her hair, & pulled her back onto me, & I told her, "YOU LITTLE RICH BITCH, YOU ARE MINE NOW!" I pushed her down on the bed, & and she went to crying & screaming for someone to help her. I told she could scream all she wanted, *NO ONE* would hear.

I tied both her hands to the bed post, then tied both her ankles to the other bed post. Then I went over to the dresser & took out all of my tools, knife, needles, soldering iron. When she seen all this, she screamed & pulled against the ropes. I took my knife & and told her, now let's get those clothes off & see what you got. She was screaming & crying.

I cut her blouse off, & she had this little pink bra which I cut off. She had a really *NICE* set of breasts. I cut her shirt off, and she was *NICE*. She had this *FULL* mound of soft brown public hair & I took my finger & pulled it hard. She was hysterical.

I then felt all of body, like fruit to see if it's a good piece, I *kneaded* her thighs seeing how *meaty* she was. I knew she was going to taste excellent. Her meat was real firm & *I knew* she would be tender.

I did her entire body like that and it freaked her out. She had *never* had a man see or touch her body.

Of course all of this was me into my sadistic desire, so I took off my clothes & she was jerking against the ropes & screaming. I climbed between her legs, took some Vaseline & lubricated her up & inserted my cock into her, & when I did, she arched her back as if to get away from me. I grabbed her by her thick hair & held her as I rammed deep in her, & she let out this blood curdling scream as I *tore* her.

It didn't take many thrusts & I released. She was crying hysterically as she just lost her virginity by rape. I bit her nipples pretty hard, & I had left bite marks. She was writhing in pain, but I wasn't through with her tender ass yet. I got straddled over her chest & I grabbed her hair & pulled her head up, & I told her to SUCK or die. I inserted the head into her mouth & she tried to gag but I put the blade of my knife to her throat & told her if she didn't suck I'd cut her throat. You should have seen the look in her eyes as I pushed deep into her mouth. I practically fucked her mouth.

Then it was time to really put something into her. So I pulled out my 18" dildo & when she saw it, she went berserk, screaming. I smeared some Vaseline over it, & worked the head of it into her bloody pussy, & when I'd gotten the rubber head in, I looked at her as I slowly pushed it deeper, deeper into her & and it ripped the flesh between her pussy & ass hole, & she was absolutely screaming again. I pushed it in at least 12 inches. I pulled it out, & reinserted it into her ass hole, & boy I had to work to get it in, but when I did, I reamed her good. She was in so much pain, she passed out, & I just took a break while she lay there. When she started coming to I had plugged the soldering iron in, & the tip was red hot. I took it and seized her nipples & clit, & this caused her to pass out again. So I figured it was *HARVEST* time. It was time to go ahead & kill this bitch and butcher her.

I had a barn where I did my butchering, it had these high timber rafters where I hung two ropes. I had a water hose so I could wash my prey down. So while she was unconscious I cut the rope loose from her hands & ankles, & re-tied her hands behind her back, just in case she came to before I got her outside to my butchering area.

I drug her outside across the ground to where I had the ropes. I then tied her ankles to each rope, and hoisted her upside down up off the ground. I pulled her up until her head was about a foot above the ground. The ropes her feet were tied to were about 10 feet apart, so it spread her legs apart.

About then she started coming to and as she became aware of her predicament she went nuts & was screaming & her jerking was causing her to sway on the ropes. I kneeled down, & I told her it was time to replace my freezer with meat. She was going ballistic, so I grabbed her by the hair, & pulled her head backwards & up, & with my knife, I reached under her and with one quick swipe I sliced her throat open,

& her blood gushed out & I held her head up until the blood drained out and as her blood poured out, her body went to quivering & vibrating as it went into the death throes, & as she died, her body just went limp. I took my knife & finished cutting off her head, and as I cut her neck meat all the way around her neck, I had to turn & twist her head so her neck bone would snap, & when it did her head dropped off, & I held it up by the hair, examined it, then set it over on a table.

I then took my knife, & stuck the blade into her pussy, and sliced her stomach open all the way down to right between her titties. I then reached in with my hands & pulled the intestines out, let them drop to the ground. I then reached back in & cut loose her liver, heart & lungs & pulled them out. I laid her heart & liver over on a table because those are delicious cooked up. I then took a hose & washed out her body cavity of the remaining blood & flesh. Then, I cut all the meat off her thighs and just left her bone. I cut off the meat from *BOTH* cheeks of her ass. Then there is a strip of meat that runs down each side of her back-bone, & I cut these off.

I cut both her titties off flush with her chest. I cut both shoulder blades off, as they are good for roasting.

I then cut the rest of her down & put in bags to burn. I then stood at the table & *skinned* her skin off the chunks of meat I cut off her.

Then after the skin was off I sliced the meat up into ½ strips & put in freezer bags.

I took her head & cut her hair off, put it in a zip lock bag to save. I cut one of her ears off. And I cut her bottom jaw off to save. I buried all the scraps. She had some school books & a purse. I buried those also.

> That night I cooked up a batch of her meat. I salt & peppered it. I floured it and deep fried it with onion, & it was absolutely the most delicious tender meat it would melt in your mouth.
>
> There was a huge SEARCH for her for weeks. Because her parents were such High Society, they spared no expense. I would sit and watch stories of her disappearance on T.V. while eating her meat☺.

In another 2000 letter, written by David Gore, he described one of his hunting expeditions for human prey. Again, what follows is published verbatim, and for the obvious reasons the victim's name has been removed from the text:

> I have to share with you a women I killed, she was in her 30s and she weighed around 180 lbs. She was the only & last large woman I killed, because she was just so heavy. I mean when you have to drag her, that 180 pounds is like dead weight. She was a lot of *WORK*. But she had a *LOT* of meat on her. Normally I never went after one her size, but on this particular day, I was hungry for a *Kill*.
>
> I had left my house early that morning, to begin a "hunt". I spent all day, driving prowling the beaches, the neighborhoods, bus stops and I just couldn't find a suitable victim.
>
> Well about 4:00 or 5:00 that afternoon the day was coming to an end. And my adrenalin & things to "DO" one was at its peak.
>
> So I decided to make a pass through a County neighborhood, before heading home. Well as I was driving down this dirt road, I passed this mobile home trailer, and the woman was getting out of her car, & going up to the

trailer. I gave her a look over, & and she wasn't bad. I saw that she was a little larger than I liked, but I was roving for one to DO, so I thought WHY NOT?, I'd try to get her. I didn't want to waste time scouting her out, so I made the decision to just attempt to abduct her right then.

My plan was going to be simple. I was going to knock on her door, and when she opened her door, I was going to just force my way in, & attack her basically. I tucked my gun down the back of my pants, got my handcuffs & rope & tucked them in my pants. And I had this baton like you see Cops carry. It's basically a nightstick I was going to use it to hit her with to stun her.

Now I did *NOT* know if anyone else was in this home with her. I really didn't care. I decided that if there was *ANYONE* else in there with her, when I forced my way in, I was going to just shoot *anybody* I saw. There were no neighbors around so I wasn't concerned about anyone hearing gunshots. So I pulled up in her driveway, and my adrenalin is pumping. When you get to this stage and you are just minutes away from grabbing one, everything in you is at such a *high*.

So I have what I need, and I'm dressed nice, clean cut, and I knock on her door. I am holding my nightstick in my right hand sort of behind me. I sort of expected her to peek out and see who was at her door. But she didn't. She just opened the door to see who was there and the instant she opened the door I lunged at her, and I swung the nightstick as hard as I could and I hit her right in the center of her forehead. I mean it struck her right above the bridge of her nose. Well, she fell backwards and when she dropped, her ass hit the floor & her head fell back & hit the floor. And when I hit her it made a *LOUD* pop sound I knew I had hit her good.

Well almost as soon as her body hit the floor I was on her, I didn't even hesitate. I reared back & hit her in the head again with the stick & she just let out this "Ugh" & lay still. I immediately pulled my gun & I was looking around, ready for anyone to be in there with her and I was sitting on her as I do this ☺.

Well fortunately she *WAS* alone. I had knocked her unconscious ☺. It happened so fast, I didn't even think she knew what hit her. I mean the second the door opened & I saw her, I was on her.

Now the large bitch is laying out on her living room floor, and the *VERY* first thing I notice is how *HUGE* her breasts are. I have *NEVER* seen breasts this large on a woman. They were the biggest ones I'd ever seen. I would guess that each breast weighed a least 10 pounds. I was so mesmerized by this size, I just reached & squeezed them. Um☺.

Well, I sat on top of her for a few minutes, with gun in hand, just listening, making sure *NO* one else was there. I then got off her, and rolled her over onto her stomach, and I knew right then, this was going to be work ☺. I pulled her arms around behind her back, & handcuffed her wrists together. I noticed she wasn't wearing a wedding ring, so I was pretty sure she wasn't married. She had on several other rings. I removed them from her fingers & put them in my pocket.

I then, took the rope I'd brought in, pulled her ankles together & tied her ankles tight.

I then rolled her back onto her back, & I went into her bathroom & got a couple wash cloths, brought them &

stuffed them into her mouth and pushed them down into her mouth. Then I took a short piece of rope and tied it around her mouth & head to hold the gag in.

I knew she was just knocked out because she was breathing. Once I had her bound & gagged I walked through her trailer, and I collected her purse, and all of her bras & panties, her perfume, and several articles of her clothes. I went into her kitchen & got her best knifes [sic] & put everything into a pillow case, & eased the door open to make sure no one was outside, then took them to my car.

When I came back in, I was going to drag her out to my car, and put her in the trunk. Well, I lifted her shoulders up off the floor, under her armpits & WOW, she was dead weight. I went to pull her across the floor out her front door & I had to just take one step, pull, one step, pull. I got her out the door, & there was like three steps you go down to the ground, so I just sort of pulled her down them, & I knew that this was my most vulnerable time. If someone drove by while I was dragging her to my car, I was busted.

So, I wanted to get her to my car as quickly as possible. My car was like 20 feet away, so I mustered up every ounce of energy I had, grabbed her by her feet & went to pulling and I got her to my trunk & worked like hell getting her up & in, and I was all out. I closed the trunk & went back & wiped my fingerprints from any place I touched & locked the door.

Then I drove to my trailer where I "DID" all my victims.

I pulled up, got out, opened the trunk to get her out. And she was now conscious ☺. She was moaning & her eyes were wide open staring at me & you could see her fear in them. She had these really blue eyes, and her hair was almost like a bleach blonde, it was short.

She was extremely pretty, she was just what I call *LARGE* frame female. She wasn't this gross fat, just large bone & and she had a layer of fat over her. Actually for a butchering & eating she was ideal.

Well, when she saw me, she trying to holler at me through her gag. I reached in, got me a handful of her hair, pulled her head up, and told her "BITCH YOU BELONG TO ME NOW!"

There this bitch was, all secure ready to be enjoyed. She was wearing a blue blouse, and these Levi type pants. I took out a knife, & cut up each leg of her pants and pulled them off. When I did this, she was mumbling through the gag & shaking her head. She was wearing these silk panties which I promptly cut off & she had the thickest bush of public hair. I mean it was thick & covered her whole area.

I ran my fingers through it. I saw tears start rolling down the bitch's face.

I then cut off her blouse & she had on this full figure bra so I cut it off & when I did, two watermelons rolled out. I was stunned by the SIZE of her breasts. I went to squeezing on them & mashing them. She just cried & moaned. She kept her eyes closed tight during the time I was violating her body. I noticed when a female does this it's her way of blocking this out. When I was enjoying the size of her breasts a thought came to my mind. I remember vividly somewhere when a man had cut off a woman's breast and took the skin of her breasts and made a pouch. I thought this breast would be perfect to try that one.

I wanted to re-position her legs so I could do a few things to, so I took & re-tied her legs so that each leg was pulled up

& back along her sides. And the ankles were tied to the bed post above her head. Like this (diagram). With her legs tied it exposed both her ass hole and pussy for torturing. I could ram a stick up her in this position & it would cause enormous pain you know, I did not have a desire to rape her, I wanted to *HURT* her. But I couldn't resist. My *male* nature just had to poke it in, so I did a quicky on her while she squirmed.

After I did it, I told her to consider herself *RAPED* & I laughed. I then got all my *tools* out, and I told her, she needed to be taught a lesson about *kicking.*

I had this *wooden* pole. It was a 2 feet long & had a diameter of about 3 inches. It was varnished so it was real slick. The end was pointed like a bullet. And I took this & put some Vaseline over the end so it would push in easy, & I proceeded to insert the end into her pussy hole & I had to really wiggle & push to get it inserted, and while I was doing that, she was jerking & screaming, trying to get away from that thing between her legs ☺.

I managed to get it in about two inches, & I looked at her and said, "KICK THIS BITCH" & gave a hard shove on it & it rammed up inside her about 10 inches, & when it did it ripped her pussy flesh between her hole & asshole & blood squirted.

Well, she lunged her whole body up & let out this blood curdling scream. I pushed her down and got the 18" dildo I had right there & shoved it up inter her ass hole, while the wooden one was still up her vagina. Here she was with two objects coming out of her pussy & asshole and she went into a seizure like state. This is when they start wheezing & their body quivers. This is from the body enduring so much pain it just acts up.

So I pulled both out of her & they had blood smeared all over them & when I saw this I wiped my hand over the sticky blood & it felt *SO* good.

She was still in that state, I pulled her gag from her mouth and the rags were soaked with her saliva. I liked that. She was sort of gasping, and, like a person does when they are in shock. And she was making this wailing sound. I looked at her and said, "What. You don't want to kick me bitch"☺.

I examined her body, mashing her thighs, ass, shoulders. I was checking her meat content ☺.

When she started groaning and crying, she looked at me and said, "Why? Why are you doing this?" I said because I'm hungry ☺. She didn't know what it meant.

I took & squeezed her nipples, & I said, "You have some big ones here." She kept asking if I was going to let her go. I said, "maybe". I took a pair of pliers & gripped one of her nipples in the pliers & squeezed & I squeezed the nipple so hard it brought blood, & I leaned down & took her bloody nipple in my mouth & sucked the blood & oh, I liked it. She was screaming & yelling & calling me all kinds of names.

I said, "You know, you have a lot of good meat on you. You are definitely US DA Choice. And when I said that, she got the death fear look on her face & just said, "Oh, God. No. Oh, God, NO."

Then she said, "Oh, God, You're going to kill me aren't you?" I said, "Well, yeah cause I am a cannibal & I'm hungry." She went crazy. She screamed like I never heard someone scream & I took that wooden pole I used to rape her with & I hit her in the head. I didn't hit her hard enough to knock her out, but hard enough to really hurt. I said, "DAMN. YOU DON'T KILL EASY DO YOU?"

Oh, she went to screaming at the top of her lungs. She would scream "Oh, God Help, He's Killing Me." I was hitting her like this on purpose. It was just another way of torture.

I'd hit her again, this time on top of her head. And each time she'd go ballistic. I did this several times. I hit her all on the head☺. I then hit each one of her breasts hard, & I just started hitting her body all over, especially her legs. I told her, "This tenderizes the meat before I kill you."

She was screaming so hard and jerking she lost her voice ☺. I said, "Damn bitch, I guess you are tender enough, I need to go ahead & finish you off now."

She just went numb. It was like she resigned herself to be killed & she braced herself for it ☺.

I wanted to try something I'd heard about, so I got an ice pick, & I took it, & I right underneath her left arm, and almost even with her breast, there's like two ribs. Well I heard if you stick someone here, it will pierce their heart. So I wanted her to die slow, & for her to *know* she was dying. So I took it & out the point against her ribs & pushed it in & when I did, her whole body arched against the rope. I pushed the ice pick in to the hilt & just left it in & she had a look on her face, that the only way I can describe it was a DEATH LOOK.

When I stuck the ice pick in, & she arched, her whole body just stiffened & her eyes glued *WIDE* open. And I knew I'd punctured her heart, & she was bleeding internally because I saw a trickle of blood ease out of the corner of her mouth. And it took probably 5 minutes for her to bleed to death internally and as she began dying her body began relaxing *VERY* slowly, and when she reached her death throes her body shook real violently. I've seen them do this at the point of death. It's like a contraction. Then after her body quivered & her eyes glazed over, she went limp, and just as she died, she pissed out on the bed. They lose their bladder when they die. I then pulled the ice pick out & cut her ropes loose.

Now I had to get the big whore out to my barn to hoist her up to be butchered. I tied her by her feet & drug her off the bed & across the floor out across the ground to where the hoist was. And I let her lay there a few minutes while I rested. She was heavy dragging.

Now, I had this frame where I had ropes hung & this was where I hung my victims to butcher.[19] I had all the instruments I needed, a water hose to wash the carcasses down with. This way I could tie the feet to these hooks, & winch her up off the ground. It was a good system. So, I had her laying there & I lowered the bar with the hooks on, tied each ankle to these then winched her off the ground to where her head was about 6 inches off the ground. The first thing I do after I have them hung, is cut their throat from ear to ear. This lets them *bleed* out so when you start butchering, it's not so bloody. Sometime I will catch some of her blood in a bottle to use to make a gravy sauce out of.

While her blood is draining, I took a razor & *shaved* her public hair off. I shaved her clean. Then I took a water hose & washed her down. Then I took my knife & cut her neck all the way around. I cut all the way through to her neck meat down to her neck bone, & then I twisted her head so it snaps her neck bone, & then her head drops off. I sat it on a table.

---

19 Gore also used this hoist to butcher the wild game he hunted down.

> I scalped her, removed her blue eyes & lips. She had these really blue eyes & I wanted to see if I could remove one of the eyeballs to save.
>
> The next thing I did was start right at her pussy hole & slice her open all the way to her sternum. Then I reached in & pull all the guts out & let them fall to the floor . . .

And so David Gore goes on, and on, and on, describing in vivid detail how he skinned this victim and prepared the meat for cooking. But apparently this woman wasn't quite to his discerning taste, for he adds: "To be honest, the best ones to get are young 13 & 14 years old, because they are small & easy to carry and you can put them into a relatively small place to transport."

Ever anxious to pass on his knowledge for the benefit of other wannabe serial killers, Gore says: "I was always very aware that women in their 30s and 40s are mature and well able to try to escape. When as a 13 or 14 year old they are pretty submissive and they just don't have the intelligence to figure out an escape. They are more scared & they just 'handle' a lot better."

Gore says that the more victims he abducted, the more relaxed he became in taking them and killing them, to the point that he would go "hunting" every day. "The sadistic urge to kill kept growing stronger," he wrote in a letter to the author, "I lived in a very dark world."

According to Gore, some weeks he would abduct three or four women, although we have to take this claim with a pinch of salt. He also says: "Then there [were] times I'd go a whole week and not be able to find one victim," so there may be some truth in his abduction claims after all.

In one of Gore's letters he enclosed a photograph of a dead woman lying on a carpet.[20] In an attached note he said, "I'd love to find a dead body like this. That would be neat ☺. I could have had a meal without all the *work* ☺."

Gore is also at pains to point out that he "did not hate women, or all girls, only certain types. Plus the fact that my ex-wife really did me dirty. So it was just convenient that my focus was on girls. I've had people ask me why didn't I just kill my ex-wife, why did I kill young girls?"

When asked why he targeted young females, Gore said:

> Many people have asked me this question & I've never answered it because you will never understood my desire to *EAT* human meat, and young girls were delicacy. So how do you tell someone the reason being that I killed young women was because I wanted to eat them. Actually, the night before I was caught I was in the planning stage of abducting a BUS load of high school *CHEERLEADERS*.
>
> I had already targeted the bus. Here is the *PLAN* I was making.
>
> There was this bus that carried Junior high school girls to OUT OF TOWN football games to cheerlead. There were probably a dozen young girls in the bus around 14 to 15 years old. There were 2 or 3 adult women on there with them.
>
> I was going to dress up in a police officer's uniform. By the way I had one of these flashing blue lights cops put on

---

20 The body was that of a young married mother of two, Mrs. Emily Patterson, who was murdered and raped in her home at 100 Riverton Avenue, Winnipeg, Manitoba, on Friday, June 10, 1927. Her body was found by her husband. The notorious serial killer Earle Nelson was found guilty of this murder and hanged on January 13, 1928.

> their dash. I was going to pull up behind this bus & turn the blue light on. When they pulled over I was going to tell the chaperone that we had a report that there might be a bomb on the bus. I'd tell her, don't tell the girls, but let's just switch busses and y'all can go on. This adult would tell the girls that we have to change buses & everyone would get off & get on the other bus. Now I would have jammed the door & window so they couldn't be opened.
>
> When everyone was on *OUR* bus, I'd stand up & pull a gun & tell them all if they tried anything they'd be shot.
>
> I had a lot of little things to work out. But I would have tried it. Having that many to enjoy would have been pure rush☺. Right off the bat I would have chose one girl and killed her in front of the others to show them I mean business.
>
> Anyway, that was my sick world ☺.

Of course, by now the reader is asking what planet David Gore came from. For his part, Fred Waterfield says that knew nothing of his cousin's insane schemes, dryly remarking, "Next, he'll be telling you that he was building a spaceship so that he could take his victims to the moon."

I am sure that Fred Waterfield will not be permitted by the Florida Department of Corrections to read this chapter. However, I do intend to make sure that a copy of this book *is* sent to the FBI and to the present governor.

***

CHAPTER 6

CHARLES "CHUCK" LANNIS MOSES—A REAL-LIFE OUTLAW JOSEY WALES

Down every road there's always one more city
I'm on the run, the highway is my home
I raised a lot of cane back in my younger days
While Mama used to pray my crops would fail
I'm a hunted fugitive with just two ways:
Outrun the Law or spend my life in jail.

—MERLE HAGGARD
"I'M A LONESOME FUGITIVE"

My friends call me "Outlaw Mosey Wales" after the movie "Josey Wales" starring Clint Eastwood. I am a true outlaw, survivalist, and a Christian God-fearing man. I love to play the guitar and sing.

—CHARLES MOSES
LETTER TO THE AUTHOR, OCTOBER 19, 2009

He goes for camping equipment and weapons. Ninety-nine percent of the time he always runs. He's good at it.

—CHIEF SHERIFF'S DEPUTY GARY STUDEBAKER
NOCONA, TEXAS

Charles "Chuck" Lannis Moses

A serial killer is a person who murders three or more people at different locations, over a period of time, with a cooling off period in between the events.

—FBI DEFINITION OF A SERIAL KILLER

IN THE MIDWEST, a fugitive drug dealer did anything to avoid capture, and his desperate flight was fueled by drugs and punctuated by gunfire, and as he barreled along from Nebraska to Wyoming, authorities united in pursuit. This is Charles "Chuck/Charlie" Lannis Moses's story, written with the assistance of Moses, aka "The Lonely Fugitive." He became notorious as one of the FBI's Most Wanted, and he relates his account exclusively to this author in letters from prison.

The record shows that Charlie Moses killed just once. Nonetheless, he did attempt to shoot dead two law enforcement officers and, had he not been caught, undoubtedly he would have committed murder again and again. So, for the purposes of this book we can call him a "serial killer in the making."

Wednesday, February 2, 2000, Lincoln County, Nebraska: The ground was as hard as a plaster cast, but now a thaw is underway with the Nebraska Weather Center logging a high of −18 degrees. The state, south of Columbus, would still need a few more days of moderate temperatures to make deep slush and mud.

It had just started to rain, and Sheriff's Deputy Stan McKnight was on a routine patrol when he saw, in his rear-view mirror, high beams gaining on him. Then a maroon Chevy pickup truck sped past leaving a filthy spray in its wake.

McKnight noted that the truck had a Texas license plate, but he couldn't read it properly. He switched on his red and blue strobes, but he was unable pursue the truck because the road was too icy, so he cautiously followed while radioing for backup.

Several Nebraska State Patrol troopers were alerted, and it soon became apparent that whoever was in the truck had no regard for his own safety. However, although the roads were empty, McKnight decided against a high-speed chase. It was not worth the risk, as McKnight recalled:

> It appeared that the driver knew the area he was in, and because he could take more chances than I would, he was able to disappear. I had called in assistance from the police department and all the State Troopers that were working. We combed the entire area to no avail.

Nebraska police sent out a lookout bulletin for the maroon pickup with Texas plates, but that night there were no further reports of the vehicle or its driver.

North Platte (pop. 23,900) Lincoln County, Nebraska: A week later, and 40 miles away in the county seat of North Platte, a farmer called the police. He had not used his barn in years, so he was surprised to find that somebody had been there recently. He was also worried by what had been left behind.

Deputies found chemicals and other farm supplies, a dangerous combination. The ingredients could have been used to make methamphetamine.

An illegal stimulant drug, "meth" is otherwise known as "crank" or "speed"; the drug is simple to make, and deputies in

Lincoln County had seen this kind of setup many times before. In recent years, the Midwestern United States had seen an epidemic of methamphetamine production, as Lincoln County Sheriff's Corporal Casey Nelms explained:

> Methamphetamine labs are a problem because it's such a rural area, a lot of abandoned farmhouses; farmsteads where people don't live anymore give these drug people the opportunity to go in and manufacture this drug undetected. The drug is addictive and extremely dangerous. Most users become aggressive and desperate. When meth labs pop up anywhere, violent crime always follows.

During the search of the makeshift lab, deputies also found several letters. They were addressed to one Charles Lannis Moses, Jr., at an address in Nocona, Texas, so they contacted the Texas authorities asking for information on the man. They were sent photographs of Moses and were told that he was wanted for firearms theft. Nebraska authorities also learned that he owned a maroon pickup truck with Texas license plates, which matched the description of the vehicle McKnight had chased the week before.

If Moses was manufacturing the drug, there was a good chance that he was using it, too, which at once explained why he had driven so recklessly. Nelms said, "The people who use this drug become very paranoid. They have no pain threshold. Sometimes they are up for days. They are just a real problem and hard to handle."

Police went door-to-door, asking if anyone had seen Moses or noticed an outsider fitting his description. A few people thought they had seen him before, but no one had spotted him during the past few days. He had no known local address.

11:30 p.m., Saturday, February 12, 2000, Sutherland (pop. 1,200), Nebraska: It had been just a over a week since the lab had been discovered. On "a pretty nice morning," Moses had found a quiet place beside the Platte River at an old farmhouse. He had a few hours to kill before meeting with one of his buddies, Huey, who was driving out from New Jersey, and Charlie was cooking a batch of meth for his pal.

After he finished cooking the meth, and with his police scanner crackling away in the cab of his truck, Charlie called up his buddy on the CB. They arranged to meet in the evening near North Platte, and Moses, now super high after cooking the meth, would be driving into "a straight-on blizzard," which was blowing in from the northwest.

"By the time I got to North Platte, snow had covered all of the highways and medians. I pulled into the Flying J truck stop, then I drove around till I met my pal's rig," Charlie recalled.

The two men chatted, and the meth exchange was completed. They then made plans for Moses to drive to Denver, where he would change the paint job on his truck, change the license plates, and alter his own appearance in an effort to keep him on the run.

Parting company, Huey told Charlie to stay cool and not get caught by "Smoky Bear." Moses responded, "If I get caught it will be the shoot-out of the century." Both men laughed and went their separate ways.

It began to get dark, and Moses followed his pal's rig 25 miles west to the Sutherland exit, the weather now so bad he could hardly make out the taillights of the truck in front of him. He turned off the interstate and into a gas station where he "pumped gas and bought a bag of Doritos chips to munch on." On the way out of the door, he spotted "this huge policeman," who was leaving at the same time.

Corporal Casey Nelms was about to start his shift, and just as he did every night, he stopped at a gas station a few hundred yards from the Interstate 80/Sutherland interchange to pick up a cup of coffee. But this night would be anything but routine.

Through the gas station window, Nelms spotted a parked vehicle that matched the description of Moses's pickup. The officer wiped the condensation from the glass and peered through. Now he was sure it was Moses, but to confirm this he needed a close up and personal look at the driver, who resembled the man police were looking for. The Texas plates—2TCB58—matched Moses's truck, so Nelms walked outside and wiped the snow from his windshield. When the driver said, "How'd ya do?" Nelms replied, "Allright."

"What are the roads like out there? Is it gonna snow all night?" asked Moses.

"Yes," came the curt answer.

Corporal Nelms then asked Moses where he was heading.

"Just heading out," said Moses, now making for his truck 100 feet away. The officer asked for Moses's ID. "It is in a bag in my truck, I'll get it."

At his truck Moses asked the cop if he could switch the engine on to warm the vehicle up. "Go ahead," Nelms agreed, while examining the driver's license in the name of Charles Lannis Moses and making a note of the front tag.

Leaping into his vehicle, Moses slammed the shift into first gear and tried to take off, but the parking lot was all ice, and the truck was just spinning out.

"You are under arrest!" shouted Nelms, as he slipped and scrambled into the still open driver's side door. The officer tried to pull Moses from his seat. He pulled on the steering wheel. The vehicle gained some traction and shot forward a few feet. Then Nelms pulled his sidearm and stuck it into the suspect's temple. "I'm gonna blow your fuckin' head off!" Nelms screamed.

Charlie Moses takes up what happened next:

> Naturally, I grabbed his gun and pushed it up to the top of the cab, and I told him, "Man, I've paid for the gas, what the fuck is wrong with you?" Then he started pulling the trigger to his gun . . . bullets and glass flying everywhere. I dumped the clutch . . . the truck took off and spun around . . . hit the gas pump . . . the cop fell down. I took off across the parking lot, my door still open. Then he unloaded his clip .40 caliber Glock pistol into my truck . . . glass and blood was flying all over.

In his report, Nelms said that, "the suspect pulled a .22-caliber revolver and bolted for his truck. I really expected that once I got ahold of him in the vehicle, I could take him out without any problem. But he was just so spectacularly strong. I couldn't do anything with him, except to keep struggling to keep his gun away from my face, and I managed to wrestle it away from him."

Nelms loosed off several shots and radioed for help. "I was pretty sure that two of my rounds hit; the second round I saw hit the back of the cab," Nelms later recalled.

Moses sped off. He knew that he had been hit but was not sure where. He couldn't move his left arm, and his right hand was "bleeding bad, so I took off like a turkey through corn. My heart was pumping, and I heard the cop on my scanner calling for backup and shouting, 'Shots fired . . . Moses is on the run . . . I think I shot him . . . all of his windows are shot out . . . there's blood in the parking lot . . . Got to be his . . . I shot him up pretty good.'"

Charlie Moses disputes the account given by Corporal Nelms, and Charlie's story seems to have a ring of truth about it:

> This cop knew straight off who I was and he knew I was wanted 'cos he had seen me before. I reckon that he had already called for backup and was told to wait for help. So, when I went out to my truck, hee could have simply pulled his gun and told me to get on the ground. But he didn't do that, and he lied about me running to my truck . . . we walked over to it together. No way would he not shot me if I had run to my truck, knowing how dangerous I was. His story is bullshit!

Nelms tried to follow Moses, but the fugitive drove south down Highway 25, past the Oregon Trail Golf Course, with the recklessness of a man high on meth. Nebraska State Police heard the "shots fired" radio call, and Sheriff's Deputy Stan McKnight learned about the chase on his radio. What McKnight now needed was a place where he stood a good chance of intercepting Moses.

McKnight: "There is an area commonly known as 'The Question Line.' It is a place where I could see three different roads intersecting with this area. From that location, I could see a mile either way along all three routes."

Now with the police in hot pursuit, Charlie Moses explained what happened next:

> I took [off] out of that parking lot like eggs through a hen. Driving down a single-lane gravel road, snow blowing in my truck from all directions, I get to the road I need to get to, and to a place I'm familiar with. I hear the police talking with each other trying to set up a parameter, and they're driving with no lights. I ran out of road but continued on through an old cornfield, through fences, corrals, then finally got behind a barn, where I stopped for a few minutes.
>
> I lit a smoke, opened the door and stepped out of my bullet-riddled truck. Not too much damage . . . all my tires were still up. My left arm was just hanging down . . . couldn't feel nothing . . . the adrenalin pumping like crazy (and probably the meth numbing the pain). My Levi jacket was soaked with blood, which was frozen by now. I jumped back into my saddle, started my girl up, took off down the highway. I went trying to make a run for the border.

McKnight had been waiting in the darkness, hoping that Moses would drive by:

> After sitting there, a vehicle did come from the west to the very road intersection where I was at. When it came past me, I turned my headlights on and saw that it was Moses's truck. He was traveling in excess of 70 to 80 mph . . . at night, in those conditions, and because of his speed, he was soon able to outdistance me quite rapidly.

Moses had also seen McKnight's cruiser. It had come out of nowhere and was running parallel to his own truck. Then the cop was behind him:

> The roads in front of me are starting to twist and turn, so I slow down. Tink, Tink, Smash, Smash. I hear pieces of my truck getting hit. I look in the mirror, an' I see muzzle flashes

> . . . bullets are whizzing by my head, hitting all around the cab of my truck.

For the second time, a frustrated McKnight thought he had lost the same pickup truck in a chase, so he decided to change tactics:

> At that point, well, he had pretty much got ahead of me, an' at the same time I had to slow down and check driveways and road intersections to make sure he hadn't turned off on me.

In fact, Moses had not pulled off the road. He was enraged, so he slipped the shifter into neutral and hit the brakes. Pulling out a high-powered rifle, he watched as McKnight's flashing high beams came toward him.

The deputy spotted Moses's brake lights in the distance. The speed freak's vehicle had stopped. McKnight slowed down, eased his cruiser to a standstill, then he called for backup. Apart from the pitter-patter of rain on his car, it was dark, misty, icy cold, and far too dangerous to advance alone, but while he waited for support, Moses, rifle-in-hand, made his move. There were two muffled reports. One bullet struck McKnight's head. Another round ripped through his hand, then the fugitive drove off.

"I tried to blow the motherfucker's head smooth off," said Moses. "I sprayed his windshield with several rounds, then I stood there and looked into what I thought were his dying eyes, at the same time calling him a back-shooting bushwhacker. Then I drove off . . . slid off into the night just as easy as a rattlesnake."

McKnight said: "Upon figuring that I had been hit by bullets, I was going to try and call the rest of the officers to let them know what was going on, only, when I reached for the microphone, I couldn't talk. My mouth was full of blood and I was starting to choke. I found some napkins in the seat, and I got them shoved up in my mouth to make the blood stop. Then I spat out, then I could talk and let them know I had been hit and that the subject had gone to the left and I would keep chasing him."

Despite his injuries, the brave deputy continued chasing Moses: "The wind was coming through the bullet holes in my windshield, blowing glass all over me. My left eye was completely shut from blood. My right eye was just blinking, but I could still see enough in my headlights to keep going down the road."

Based on the coordinates that McKnight radioed, Nebraska State Troopers staked out the area. They drove without headlights and indicators so they would not alert Moses; two police cruisers positioned themselves on a dark country road and waited. Minutes later, high beams appeared over the brow of a hill. It was the fugitive. One of the troopers spotted a gun, so he fired at Moses. In the following exchange, a round penetrated State Trooper Jeff Crymble's body armor. He started to lose blood fast. With his life at risk, a colleague called for an ambulance. Paramedics stabilized Crymble, and he was rushed to the hospital.

Nebraska State Patrol Sergeant Lynn Williams, who stayed at the crime scene, reports:

> We secured the area, and then our major concern was obviously the gathering of evidence, so we collected the trooper's service pistol, his duty gun belt, spent shell casings, and we also took 35mm photographs and videotaped the scene.

> Moses had fired several bullets. The reflective police crest on the officer's car was one of the few things visible on the dark prairie, and that took a direct hit. The bullet that had passed through the door of the trooper's patrol car had struck him in the abdomen, piercing his bulletproof vest, as well as traveling through his body. It was obvious that the weapon was a high-powered rifle, so we were looking for something like an assault rifle . . . something large-bore, high-powered.

Police took the spent rifle slugs to their ballistics lab, where technicians measured the size, weight, and metal composition of the bullets. They were, indeed, high-velocity rounds, probably fired from a 7.62mm SKS military semi-automatic carbine; with a ten-round clip, an effective range up to 433 yards and a muzzle velocity of 2,149 feet per second, this was deadly weaponry designed for use in war.

Trooper Crymble and Deputy McKnight were taken to the Great Plains Regional Medical Center in North Platte. Crymble's condition was listed as serious, but he stabilized in the ICU. Deputy McKnight was transported to Omaha for reconstruction on his hand.

> Police Emergency Bulletin
>
> Suspect, Charles Lannis Moses, Jr., was last seen traveling southbound on Highway 25. Moses is a white male, 31-years-old, 5'9", 150 lbs., with brown hair and brown eyes. He is unshaven with a goatee and mustache. He was wearing a light-colored heavy winter jacket and blue jeans. He was last seen driv-

> ing a maroon 1995 Chevy short box 4x4 pickup. The pickup has a Texas license number 2TCB58. Moses is wanted in Texas for probation violation, possession of a prohibited weapon (illegal explosives).
>
> Anyone who sees Moses, or the maroon pickup, should contact authorities immediately. Citizens should not try to make contact with Moses. He is armed and extremely dangerous.
>
> —Nebraska State Police

Because the case involved the shooting of two law-enforcement officers, the FBI was recruited to help capture Moses. Special FBI Agent Ron Raywalt took the assignment, later recalling, "Our caseload, primarily, is in the area of white-collar crime, and it is not very common that we get called in to assist in investigations of violent criminal activity."

Nevertheless, Raywalt pulled together what he needed to obtain a federal arrest warrant against Moses, and in this particular case he anticipated that Moses would flee Nebraska.

Hoping to catch Moses before he left the Cornhusker State, the authorities set up a command center at a police barracks. Officers from virtually every law-enforcement agency in the state shared information on Moses. Several had had run-ins with him before in connection with clandestine methamphetamine labs, and they knew that he had a history of using abandoned farmsteads, not only for manufacturing the drug but for living and hiding as well. So, the cops targeted those areas to search, and hundreds of police and FBI agents started looking for any sign of Moses and his maroon pickup truck in the sprawling, rural landscape. Finding him would not be easy.

Monday, February 14, 2000, Dickens, Lincoln County, Nebraska, and 30 miles south of the shoot-out: Around mid-morning, a young farmer found tire tracks leading to his garage. His parents' car was usually inside, but it was gone. In its place was a maroon pickup. The farmer recognized it from the television news, and investigators soon confirmed that it belonged to Charles Lannis Moses. Bullet holes showed that officers had hit the vehicle when returning fire.

Nebraska State Patrol Sergeant Lynn Williams reports:

> The license plate we were looking for was still displayed on the vehicle registered to Mr. Moses. It had evidence that it had been shot at. The bullet holes were in the back portion of the cab. They had shattered the back window. Some of them had lodged in the dash of the cab, and others had passed out through the front windshield.

Charles Lannis Moses to the author:

> Over 140 bullet holes were in my truck, and I survived. I was driving through many gauntlets with a barrage of bullets whizzing by. Oh! What a rush.

Police also found blood. Moses had been wounded by at least one of the shots fired at his truck. But if he was injured, meth was the perfect drug to ensure that he would remain alert, pain-free, and aggressive so he could keep on running.

Lynn Williams said:

> There was a tremendous amount of paraphernalia located in his pickup that deals with cooking and/or manufacturing methamphetamine. Moses virtually had a lab in the back

> of his truck. We also found survival gear, police radios and scanners, and weapons in the cab. What we didn't find was the high-powered assault rifle used to shoot the two police officers.

Ogallala (pop. 4,950), Keith County, Nebraska: An hour after the pickup was found, nearly 60 miles northwest in Ogallala, a state patrolman responded to a 911 call from a man who said that he was an acquaintance of Charles Moses. The man said that he had seen the fugitive 15 minutes earlier. Moses had spoken to him at a rest area, and he was driving a vehicle that fitted the description of the vehicle missing from the farm in Dickens. The man told the officers that while he and Moses talked, a news flash on the car radio reported that police were looking for Moses and the vehicle he was driving. Moses then panicked and sped off. The man said that he had waited 15 minutes before reporting the incident because he was afraid of Moses. He knew from the radio warning that the fugitive was armed and dangerous, so he feared for his own safety.

Now, police were worried that Moses would change vehicles yet again to throw them off his trail.

Paxton (pop. 614), Keith County, Nebraska: Two hours after this sighting, and 20 miles west of a rest area in the village of Paxton, 48-year-old farmer Robert Sedlacek found fresh tire tracks outside a house on his land. He stopped to check them out because he knew the place was empty. Then he telephoned his son-in-law, Paul Fisher, to ask if anyone had been to the property. Paul answered, "No," but explained that he had heard reports of a dangerous fugitive in the area. He told Robert to get out of the place immediately.

On the other end of the phone, the farmer could then be heard talking to somebody. "I heard my father-in-law say: 'What are you doing here?' " Fisher recalled. "Then there was a gunshot . . . then silence."

Charles Moses had claimed his first murder victim. The fugitive was still on the run, but now more desperate and deadly than ever.

Just 36 hours after Moses had seriously wounded two police officers, a homicide investigation was started. Investigators now had to piece together the murder from the crime-scene clues.

Based on this evidence, Sergeant Lynn Williams believed that Charles Moses was the killer:

> We had learned that the victim had driven a 1999 blue pickup, with the Nebraska license plate, 21-3428, onto his farmland to check on tire tracks he'd observed. He surprised Moses, who also acted with surprise and shot him. He dragged the farmer out of his vehicle, then climbed in and Moses fled the scene.

Behind a barn on the property, investigators located the car that had been stolen from Dickens. It had been hastily abandoned and partly covered with a tarpaulin and branches. In the back seat, officers discovered chemicals, knives, and several firearms. Troopers also found tire tracks from Sedlacek's pickup and broken glass on the side of the driveway. It appeared as if the driver's window had been shot out.

FBI Special Agent Ron Raywalt knew that this was an important clue:

> I anticipated that Moses would try and use a defense, stating that he was returning fire from someone shooting at him. I knew that I could determine how many shots were fired and the direction that the shots originated from.
>
> When a high-speed projectile hits a piece of glass and the glass breaks, physical characteristics are left in the glass. This answers questions for the crime scene investigator. It tells him which bullet hit first and the direction of travel the bullet took.

Moses had been desperate to switch vehicles once he knew the police were onto him. Investigators had found the victim's ID but could not find the mobile phone he was using when he was shot. The cops now believed that his killer had it with him in the farmer's blue truck.

Investigators issued an alert for the stolen vehicle and worked to track the cell phone's signal. When switched on, cell phones constantly search for the nearest transmission/receiver mast to use. Police can flag a specific phone number and learn which tower is serving it. They can then narrow down the location of the phone.

Two hours after the farmer's murder, a cell tower in Oshkosh, Nevada, picked up the signal from the missing phone, but before the police could respond the phone went dead. Moses had heard the phone ring and thrown it out of the truck.

The FBI had also been studying the glass fragments from the crime scene and had determined that only one bullet had been fired from outside the truck, and it had gone straight through the victim and out of the opposite side of the vehicle. This was not self-defense, this was murder. Charles Moses was crisscrossing the state, armed and out of control.

Nebraska, just east of the Wyoming border: That evening an elderly woman was enjoying a quiet evening at home when she heard someone breaking in. She could hear an intruder walking through her house toward her bedroom. It was too late to escape, so she did her best to hide. Someone was rifling through her drawers and cupboards. She had heard about the fugitive on TV, and she feared for her life; then, moments later, the intruder left. The woman rushed to a neighbor's house, where she called the police. She told them what had happened but that she hadn't seen the intruder's face. Tire tracks matching those from Robert Sedlacek's stolen truck were found outside the house, and there were bits of glass near the left tire track. They had come from the driver's window, which investigators believed Moses had shot out while killing the farmer.

The local police immediately contacted the FBI with their findings. The FBI, in turn, notified the Wyoming authorities that a cold-blooded killer might be heading their way. The search for Charles Lannis Moses had become the largest manhunt in Nebraska's history.

Tuesday, February 15, 2000, Lusk (pop. 1504), Wyoming: The small town of Lusk is about 20 miles from the Nebraska border, and Lusk Police Department Chief Cary Gill received the FBI's "Wanted" bulletin. Chief Gill says, "That morning we heard about Charles Moses from our dispatch. He was driving a Nebraska-plated pickup, blue, and he could be headed in any direction."

The media alerted the public that a dangerous fugitive could be loose in the area, and, at around 1 p.m., the publicity paid off. Says Chief Gill:

> A caller reported that the blue pickup was at the south-end corner of "The Outpost" truck stop in Lusk. I went with Assistant Chief Dusty Chrisman, and there were several vehicles in the parking lot that fit the description. We knew that one of them might conceal the dangerous suspect and we were looking at license plates. Then we spotted one that matched the description. We decided to block him off if we could.

Someone was inside the truck, but the officers couldn't tell if it was Moses. The driver's side window appeared to be missing. If it was Moses, he might have finally come down after a long methamphetamine binge, exhausted.

Chief Gill called for backup and waited for other units to arrive. Then the driver woke up, but Assistant Chief Chrisman's view was obscured; he wasn't exactly sure it was Moses, so he couldn't risk firing his sidearm. It now meant another yet another chase as Moses fired up the engine and tore out. He headed north along Main Street through the town's business district, and there was the very real fear of losing the fugitive at the town's limits as he headed along Highway 85.

Although the officers were in hot pursuit, Moses got away from them after careening onto a ranch road, where the two-wheel-drive cruisers could only bounce and skid along, while the 4x4 could go almost anywhere. Driving like a man possessed, Moses sped up over an old dam into pastures where the Niobrara County cops couldn't chase him.

Sheriff Samuel Reed suggested cutting off a ten-mile area in an attempt to trap Moses: "The perimeter was a very large area. It kinda sat in the middle of three major highways, an' we had another county road that kind of dissected it in the middle."

Every law enforcement officer in the vicinity manned road-blocks to look for Moses. The media warned the public to keep away from him, while cops visited people living in the cordoned-off area, asking them to call police at the first sign of any suspicious activity. Sheriff Reed:

> I had a very deep concern and I knew that if we didn't apprehend Moses before dark, we could have a terrible, terrible time finding him. I knew the rancher people who lived there. I was very, very concerned for their safety if he entered a house at gunpoint, holding them hostage, shooting them and taking their vehicle and leaving the area.

Although Moses was effectively confined within the ten-mile area, it was too dangerous for officers to go in on foot, for they would be vulnerable to ambush or sniper attack, as Sheriff Reed explained:

> For officers to go in would have been extremely difficult. There are a lot of pine trees, deep draws, and ravines. It would have been very, very difficult to go in there and find himin the dark, almost impossible.

FBI Special Agent Ron Raywalt assisted the Wyoming authorities by contacting Nebraska Governor Mike Johanns, who authorized the immediate use of two unarmed National Guard UH-60 Black Hawk helicopters to survey the state highways and rural roads, trying to locate the vehicle Moses was driving.

The choppers wheeled and clattered overhead, and the observers soon spotted the truck. It looked like it was stuck in a muddy ravine. A SWAT team was sent in. They knew that the hunted man was armed with a high-powered semi-automatic assault rifle. The elite cops had to move cautiously. The dangerous, drugged up killer could be behind any rock or tree.

Straight from a scene in *Rambo*, the authorities positioned themselves among boulders and scrub above the truck, but they couldn't see Charles Moses. They feared that he might be watching them—that he had already zeroed in on them, his finger caressing the trigger, just waiting for that first clean shot.

The SWAT team started at the truck after firing a "flash-bang" to stun anyone nearby. Moses wasn't there. Fanning out, a cop discovered boot prints in the mud, and the officers began to follow them, but among the trees, and without a tracker dog to sniff Moses out, the trail went cold.

That night, Moses would surface yet again. He had wrecked the truck at the top of a steep slope. It had come to a stop, engine running, against a huge granite boulder, and now the vehicle was balanced precariously with only a tree preventing it from plunging into the small ravine. When he climbed out, Charlie slipped. He plunged down the steep slope, like a ball in a pinball machine:

> I hit a rock, bounced off a tree . . . rolling . . . turning . . . flying . . . sliding, and finally I hit the bottom of the ravine with a hard and abrupt thud. I looked up at my truck just hanging there over the edge, almost in thin air. The front bumper hung to a tree and the back bumper was wedged against a hard granite rock. My head hurt, my body was pretty fucked up. Nothing seemed to be broken.

I had torn loose the bandage on my arm. My wound was bleeding pretty good an' I could feel the sticky blood running down my arm. It didn't take long to soak my jacket. I climbed back up that wintry hill of ice, snow, rock, and tree, back to the truck. I managed to climb back inside, grab what I could of my provisions . . . everything was pretty much on the front floorboard of the passenger side. So I had to climb over the seat and console, hoping the whole time I don't dislodge the truck.

I gathered what I can, drop it outta the door as I climb back out. The engine is still racing, and I'm thinking, "are you gonna blow or not?" Then pretty much the same way as before I go down the slope again. I get to the bottom, gather up my stuff: sporting scope, scanner, bottle of coke, couple packs of Marlboros, shells, and a blanket. My 357 was in my pocket; my rifle was somewhere in the snow. I found it . . . cleaned the barrel. Then I rolled all the stuff into the blanket, picked up my dope case, put on my hat, and began to hike away from the truck. I had to put as much distance between [me and] that crash scene as I could.

At the bottom of the ravine ran a river, which was pretty much empty except for where I needed to be. So, I walked through the river, ice, snow and gravel for several miles. I'm a sitting duck out here . . . no cover at all.

Bzzzz . . . I hear an airplane flying over pretty low. I get up next to the bank and try to blend in best I can. It flies over. Chop, chop, I hear the rotor blades of a Huey. I quickly take off running. Just around the next bend . . . my sanctuary . . . a huge evergreen tree right in the middle of the riverbed. Boy, I ran over to it, climbed up and covered myself with the branches, careful to conceal my whole body

> the best I could. A few more minutes . . . here comes the chopper flying about 50 feet above the ground. A man was hanging out strapped to the helicopter and holding onto a big machine gun. A .50 cal, I presume, an' he's looking all over for me. I stayed under cover and hid all the while they searched with a couple helicopters and two or three planes.

It was now getting dark, so Moses felt it was safe enough to leave his hideout and move on, but his rolled-up blanket had come undone, and his supplies and dope were missing. He needed his dope. He started to panic, asking himself how was he to keep going?

Backtracking as carefully as he could, Moses then spotted hundreds of lights along the rim of the ravine. Dozens of headlight beams illuminated the area. Then there was a loud explosion followed by gunfire. This was the flash-bang thrown at his truck. Then even more shots riddled the vehicle.

Taking off in another direction, he stumbled along the riverbed in almost complete darkness. He found a clearing, pulled a cigarette from its pack, lit a smoke, and sat down to consider his options, which were fast running out. In the distance he could see lights. Maybe the lights of a ranch. It was about a quarter of a mile away, and he could hear people talking:

> I couldn't hear what was being said, and had hoped they hadn't heard me crunching across the riverbed. I prayed to God. If he would let me phone my family, I told him I would throw away my guns. Anyway, what could I do next . . . steal another vehicle . . . hold someone hostage . . . what am I gonna tie 'em up with . . . am I gonna have to kill them? All this shit and more kept racing through my mind.

Then the people I had heard talking got into vehicles and drove off so I quietly as possible made my way toward the light at the ranch.

As I approached, all kinds of thoughts were running wild in my mind. How was I going to handle these people . . . go in shooting . . . sneak in . . . or should I pass them by and keep going? I had to find transportation soon, but I knew that all roads were blocked by now. A perimeter set-up for a good ways . . . too far to make it on foot in the shape I was in. The sky was clear, the moon shone brightly, stars were dancing in the heavens, the air was chilly. It was just too bad my body had become fucked. I was soaking wet. I had been walking and stumbling for miles, hiding out for hours, running for days while bleeding profusely, although it had stopped for now. I had plugged the wound as best as I could after the fall. Hypothermia was setting in . . . no food other than a thin piece of beef jerky. I am down to a couple rounds for the rifle and a box and two speed-loaders for the .375 Magnum.

After seeing and hearing all those gunshots earlier, I knew this was a different game now, so I had to come up with a different plan. I walked up the steep hill, quiet as a church mouse, and up to a fence. I crawled through, into an area fenced off to bales of hay.

I looked around and lit up a smoke, then I nuzzled down in between a couple of bales, had a good, long smoke. I did some praying. I did a weapons check. All was good. Then I did some recon from my position.

For a short while, Moses crept around the outbuildings and a number of old vehicles parked nearby. In the ranch house, dogs were barking. In front of a barn was a green Explorer. There were no keys in the ignition. Then Moses took the bull by the horns, walked up to the front door and knocked.

"Is anyone at home?" he asked.

There was no answer, so he tried the doorknob. It was locked.

"I didn't dare break in," says Moses, "but I needed refuge and supplies if I was to continue on foot . . . then two vehicles came down a track towards me. I had no option but to run into the barn."

8.30 p.m., Tuesday, February 15, 2000, near Lusk, Wyoming: Rancher Jim Kramers and his son Justin returned to their ranch in different vehicles, then went inside. Justin, heard their dogs barking at something behind their house, so he grabbed his rifle. Both men went outside, and from their porch they could see a man who they thought was Charles Moses—the fugitive that *had* to be stopped—skulking in the darkness.

Jim whispered to his son to sneak around back and quietly draw a bead on Moses, telling him to do what he had to do—shoot to kill if necessary. Jim then found himself in a standoff with a desperately cold and hungry man who had committed cold-blooded murder, But the rancher had a plan he hoped would work. "I was totally unarmed," Jim later told police, adding, "Moses had a rifle and a pistol in his hands, and that pistol was pointing straight at me."

With remarkable presence of mind, Jim Kramers quietly offered Moses a deal. He knew that the fugitive had been exposed to the day's pouring rain and freezing cold. If Moses would drop his guns and come inside the warm ranch, Kramers would give him a hot meal and throw his soaking clothes in the dryer.

At first, Charles Moses refused the offer, but Kramers told him that this was the only way they could work together. The plan, if it worked, was then to secretly call the police.

By now, Justin had the fugitive in his sights, and Moses looked like he was going for the plan, but it could go either way. For his part, Jim hoped that his son would not be drawn into violence. "I was concerned throughout the ordeal that my son would not have to shoot someone. Justly or unjustly, I did not want him to go through life knowing that he had killed a person," Jim later told reporters. Today, Justin Kramers recalls: "One of the fears I had was if I had to shoot at him and I would miss. I only had one shot, and he had a six-shot pistol."

After weeks on a methamphetamine-fueled rampage, Moses had finally slowed down. With a sideways glance, he could make out the muzzle of Justin's hunting rifle aimed at his head. "I knew he had zeroed in on me," recalled Moses. And, although the young rancher was scared he might miss, his aim was as steady as a rock. The fugitive dropped his weapons, and after a two-hour standoff he walked into the house.

Once inside the warm property and out of his wet clothes, Moses concentrated on his first hot meal in days while Justin slipped out through the front door and ran to his brother's place a short distance away. He placed a call to the sheriff, and when he returned, Moses hadn't even realized he'd been gone.

A Lusk police officer and a Wyoming game warden arrived within minutes. Because of Jim Kramers's plan, the wild fugitive was without his guns. After a staggering chase across hundreds of miles, after burglaries, car-jackings, gunfights and murder, Charles Lannis Moses was hogtied, cuffed, and dragged into the snow, finally in custody.

Charlie Moses said that he would have given anything to shake the rancher's hand properly, for he believes that the man saved his life. He is convinced that if the game warden hadn't taken charge of his arrest, he would have been shot dead by the cops or the FBI, who he believed had orders to shoot to kill on sight.

As law enforcement had suspected, Moses had been wounded. At the Cheyenne Regional Medical Center, he was treated for a bullet wound to his shoulder, a fragment of lead in his thumb, dehydration, and exhaustion. The police chase had run him into the ground.

> Now remember, when things look bad and it looks like you're not gonna make it, then you gotta get mean. I mean plumb, mad-dog mean. 'Cause if you lose your head and you give up then you neither live nor win. That's just the way it is.
>
> —Clint Eastwood
> *The Outlaw Josey Wales*

Back in Nebraska, Moses initially fought the charges against him, but when confronted with the overwhelming evidence, he accepted a plea bargain. He pleaded "no contest" to second-degree murder and two counts of assault on police officers. He was sentenced to 190 years in prison and is currently incarcerated at the Tecumseh Correctional Institution.

The police officers whom Moses shot eventually returned to full duty.

Methamphetamine is still the biggest drug problem in the Midwest, and law enforcement officers are determined to fight it, whatever the cost.

Tecumseh Correctional Institution, P.O. Box 900, Tecumseh, Johnson County, Nebraska: Today, Moses attempts to deny killing the farmer:

> The police killed the farmer [Robert Sedlacek] and framed me for it. Interesting? By the first police report I read, I had shot a cop in Texas, shot a cop in Lincoln, Nebraska, a bank teller, and an innocent bystander, shot a sheriff, a highway patrolman, and a farmer.
>
> So I do want to tell the world what I believed happened with the farmer. The cops had a BOLO[21] on me as being armed and dangerous . . . do not approach . . . if possible shoot on sight if spotted.
>
> Now, I know that when I left Sedlacek's farm, I saw *no man*. Yes, I stole a truck. I busted his window with the rifle butt, got in, and drove off. Then I passed by a cop heading for the farm. That cop pulled up, and when the farmer walked out of his place he was gunned down by mistake.

Indeed, Charles Moses has a lot more to say about his innocence in this murder, but it was proven to the satisfaction of the court that he had murdered the farmer in cold blood.

As a footnote to this chapter, the author submitted a draft to Chuck Moses and received a very strong letter from his mother, by way of a reply, for she is completely convinced that her son

---

21 An all-points bulletin (APB) is a broadcast issued from one law enforcement agency to another. It typically contains information about a wanted suspect who is to be arrested or a person of interest whom law enforcement officers are to look for. There are usually dangerous or missing persons. As used by the police, the term dates to at least 1960. An all-points bulletin can also be known as a BOLO or BOL, which stands for "Be on the lookout." Such an alert may also be called a "Lookout" or ATL (Attempt to Locate).

is a *totally* innocent man. Indeed, the lady is furious with me, for she argues that the cops framed Chuck.

For reasons of her copyright law, I am unable to include her letter of complaint in this chapter, but I can publish my reply to her. I think my reply deals with everything and I have not heard a peep from Chuck, or his mother, since I sent this letter:

Dear XXXXXX

Your letter dated 29 January 2010 arrived today. I am sure that you have the year wrong but I have copied your front page and have attached it to this letter.

Having read through your letter, I apologise if Chuck's chapter does not suit you. Nevertheless, I double-checked with most of the other parties involved in the programme and I have no doubt that they were all completely truthful.

Thereafter, I wrote to Chuck and asked him for his version of the events that led to his final arrest. I then inserted his comments into the body text of the chapter.

I can, if you allow me, put some of your letter into the chapter, especially Chuck's problems up until he was bailed.

When I get a sniff that a convicted man may be innocent, I ask that inmate to send me any court documents, witness statements, forensic reports, etc., so that I may investigate further. Quite often, I receive hundreds of documents, as was the case of Fred Waterfield; serving life for serial murder—murders for which he is entirely innocent. I did exactly the same thing with Douglas Clark, aka "The Sunset Slayer."

If an inmate, at his or her expense, is able to provide me with the material I ask for, I can then take the case apart piece-by-piece.

Chuck was unable to send me the papers concerning his case, so I have to go with what I have at hand.

I hear what you have to say concerning your own private beliefs, but while I can incorporate your thoughts into Chuck's chapter, you will understand that unfortunately it will be deemed as hearsay.

Officers Nelms and McKnight.

The facts are that discharging a firearm at police officers with intent to kill carries a maximum tariff of life imprisonment in Nebraska. Therefore, notwithstanding the Robert Sedlacek incident, Chuck would have received a life sentence in any event. Had one of the officers died, in all likelihood Chuck could be now be awaiting execution.

However, *what is crystal clear* is that Chuck was prepared to shoot to kill in his attempts to avoid arrest, and he admits this himself.

Robert Sedlacek.

Eunice, Chuck signed a plea bargain agreement to avoid the death penalty and pled "no contest" for the second-degree murder of Mr Sedlacek. That, today, Chuck says he is entirely innocent of killing Mr Sedlacek does not change his "no contest" plea at all.

As far as the forensics evidence is concerned, one has to look at probabilities here and the law concerning "circumstantial evidence."

It is the cumulative effect, the "arithmetic of circumstantial evidence," which causes so many juries to say that even though the evidence before them is entirely indirect they are "satisfied beyond any reasonable doubt," of the safety of convicting.

I am fully familiar with the subject of gunshot residue (GSR), also the use of "field test kits," and of paraffin testing of an alleged shooter's hands, arms, and sometimes the face, in ballistic science.

You quote from the coroner with regard to GSR, saying that if Mr Sedlacek *had merely handled* a firearm that morning, GSR would be confined to the inside of the hands. Unfortunately, you, or the coroner, are erroneous here. I think that you are referring to paraffin testing, not a test for gunshot residue, which are entirely different tests.

You have also been misled when you state that *if* Mr Sedlacek had fired his gun, then gunshot residue would have been confined to his thumb and forefinger, when, in fact, GSR would have been present all over his shooting hand, perhaps even on the sleeve of his clothing.

That these ballistic tests were not carried out on the deceased person does not surprise me at all. There is no doubt that Mr Sedlacek, a completely honest and hardworking man came onto his own property and surprised Chuck, who was carrying a firearm.

You will recall the previous shooting at two law enforcement officers, and you will remember how Chuck threatened rancher Jim Kramers with a gun. So, why should Mr. Sedlacek have been treated otherwise?

Further to all of this, you will recall that Chuck *did steal* Mr Sedlacek's truck. That Chuck drove the vehicle to the home of an elderly lady in Nebraska, where he admits entering the property with intent to rob.

Police found tire tracks that matched Sedlacek's truck outside of the woman's home, and forensic testing using Refractive Indexing and Emission Spectrometry proved, beyond any doubt, that shards of glass found on the ground matched, in every respect, the glass from the shattered driver's side window of that truck, and on the dead man's clothing.

And, you will also know that forensic ballistic examination of the driver's-side window proved that the window had been closed prior to the shooting—with a bullet entering through the closed window (which imploded) before killing Mr Sedlacek, all of which confirms that the farmer *did not* fire a weapon at all.

Chuck's Injured Hand.

You bring up the matter of Chuck's injured hand—that using just the one good hand, he would have been unable to cover the top of the stolen vehicle taken from a Dickens' farm with a tarpaulin and brush, least of all drag a heavy-built deceased man from his truck.

By his own admission, Chuck says that he was high on methamphetamine at the time. It is a universally recognised fact that people high on this drug are capable of enormous strength and have an unusually high tolerance to pain. On this subject I will say no more.

In Summary.

You state that the whole story has not been told, while indeed it has been from the moment from which Chuck entered his plea bargain deal to avoid the death penalty, and Chuck would not be the first convicted man to change his story to something different afterwards, and to nitpick at issues in a case which would not change the result at all.

But you have to understand that even without the killing of Mr Sedlacek, Chuck would be serving a life sentence for shooting at police, anyway. I do not wish to sound impertinent, but it is a no-brainer to think otherwise.

Of course, perhaps a judge should have ordered Chuck into drug rehab. He didn't, but it would be quite wrong for one to blame the judge for the tragic events that followed.

I would add that not all police officers are perfect, and law enforcement accepts this. However, it is a somewhat derogatory remark to label two of these officers as "rookies" when they have chosen a profession which concerns itself with protecting people like you and me.

I also think that one has to realise that Chuck chose to do drugs which ultimately led to his downfall. He made this decision, Eunice; nobody else made it for him and for this he has to, like a man, shoulder full responsibility.

It was Chuck who fired at police; with Officer McKnight, there was a clear and brutal intention to kill.

It was Chuck who stole other peoples' vehicles, unlawfully trespassed on their property, and invaded the home of an elderly lady which terrified her witless.

And it was Chuck who shot and killed Mr Sedlacek in cold blood, then stole the man's truck to flee the scene, leaving behind a grieving widow and loving family.

I get on well with Chuck. He is paying the price for his crimes and, really, if there is no solid evidence to say otherwise, then the chapter stands as is written.

I hope you are keeping well. Please pass on my regards to Chuck, too.

Kind regards and best wishes,
Christopher

***

CHAPTER 7

MICHAEL TYRONE "BIG MIKE" CRUMP—ORAL FOR $20, THEN INSTANT DEATH

> *Mike was a slow learner at school. He was kind and considerate, thoughtful and playful, friendly and outgoing, and helped anyone who needed help.*
>
> —MITTIE RENDER, CRUMP'S MOTHER

THE DRAMATIC THEATER FOR MURDER MOST FOUL seems always set in steamy swamps, and the killers are human bottom-feeders who trawl the murky depths. Center stage: a dark, damp graveyard in the dead of night. In the wings are trees, black, bereft of leaves, their spindly branches pointing accusingly like a dead crone's fingers at the waning moon spotlighting the still-warm body that has been hastily interred in a hole in the ground, with the sides slowly falling in.

In Tampa, Florida, black women became a sadistic killer's prey, and cemeteries, his personal dumping ground. And as the body count rose, homicide detectives Bob Parrish and Gerry Onheiser confronted a serial murderer, using forensic science as their only weapon.

Areba Smith

A gray damp start to the day, it was just 7 a.m. in the homicide office at downtown Tampa Police Headquarters, and a red-eyed Detective Robert "Bob" Parrish was gazing out the window while sipping coffee from a Styrofoam cup. The weather was typical for Tampa on Friday, October 10, 1986. The average temperature would work out to 77.2°F, the wind a steady 3.9 miles per hour. Fog blanketed most of the city, light drizzle and thunder were in the air.

Parrish's longtime partner, Detective Gerald "Gerry" Onheiser, was hunting and pecking at "Clyde," his ancient typewriter, with the portable radio on his desk squawking: "Detective Onheiser, the press are here . . . Come to the sergeant's office, please." Ignoring the female dispatcher, he grumbled silently before ripping a report sheet out of the machine, crushing it into a ball and throwing in the general direction of an already overflowing trash bin.

"Detective Onheiser, please pick up your phone . . . Detective Onheiser, your phone, please."

The cop picked up the handset. "Yeah and *no*!" he shouted into the mouthpiece. There was a pause before, "Whaddaya think I am . . . *a fuckin' crystal ball?*" followed with, "Me and Bob are working this shit night an' fuckin' day. You need a comment, then go through the proper channels . . ." another pause, then, ". . . go give Public Relations a pain in the ass."

Gerry Onheiser slammed the radio down and angrily returned to Clyde. For the record, Clyde was a permanent fixture on Gerry's desk. Clyde was also a legend in homicide: a decade past retirement date, the battered IBM Selectric golf-ball machine should have been consigned to a dumpster years back, but budget restrictions on purchasing new equipment kept Clyde alive.

Next the phone on Parrish's desk rang, a red light on the handset blinking red. The officer turned away from the window, popped a mint into his mouth, and answered it. Making a few notes and recording the time, he replied, now looking at his buddy:

"Okay. Yeah . . . I got southeast corner of Ola and West Indiana . . . black female. I need CSI down there now, and keep the uniforms *outta my crime scene*."

Ronald Denney had been out on his early morning jog, which daily took him down North Ola Avenue, through the wrought iron, Gothic-style gates of the Old Centro Asturiano Cemetery, along a couple of gravel paths, and out onto West Indiana Avenue. On this day, in the southeast corner of this mist-shrouded marble town, in a field bordered on one side by a tree line, Ron had the shock of his life, for he discovered the nude, dead body of a black woman. It wasn't six feet under, but lay about three yards from the cemetery fence. Ron called the police.

Parrish and Onheiser didn't have to be Sherlock Holmes and Doctor Watson to figure this one out. A sightless cop with no sense of taste or smell could tell that the naked corpse was a black female. Her fingers had long, well-manicured nails, painted crimson; on one finger was a yellow metal ring with a glassy rock.

Detective Parrish reported:

> We found no signs of cutting or stabbing or anything like that. But she did have a fine mist of blood on her right side,

which appeared to come from her navel area. This indicated that she'd died in the cemetery from blunt trauma or by asphyxiation.

Based on the condition of the body, it appeared that she had been murdered less than 12 hours earlier, giving the killer more than enough time to flee. From his experience, Parrish knew that this would be a difficult case to solve.

As the victim was being photographed, the investigators noticed that she was barefoot, and oddly, the soles of her feet were clean. The ground was moist, and unless she had levitated across the graveyard, she could not have walked to this position; moreover, there was no evidence to indicate that she had been dragged.

The dead woman's personal effects were scattered all over the area. Each item, including her panties, top, a wig, and a pair of shoes, was bagged and tagged as potential evidence. There were also empty beer bottles and a cigarette pack, but there was no purse or driver's license to identify her.

Not far from the body, the cops found fresh tire tracks in the dirt, so Parrish surmised that the woman had been killed someplace else, then dumped in the cemetery. A large vehicle, maybe a truck or an SUV, had made the tracks, so evidence technicians made casts of the imprints.

"Where is this witness?" Parrish snapped impatiently.

A uniform pointed to a scrawny little guy with a face the color of asparagus. "Over there," said the patrolman. "Yo!" shouted Parrish."Yo, there." He waved the man over. "What's your name?" he asked.

"Ronald Denney."

"Okay, Ron, whad'ja see?"

"I was just jogging by. Ya know. I was just running, see."

"What else?"

Denney removed his baseball cap and scratched his head, which was smooth and shiny, the style of a balding man who'd decided it was easier to shave what hair he had left than comb it. Parrish looked down at his own shiny, now soaked shoes, then at the jogger, noticing that the guy's hands were shaking real bad, and they, like the zipper area of his pants, were wet.

"I jog every day . . . same time . . . same route . . . never see anyone."

"And?"

"Well, I was jogging by, and I see this fuckin' body there. An' I ran some more, an' stuff. Holy Shit, man, ya know. Then I thinks, 'Holy Shit! That was a dead body back there.' So I calls the *po*-lice. I reckon I done you a favor."

After giving his details to a patrolman, Denney was allowed to go on his way. Then, after processing the scene, officers led by Sergeant Price canvassed the neighborhood hoping that someone might have seen or heard something the previous night. Nobody had.

The morgue is a human warehouse storing perishable, out-of-sell-by-date goods. The stuff is unpacked, signed for, examined, chilled, made ready for disposal, and then trashed. The staff are shippers and packers of human remains consigned on a one-way ticket to ashes or a hole in the ground.

A body deposit entails completing the "Body Log" Form 6B Information Sheet: four pages in quadruplicate with a case number describing name and address (if known), time of arrival, source of discovery, method of conveyance, approximate age and weight, body temperature on arrival, hair and eye color, race or ethnic origin, details of external trauma (if any), and clothing/personal effects (if available), itemized. The four copies of the Log are distributed as follows:

> Copy (1): onto the morgue supervisor's or medical examiner's metal desk.
>
> Copy (2): into a battered green filing cabinet marked "Disposals—City/Private (delete where applicable)." It has to be one or the other—a cardboard coffin in a pauper's grave in the city bone yard or a silk-lined $5,000 casket with all the fancy furniture, flowers, plot, and a headstone; or the crematorium.
>
> Copy (3): into a buff envelope rubber-stamped "URGENT—Hospital Records Only"—then fired up a tube to the 15th floor.
>
> Copy (4): law enforcement (when applicable).

Life reduced to 16 sheets of paper that yellow with time and, like the ink, slowly fade away. That's it. What more do Mr. and Mrs. Joe Public need to know, except that the warehouses around Tampa were getting busier than they had a right to be—a serial killer was off of his leash.

At autopsy, associate medical examiner Dr. Lee Miller, reported on the Jane Doe recovered from the cemetery:

> Deceased is black female. She is 5' 8" tall, weighs 120 pounds, and is about 30 to 35 years old. Her cause of death

> was strangulation. She has scratches on both sides of her neck, and a fractured hyoid bone. Pinpoint hemorrhages, characteristics of strangulation, are found in the whites of her eyes. The only other injuries are a slightly scraped bruise over the right eye and a set of narrow abrasions around the wrists, indicating that the wrists had been tied. There are two lines across the back of each wrist from one side to the other side, about a third of an inch wide, with a loop on top of one hand. No marks are to be found on the inside of the wrists.

Dr. Miller found evidence of a nosebleed, which is often present in cases of strangulation. A blood test showed evidence of alcohol. Bowel contents were found over the woman's anus and vaginal area. Dr. Miller took vaginal swabs but did not see any sperm cells. Her vaginal exam did reveal a "wadded-up piece of paper." The inner two-thirds of the vagina was "lined with an unidentified while cheesy substance."

Based on the amount of rigor mortis and insect activity, it was confirmed that Jane Doe had been murdered less than 12 hours before discovery. Among other intimate body samples, strands of the woman's hair were collected, and if a suspect emerged, it was possible that some of her hair might be found in a vehicle, or on or about the suspect's person.

Identifying the dead woman became the detectives' next priority. Her fingerprints were taken and run through the Tampa Police database. Within hours Parrish found a match—Jane Doe was 34-year-old Areba Smith.

Detective Parrish said, "After I confirmed her identity, I contacted her mom and got as much information as I could about her and her habits, who she was seeing, and any steady boyfriend."

From Areba's mother, Parrish learned that Areba had been a pretty girl with a ready smile and bubbly personality. She had been outgoing until the lure of crack cocaine had reduced her to a life of painful addiction and cranked her once-full figure down to very thin. To pay for her habit, Areba had turned to hooking.

Detective Parrish continued: "There were four different bars in what we call the West Tampa area that Areba frequented, and as the principal investigator I had to go to these bars, find out who she knew and just do some good legwork. I found out that everyone spoke very highly of her. All the people I interviewed said she was a very good girl, and a very good individual."

Areba's life on the streets had placed her in contact with a lot of unsavory characters, but no one the police talked to could point to a suspect in her murder.

Detective Parrish had hit a dead end, so he started looking for clues in other unsolved homicide cases, not only in Tampa, but also in Hillsborough County and nearby cities.

It took Parrish a week to review two years' worth of homicides, looking for similarities, and, in the end, he was stunned by what he found. Other detectives had been working on reports of previous murders, and similar types of victims. Other jurisdictions had African American females, all prostitutes, their bodies found naked in cemeteries. Lavinia Palmore Clark, Joyce Madison, Shelley Wate, Glenda Trotter, Shirley Mason, and Shania Simons had been strangled, and all had ligature marks around their wrists.

Lavinia Palmore Clark

On December 12, 1985, the naked body of 28-year-old black prostitute Lavinia Palmore Clark had been found on the north side of Idlewild Avenue. The corpse was on the shoulder of the road, adjacent to the Shady Lawn Cemetery. It lay about 25 to 30 yards from the nearest tombstone.

With this collation of information, Tampa detectives and investigators from the Hillsborough County Sheriff's Office pooled their resources. Even considering Tampa's high homicide stats, things were getting out of hand. Along with other agencies in the area, they formed a task force to find and stop a killer. However, the lack of physical evidence found at the crime scenes, combined with the lifestyles of the victims, would make them difficult cases to solve.

Then came a break, and it landed in Parrish's backyard.

News reports about Areba Smith had caught the attention of a potential witness, a man named Wayne Olds, who contacted the police. He said that he had known Areba from the Tampa bar scene. He had seen her the night before her body had been dumped in the graveyard. He claimed that a dark truck had approached her on Columbus Avenue, in a rundown area known as the "hole" or "dope hole."

Olds described the truck as either dark brown or black. It was a "wrecker-type" without a boom in the back. It had rotating lights on the roof; one light was broken, and the amber yellow metal cap that fitted on top of the light was missing. The truck had tinted windows, and the wheels wore huge 4x4 tires. Areba had talked to the driver. Olds said that he had seen the vehicle in the neighborhood before, but he didn't know to whom it belonged.

For investigators, the reference to a dark truck rang bells, so they searched their files once again. Eight months earlier, a prostitute had claimed that a john driving a dark truck had tried to kill her. The woman had been afraid to press charges, but she agreed to speak with police about the incident. She told the cops that a large man, whom she knew as "Big Mike," tried to pick her up one evening.

They started talking about a price for sex—was it going to be "around-the world" for a hundred bucks—maybe down to $50 if work was slow, or a ho's strip with a blow job for $20 and a handful of green stamps? Then, as the negotiations continued, he suddenly grabbed her around the throat and started to choke her. She reached for the doorknob, jumped out, and started screaming for help. The police had been called, but by then her attacker had fled.

The hooker gave police a description of Big Mike: "big black motherfucker, around 266 pounds, brown eyes, six feet tall, balding, strange oblong-shaped head topped dome-like. He had a bullish neck set on equally powerful shoulders. His hands were the size of dinner plates."

"This was one guy you would not invite home to meet your daughter," the investigators thought among themselves.

The investigators again checked their files. Big Mike was a real piece of work. His real name was Michael Tyrone Crump, and he had a rap sheet as long as a giraffe's neck, which included a five-year prison term for aggravated battery intended harm, and aggravated assault with a weapon—no intent to kill.

Police went to Crump's home and hammered on the door. The suspect was not around, but a dark truck matching the witnesses's description was parked in the driveway. Parrish photographed the vehicle, then phoned Wayne Olds, asking him to return to the police station, where he was shown a photo-pack of six different trucks, including the suspect's vehicle, which Olds immediately picked out.

Tampa police now believed that Crump had committed at least two serious crimes, but they did not have sufficient evidence to arrest him. However, based on their two witnesses, they did have probable cause to believe that the crimes had been committed in his truck, and once they had obtained a warrant, they would have authority to seize the vehicle and determine whether it had been used in any illegal activity and contained evidence of those crimes.

Detective Parrish decided to seize Crump's vehicle on a public roadway:

> We stopped the truck on a city street, and we informed the driver, who turned out to be Michael Tyrone Crump, that we needed his vehicle for evidentiary purposes on the belief that it had been used in a recent crime.

Crump remained calm, even when he was asked if he knew Areba Smith. He said he did not. The police told him that he was not under arrest, and that he was free to go.

The truck was taken to the Pinellas County Sheriff's impound lot, where it was examined by trace evidence specialist Timothy Whitfield, who said, "As a part of searching a vehicle, we are charged with finding any, or all evidence that might be visible or invisible to the naked eye, and I first processed the truck for visible evidence."

Whitfield found a woman's earring on the floor of the cab. He also found a wooden device with a noose attached. It was a form of garote, and Whitfield had no doubt as to its purpose. "This was most unusual," he later explained in court, "because not everybody had one of these in their vehicle. And you have to ask, what are you using this for if you are not using it as a restraining device?"

Hidden between the passenger side rubber floor mat and the tire wall, investigators discovered another clue: a driver's license belonging to Lavinia Palmore Clark. She was one of the young women killed prior to Areba Smith. Because Clark was a known prostitute, and Crump was a known john, the item itself could be explained away. But to Whitfield, the location of the license was incriminating. In his evidence he stated: "Either it [the license] was intentionally placed there by the suspect to hide it, or, perhaps the victim had placed it there in the hope that in the days to come someone would find part of her in that truck."

Then the forensic team started searching for evidence invisible to the human eye. They used a chemical called Luminol to test for the presence of human blood. A blue glow revealed a fine spray. The pattern was familiar in that it matched the blood spatter from Areba's nose. Unfortunately, the droplets were tiny, no larger than pinpoints. There was no way to prove that they had come from the victim, as Timothy Whitfield explained:

> There was nothing I was able to do due to the microscopic nature of the blood. This was, of course, prior to the days

of DNA, and you needed quite a bit more blood to do complete workups.

Investigators vacuumed the interior of Crump's truck, searching for any hairs or fibers that might link the suspect to his victims. One intriguing find was a long machete hidden behind the front seat.

In the laboratory, examiners determined that the rope of the garote, was the same diameter as the rope marks on the wrists of the victims. However, one of the most important pieces of evidence was a long strand of hair that could not have come from the suspect. Analysis of the root showed that it just hadn't fallen out—it had been ripped out of the scalp. This hair sample was compared with hair taken from Areba Smith, but the color and texture did not match. However, when it was compared with Clark's hair, there was a positive match, for both samples were colored with a chemically identical hair dye. The forensic technicians were confident that both samples had come from the same person.

While the evidence from inside the truck was solid, all it proved was that Lavinia Palmore Clark had been inside the vehicle. Now, detectives needed to tie Crump's truck to the murders. They sent the tire casts, made at the Old Centro Asturiano Cemetery crime scene, along with the vehicle's tires, to the Florida Department of Law Enforcement, where examiner Oral Woods studied the treads to see if the truck matched the impressions found near Areba's body. Woods was surprised to see that Crump's truck had three different types of tires; the two front tires had similar treads, the rear tires had two different tread designs. Two of Crump's tires matched the impressions in the casts.

Oral Woods said, "I told Detective Parrish that we were definitely in the ballpark, and that we could definitely do something with them because there were class characteristics present in the casts, as well as some matching individual characteristics in the treads."

Class characteristics, like tire size and tread design, can indicate a specific manufacturer. By carefully comparing photographs, Woods determined that the tire tracks found at the Smith crime scene had identical class characteristics to Crump's rear tires. He then analyzed the casts and the tires for individual characteristics like nicks, tread wear, or embedded pieces of gravel, all of which can make a tire track as unique as a fingerprint. On the right rear tire, Woods found what he was looking for:

> I found one area on the tire that had some cuts and nicks that I was also able to find on the plaster cast poured at the crime scene. I went one step further. I made a plaster cast of that area and recorded the same characteristics, so I was able to confirm that the tire impressions made in the cemetery came from the suspect's right rear tire.

On Saturday, February 7, 1987, Michael Crump went to the Tampa Police Department to ask about getting his truck back. But first, Detective Parrish had some important questions for him—about how a woman he had been seen with was found dead the next day, and why his tire tracks were found several feet from her body.

Crump again denied knowing Areba Smith. He claimed that he had been working in the area and had cut through the cemetery the night before the murder. But, when the detective brought out one more piece of evidence in the form of Lavinia Clark's driver's license, Crump sensed that he had been caught.

> I picked her up because it started to rain and she wanted a ride to the Boston Restaurant and Sports Bar, at 9316 Anderson Road [about a 17-minute drive north from where her body was found]. During the ride, we discussed sex and we agreed on a price of ten dollars. She proceeded to give me a blow job. Then she became frustrated because I was taking so long. She pulled a knife on me, so I choked and killed her.
>
> —Michael Crump

Detective Parrish explained that, "He's a big guy, and he slumped his shoulders and looked down, which indicated to me that when I showed him the license it struck a nerve."

Crump then admitted picking up Areba Smith on the night in question. He claimed they fought and that she tried to stab him. He admitted that he had strangled her but swore it was in self-defense.

To the detective, Crump's version of her death could not explain away the restraint device found in his truck and the ligature marks left on the victim. The evidence pointed to a well-planned MO, one he had used before.

Officers next questioned Crump about the murder of Lavinia Palmore Clark. He claimed that he had once picked her up, but she had left him within minutes. He said that he knew nothing about the other seven victims, but the investigators did not buy his weak explanations.

On July 16, 1987, Crump was found guilty of the murder of Areba Smith. On March 31, 1989, he was found guilty of the murder of Lavinia Palmore Clark. He was sentenced to death, later to be reduced to life sentences.

It was perhaps obvious that Crump would appeal against the death sentences on a number of grounds, which included the alleged wrongful admission of evidence by the state and the claim that he had committed murder while his mind was disturbed.

Dr. Maria Elena Isaza, a clinical psychologist and adjunct professor at the University of South Florida, spoke for the appellant. She had been provided with raw data and test results from a Dr. Berland, a psychologist who had examined Crump earlier. Then Dr. Isaza did three-and-a-half hours' additional testing on her own.

"Mr. Crump was more of a do-er than a thinker," she told the Supreme Court of Florida. "His judgment was consistently poor. He had poor impulse control; he acted first and reflected later." Adding that old mental defense chestnut: "Because he was not capable of much planning, if he killed someone, he would have done it on the spur of the moment."

The fact that Crump had murdered on at least two occasions, that he carried a garote type of device in his truck, and that he was suspected of at least another seven "spur of the moment" killings doesn't seem to have affected Dr. Isaza's opinion at all.

Dr. Isaza further told the appeals court that Crump had grown up without a father figure, and "although he comes across as a very mean, tough, and intimidating individual, when you talk to him he has the capacity to be very warm and caring. He is only comfortable, however, when he trusts someone," added the psychologist. "If he perceives a threat, he feels persecuted or exploited, and he anticipates that he will be diminished.

"He is very sensitive to rejection," Dr. Isaza continued, "and any criticism, especially from women. When he feels threatened, he may act in a violent way, impulsively and without reflection." Dr. Isaza concluded that Crump suffered from "hyper-vigilance," a sense of feeling threatened. She found some indication of sporadic hallucinations and of hearing "God voices" talking to him. He had difficulties—"a feeling of sexual inadequacy or a feeling that his manhood depended upon his sexual performance." Her diagnosis argued that Crump's symptoms were "precursors, or consistent with a paranoid personality disorder."

According to Dr. Isaza, Crump was, "under the influence of extreme mental or emotional disturbance at the time of the Lavinia Palmore Clark murder," that his "capacity to appreciate the criminality of his conduct or to conform to the law was substantially impaired." She opined that, if Crump was with a prostitute and it was taking too long, "this would trigger the impulsive reaction he suffered from . . . He would become delusional, believing that he was threatened, being abused, or mistreated."

Yes, brother, you may live:
There is a devilish mercy in
the judge, If you'll implore
it, that will free your life,
But fetter you till death.

—ISABELLA TO CLAUDIO,
MEASURE FOR MEASURE,
WILLIAM SHAKESPEARE

And it is not as if using the services of prostitutes was a new experience to Big Mike, for he had used hookers since the age of 16. "I went with them 'cause I was shy and had difficulties establishing relationships with women," he has said. He most certainly *did,* for he killed at least two of them.

By now convinced that the murders were not premeditated, the court of appeals bought this entire mitigation package, hook, line, and sinker. With premeditation kicked out the window, they overturned his death sentences, replacing them with life with a possibility of him serving around 25 years. I will leave the last words to the prosecutor, who had this to say at one of the hearings:

> Michael Crump comes to you having been sentenced back in July '87 for the killing of Areba Smith. You look at him today. You've observed his demeanor today. This man is undergoing the punishment of prison life. He appears to be prospering. Life in prison is just that. It's life. You can read in prison. You can write in prison. You can make friends in prison. You have daily contact with other human beings. You can watch television. You can follow sports. You can follow world events. You have contact with people in the outside world. Life in prison is life. It's living. And in prison, by serving a life sentence, you can hope. You can even hope that one day your sentence will end and one day you can be released.
>
> Lavinia and Areba don't have such a hope. People want to live. Michael Tyrone Crump wants to live. Michael Tyrone Crump wants you to show him mercy and spare his life even more. He holds his life more precious than he holds the life of others. But, in the end, it is not you who are responsible for him. In the end, it's Michael Tyrone Crump who's responsible by his actions, and he alone.

But, now to a really bad man indeed.

***

CHAPTER 8

JOHN EDWARD "J.R." ROBINSON—SLAVEMASTER

There are some of us who live in rooms of experience that we can never enter or understand.

—JOHN STEINBECK

I SUGGEST THAT JOHN EDWARD "J.R." Robinson is one of them, for his overinflated ego has a front larger than any major Main Street department store. At face value, the facade is impressive, hinting at an honest deal to be had within. "Integrity" shouts at one peering through the glass windows, but it is not until one steps through the door and walks around the displays inside that one realizes, all that glitters is not gold.

J.R. Robinson, the owner of the store, is the ultimate con artist. A self-proclaimed businessman, unqualified by anything beyond his own bravura, he is the "quack" of old, peddling phony medicines and goods at expensive prices, passing off "Mickey Mouse" Rolex watches as the real thing. And if you purchased an item from the J.R. Robinson store and complained afterward, would you get a refund? Don't hold your breath.

In a warped way, that is why I was attracted to J.R., the ultimate "I-don't-give-a-fuck merchant," a sort of homicidal Del Boy (a fictional confidence man in a popular British sitcom), whose history and character no imaginative screen writer could ever invent.

For me, the challenge was to open up a dialogue with a heinous serial killer who had never before cooperated with an author, or pretty much anyone else for that matter. I didn't expect him to admit to a single wrongdoing, either. You see, J.R. is "innocent," or so he now says. And, actually, if the truth be told, I did not even expect a reply from my first letter to him.

> I want $400,000, although that amount may be adjusted, depending on need. My attorney will control all information and distribution of funds.
>
> —John E. Robinson
> letter to the author,
> February 20, 2008.

Nevertheless, I baited my hook with all the goodies that this particularly nasty little man might find attractive, and then, like the ever-optimistic fisherman, I cast my line, waited, and waited, and waited some more. I guess that J.R. sniffed at my lure, swam around it a few times, and sniffed again. The temptation was too much for this murderous con man, for they say that the easiest person to con is the con man himself. J.R. took the bait and ran with it, and he ran hard. Then, like any fighting fish, once firmly hooked, he tried to spit the barb from his mouth. The shiny lure was not all that it appeared . . . all that glittered was not gold.

For a short while, I had landed one of the most twisted serial killers in criminal history. Then he jumped ship, and the record of what happened is published here.

John Robinson is like a bloated, blood-filled leech, and the heinous killer sweats hatred, the copious secretions dripping out of every pore of his aging skin. Having pleaded guilty to a number of shocking murders to escape the death penalty, John E. Robinson is now demanding $400,000 to prove his innocence. His letters, featured in this chapter, explain that if he is not funded, he will use college students to publish his poetry to raise the money.

The bespectacled inmate squinting into the Olathe Police Department booking camera lens was that of a flabby-faced bank manager look-alike who sold his soul to the devil. This is John Edward Robinson, a depraved sex-sadist who tortured and murdered eight young women, then stuffed their corpses into steel drums to marinate in their own bodily juices until they were discovered by sick-to-the-stomach police.

An outwardly honest businessman whose shady dealings had taken him to prison several times before, John Robinson has since admitted to five murders in order to escape the death penalty, and he has recently been charged by the federal authorities for committing murder across state lines. My question to him was simple:

"John, can you please, *please* explain to me why the bodies of five women you knew very well ended up in steel barrels, three in your storage locker and two more on your land?"

He replied, in a letter to the author, January 10, 2008:

> I received your January 2 letter. At first I was simply going to forward it to my attorney to place in the file of vultures flying overhead wanting to pick my bones for personal profit.

With the aliases "Anthony Thomas" and "James Turner," J.R.—as he is known to the few friends he once had—was born December 27, 1943 in Cicero, Illinois, a working-class suburb of

Chicago. Standing 5 feet 9 inches tall, weighing 167 pounds, he is now balding with partially gray hair.

Although he refuses to discuss even his childhood without receiving large sums of money in return (the aforementioned $400,000, to be precise), we know from official sources that he was one of five children in a devout Roman Catholic family raised at 4916 West 32nd Street, two blocks north of the site of the now-demolished Sportsman's Park Race Track in Cicero. His father, Henry, worked as a machinist for nearby Western Electric's Hawthorne Works manufacturing complex, and, although a nice enough guy, he was given to more than the occasional bout of heavy drinking.

> He [Robinson] didn't talk a great deal, but when he did talk, it was to produce an effect that he wanted. He was shrewd. He was aspiring to more than he was capable of, quite frankly.
>
> —Richard Shotke
> Former Eagle Scout public relations officer to the *Kansas City Star*

John's mother, Alberta, was a disciplinarian, the backbone of the family, and ensured that the couple's offspring had a decent upbringing. Little else is known of her.

At age 13, John became an Eagle Scout.[22] In November of 1957, he was chosen as the leader of 120 Scouts who flew to London to appear before Queen Elizabeth II and the Duke of Edinburgh at a Royal Command Performance at the London Palladium. Therefore, I asked J.R. if he could tell me a little more about this memorable experience. His reply was:

22 A Scout with the highest rank attainable in the program of the Boy Scouts of America (BSA).

> I have never discussed this with anyone before, and I will not discuss it with you now. This is very valuable information to me. Your British readers would be very interested in my appearing before the Queen. If you send me $500.00, I will give you the exclusive story, which you can sell to the media and make a lot of money.

Three days later, I copied a press cutting of this Royal Command Performance from the internet, posted it to J.R., and at once politely declined his generous offer.

What I also already knew was that backstage J.R. had chatted with Judy Garland and told British actress Gracie Fields that he planned to study for the priesthood. After the show, the Queen said to Judy, who had sung "Rock-a-Bye Your Baby," "We missed you. Don't stay away so long next time."

With that bit of trivia out of the way, it is known that Robinson was a motivated youngster whose ability didn't match his drive. He told his peers that he was planning to become a priest and someday work in Rome, but no one, probably not even John himself, knows whether this was what he truly wanted to do with his life or was just his way of getting attention. Anyway, maybe the facts speak for themselves: As a freshman at Quigley Preparatory Seminary in downtown Chicago, he was a poor student and a discipline problem. He did not return to Quigley for his second year of study, and it is believed that he was denied admission as a sophomore due either to his academic or behavioral deficiencies.

After high school, in 1961, Robinson went to the Morton Junior College in Cicero. Then he met Nancy Jo Lynch, whom he married in 1964. She was to become the mother of his children.

They divorced on February 25, 2005, by which time Nancy knew of his many notable shortcomings: One of which was that he had never done an honest day's work in his life, the other being that any young woman who fell into his clutches would, more likely than not, would end up dead.

After their marriage,the Robinsons moved to Kansas City, Missouri, where J.R. attended a trade school to learn the radiology profession. True to form, J.R. never finished his training, but this did not prevent him from getting a job at a children's hospital, where he papered the walls of his office with fake diplomas and certificates. Based on his lack of skills with the infant patients, his colleagues suspected that he was either a fake or one of the most incompetent technicians ever to practice his craft. Although hospital staff remembered him as being a nice enough young man, they knew that in no way was he a certified technician.

Josephine Bermel, who worked with Robinson, said that he simply couldn't cope with young patients. "We had to teach him how to do things properly," she said. This downright incompetence cost him his first job. He was 21 at the time, and his wife had just given birth to their first child.

Undaunted by this setback, and using his phony diplomas and certificates, J.R. soon found work as a "certified" X-ray technician at a medical practice in Kansas City. Here, he was employed by retired Brigadier General Dr. Wallace Harry Graham, who, for many years, had been the personal White House physician to President Harry S. Truman and his wife, Elizabeth.

In the spring of 1944, as a member of the First Hospital Unit of the First Army, Captain (later Colonel) Dr. Graham had waded ashore at "Easy Red" Omaha Beach four days after D-day. With the battle raging just a few miles ahead, he treated the wounded in the thick of combat, and by nightfall his tents, with 400 beds, had taken in close to 900 wounded. Moving across France and Belgium, then into Germany, his unit saw some of the war's most bitter engagements, including the Battle of the Bulge, where Graham was wounded. He was awarded the Bronze Star and other decorations, as well as medals from France, Britain, the Netherlands, and Belgium.

> The Trumans were healthy. I felt like the country's most disemployed doctor.
>
> —Dr. Wallace Graham interviewed in *The New York Times Magazine*

While in the White House, Dr. Graham had a ground-floor suite of offices filled with the latest in medical technology. In addition to the President and First Lady, he also treated some of the senior staffers and later became a temporary Major General of the Air Force. He continued to look after the Trumans in their hometown of Independence, Missouri, after President Truman left office. When the 70-year-old president was rushed to Kansas City Hospital for emergency surgery in 1954, it was Dr. Graham who removed his gallbladder and appendix. He earned his medical degree at Harvard Medical School. He developed a lifelong interest in botany and also boxed. It seems that the doctor's only misjudgment throughout his distinguished career was taking on John Robinson.

Quite how Robinson managed to con his way into working for Dr. Graham as a lab technician and officer manager is a question for another day, because the doctor was patently no fool. Dr. Graham later recalled that he had been impressed with

Robinson's achievements as an Eagle Scout and his "extensive credentials" in radiology. Nevertheless, highly regarded in the community, Dr. Graham was a trusting man, so he turned out to be an easy mark for a pathological and plausible liar like Robinson.

Soon after taking up his new appointment, John made a somewhat astute discovery, which developed into an abiding, lifelong attachment to the buoyant pleasures to be had from fleecing almost everyone he came across. The upshot was that he developed the disagreeable technique of making himself wealthy at the expense of others whom he made extremely poor. From then on, even up to today, dishonest thoughts occupied every space in John's head, and he pushed honesty completely to the back of his mind.

Robinson started his criminal activities in 1967, but soon came unstuck and was placed on probation for three years for embezzling $33,000 from the 57-year-old Dr. Graham. He had begun by stealing and taking liberties in the practice's medical office. He boasted to friends and colleagues about a house he had bought. In addition, he engaged in sexual liaisons with both office staff and patients—convincing one patient to have sex with him in the X-ray lab by pretending his wife was terminally ill and unable to accommodate his priapic needs.

How did J.R. find the money to buy the house? The answer is simple: He drained the practice's bank account to the extent that, just six months after he had been taken on, a bewildered Dr. Graham was unable to pay Christmas bonuses to his staff. This unexplained loss of revenue prompted an audit of the practice's books, and accusatory fingers all pointed toward Robinson. J.R.

was arrested and marched away in handcuffs while feigning sincerity and remorse, hoping that this would get him nothing more than a slap on the wrist from the criminal justice system.

In 1969, Robinson was convicted of the theft. It was his first offense, and he pledged restitution, so a Jackson County judge exercised leniency, sentencing him to three years' probation. Dr. Graham never saw a cent of the money J.R. had stolen from him.

> Robinson? I wouldn't leave him alone in my yard to wash my truck. That sumbitch would steal the car, the hose, the faucet, and carry away as much fuckin' water as he could carry.
>
> —JEFF TIETZ, FORMER KANSAS CITY POLICE OFFICER

J.R.'s next career move was as the manager of a TV rental company. He soon tuned in to stealing merchandise from this employer, too. When he was exposed, the company did not prosecute him, but they most certainly did fire him.

During the next decade, Robinson, of whom one employer said: "He gave a very good impression, well dressed, nice looking . . . seemed to know a lot, very glib and a good speaker" was often in trouble with the police. He defrauded tens of thousands of dollars from various companies to help him along the way. Despite being on parole for most of this time, he managed to prosper.

To give credit where credit is due, if John Robinson was anything, he *was* pathologically persistent. For the next 20 years he bounced from job to job, managing to keep out of prison by crossing his fingers, crossing jurisdictional boundaries, and convincing employers not to press charges when he was caught.

In 1977, J.R. bought a large waterfront house. It was set in four acres of prime real estate in Pleasant Valley Farms, an affluent neighborhood in Johnson County, Kansas. By now, he and Nancy had four children and it was here, in picturesque rural surroundings, that the confidence trickster and embezzler formed a company called Hydro-Gro Inc. The firm ostensibly dealt in hydroponics, which is a method of growing plants using mineral nutrient solutions and a great deal of water instead of soil.

J.R.'s own publicity literature, a glossy, 64-page brochure, portrayed him as a "sought-after lecturer," an "author," and "one of the nation's pioneers in hydroponics." This claim would have certainly come as a surprise to the ancients, for the hanging gardens of Babylon, the floating gardens of the Aztecs of Mexico, and those of the Chinese are examples of hydroponic culture. Egyptian hieroglyphic records dating back several thousand years BC describe the growing of plants in water. So, hydroponics is hardly a new method of growing plants. But by the 1970s, not only were scientists and analysts, many of whom worked for NASA, involved in hydroponics, but also traditional farmers and hobbyists had begun to be attracted to the virtues of hydroponic growing. However, John E. Robinson was not—and this will come as *no* surprise—among them.

Hydro-Gro Inc. was, of course, a bogus enterprise, and in setting it up, Robinson swindled a friend out of $25,000. The man had invested because he hoped to get a better return on his money, to pay for his dying wife's medical care.

With his phony resumé in radiography and hydroponics richly embroidered in merit and distinction, this devious jack-of-all-trades and master of none also managed to engineer his appointment to the board of governors of a workshop for disabled people. It was a position he occupied for scarcely more than two months when the self-proclaimed philanthropist, with an almost religious desire to help the developmentally disabled, was named "Man of the Year" for his work with the handicapped.

Amid much publicity, the *Kansas City Times* extolled Robinson's virtues, and at a special dinner and presentation ceremony, J.R. was given a grandiose gesture of approbation in the form of a certificate signed by the mayor and a Missouri state senator.

According to Robinson, he had "no idea" that when he had been invited to this dinner they would be honoring him. However, feigning surprise when the winner was announced, he humbly accepted what amounted to a rigged award as members of the organization's board sat in stunned silence.

A short time later, however, the meritorious award was exposed as having been obtained fraudulently. It had been granted as a result of faked letters of commendation received at City Hall, all written by none other the Man of the Year himself, John E. Robinson Sr.

Robinson's plan backfired big-time when the city fathers, whose names Robinson forged on the letters of recommendation, read about the event in the local press. One man was outraged because on "his" letter supporting Robinson, his name had even been misspelled. The *Kansas City Times*, stung by the scam, took its revenge by exposing Robinson two weeks later as a fraud. His children were ridiculed at school, and his wife, who says today that her husband was unfaithful to her for at least 20 years of their 38-year marriage, was reluctant to show her face in public. But how did John react? One might have thought that he would have wished he could have become invisible. The fact was, however, J.R. couldn't have cared less.

By now the reader will have come to the inescapable conclusion that Mr. Robinson is a most disagreeable fellow, not a man to trust, least of all the type to enter into any form of agreement with, so it came as no surprise to this author when J.R. penned the letter of February 20, 2008, demanding $400,000.

In 1980 Robinson was given the position of director of personnel by another company, and very soon he honed in like a heat-seeking missile on his employers' checkbook and money, using the former to direct quite a lot of the latter to his own bank account. After laundering $40,000 into PSA, a paper company he owned, he yet again found himself placed on probation, this time for five years.

> He had no real employment, unless you consider figuring out ways of scamming people out of their money to be real employment.
>
> —District Attorney Paul Morrison
> Robinson's murder trial

Between 1969 and 1991, John Robinson was convicted four times for embezzlement and theft, earning himself the notable distinction of being barred for life by the Securities and Exchange Commission from engaging in *any* kind of investment business. Some of his thefts were minor—he lost his job with Mobil Corporation for pinching $300 in postage stamps—while others were more significant.

For his part, Robinson soldiered on unfettered and undeterred, founding another firm, Equi-Plus, to add to his impressive portfolio. This newcomer to the Robinson stable specialized in "management consultancy" and was very soon engaged by

Back Care Systems, a company that ran seminars on the treatment of back pain. And, by golly, give the company a pain John surely did!

Equi-Plus, aka John Robinson, was commissioned to prepare a package that included a marketing plan, printed publicity material, and videos. However, what Equi-Plus *actually* provided was a string of inflated, and in most cases bogus, invoices. Once again, a criminal investigation was begun into the business activities of the energetic J.R., who responded by producing a series of faked affidavits, all attesting to the legitimacy of the invoices submitted to Back Care Systems.

While the investigation continued, this slippery eel founded Equi-II, an Overland Park corporation run by Robinson, who at the time described himself as a "consultant in medical, agricultural, and charitable ventures." And it was while he was at the helm of this new outfit that he moved into a sphere of activities far more sinister than embezzlement and fraud.

With the $40,000 in stolen funds, J.R. acquired an apartment in Olathe, a town south of Kansas City. Here he was able to enjoy sexual affairs with two women, one of whom is quoted as saying, "John kind of swept me off my feet. He treated me like a queen and always had money to take me to nice restaurants and hotels."

But there is no such thing as a free lunch, and retribution loomed on the horizon for the thieving and libidinous Robinson. He was convicted of the theft, and given his criminal record, this time he faced a possible prison sentence of seven years. However, he only had to spend only a couple of months behind bars and once more found himself placed on probation for five years.

Paula Godfrey

> John Robinson took away from our family our oldest daughter that we all loved so much. After she disappeared, my wife was a changed woman. A big part of her was ripped away.
>
> —*William "Bill" Godfrey, Paula's father*

In 1984, an attractive, dark-haired young woman named Paula Godfrey went to work for J.R. as a sales rep at Equi-II, after graduating from Olathe North High School. Her new boss told her that she was going to be sent to Texas to attend a training course paid for by the company. Robinson collected Paula from her parents' home in Overland Park to drive her to the airport. Her family never saw her again.

Having heard nothing from their daughter for several days, Paula's parents became anxious and eventually contacted the Overland Police Department to report her missing. The police questioned Robinson, but when he professed ignorance of Paula's whereabouts, they went away satisfied with what he had told them.

Not long afterward, the police located a letter bearing Paula Godfrey's signature which began, "By the time you read this, I'll be long gone. I haven't decided on Cleveland, Chicago, or Denver, oh well." In the rest of the letter, Paula seemed to be saying that she was perfectly fine but didn't want to remain in touch with her family. The neatly folded letter had been found in the bottom of a briefcase belonging to one Irving "Irv" Blattner, an ex-con associate of Robinson, who had been arrested on an entirely unrelated matter. The one-page letter was a photocopy and accompanied an original letter from J.R. addressed to Blattner in an Equi-II business envelope.

After reading the letter, the police closed their investigation. But Paula Godfrey was to become J.R.'s first murder victim. The truth of what happened to her would not come out until 2003.

It seems that Paula, an excellent ice skater, had gotten into some kind of domestic trouble, and Robinson helped her out by loaning her some money. For his part, Irving Blattner helped her find places to stay in Belton, on the Missouri side of the state line, where her boyfriend couldn't find her. One night, Robinson drove to a Belton motel where the young woman was staying, and for reasons known only to the tight-lipped J.R., he hit her in the head with a lamp while Blattner blocked the doorway so she couldn't escape.

Notwithstanding this, following his new vocation as a philanthropic helper of young women, J.R. approached the Truman Medical Center in Independence, a small city in Montgomery County. There, he spoke to social workers, telling them that he, together with some other local businessmen, had formed "Kansas City Outreach." This, he explained while patronizingly peering over the top of his glasses, was a charitable organization that would provide young unmarried mothers with housing and career training along with a babysitting service. The Truman Medical Center smelled a rat. They refused to help this patron saint of lost causes, so the next Saint Jude moved on and pitched the same story to Birthright, an organization that gave help to young pregnant women. Birthright, in turn, pointed Robinson in the direction of Hope House, a refuge for single moms.

According to writer David McClintick, J.R. told both organizations that Kansas City Outreach was likely to receive "funding from Xerox, IBM, and other major corporations," which would have been news to them. In any event, the great philanthropist asked the social workers to submit candidates they felt would be suitable for the KC Outreach program, and in early January 1985, Robinson was contacted by the Hope House shelter and put in touch with Lisa Stasi.

Lisa Stasi

Poor, uneducated, and unworldly, 19-year-old Lisa Stasi was cute. With long, dark hair, and trusting eyes—and a four-month-old daughter, Tiffany Lynn—she was homeless and living at Hope House, the shelter for single women. Sadly, her marriage to Carl Stasi had fallen apart and he'd left his wife and baby to rejoin the Navy at the Great Lakes Naval Base outside Chicago.

Carl later testified that he'd met his wife through a friend. They had married in Huntsville, Alabama, in August 1984, where Lisa had been raised. Lisa was eight months pregnant at the time. "We were going to stay there and start our lives there," Carl Stasi later testified, "but I didn't have no insurance and the baby was due, and so we came back here [to Kansas]."

Tiffany Lynn was born a few weeks later at the Truman Medical Center, a hospital well known for its care of the indigent. Nevertheless, broke and homeless, the Stasis's marriage quickly fell apart. "It was shaky," Carl explained. "I was irresponsible and I wasn't working at the time. It was going downhill from there."

He and Lisa separated in mid-December, and he returned to the Navy a few days after Christmas.

John Robinson, using the name John Osborne, now arrived on the scene. Using his phony credentials, he offered Lisa free accommodation and career training. He explained to her that this involved helping her to gain her High School Equivalency Diploma, after which he would arrange for her to go to Texas to train as a silk-screen printer. After she had completed her training, he said, there would be job opportunities for her in Chicago, Denver, or Kansas City. In the meantime, her new mentor told her, he would not only pay for her accommodation and living expenses, but also he would give her a monthly stipend of $800.

I fed her [Lisa] and the baby. She slept a long time, she took a bubble bath.

—CARL'S SISTER, BETTY, TO THE COURT AT ROBINSON'S TRIAL

It was an offer she couldn't refuse.

The kindly benefactor took Lisa and Tiffany from the refuge and installed them in Room 131 at the Rodeway Inn, a motel in Overland Park, telling the young mother that she and the baby would be traveling to Chicago within a few days.

When J.R. left the motel, Lisa went to see her sister-in-law, Betty Klinginsmith, to discuss matters with her. She stayed the night, and the following morning, Wednesday, January 9, 1985, Lisa telephoned the front desk at the Rodeway Inn and learned that an irate "Mr. Osborne" was looking for her. She left a message for Osborne with the clerk, asking him to call her at Klinginsmith's home. A few minutes later the phone rang, and Klinginsmith gave Osborne directions to her house.

"He [J.R.] came to my door about twenty-five minutes later and rang the doorbell. I went down to the door with my son, who was five," Klinginsmith later testified at J.R's trial. "Lisa put on her coat. He didn't waste any time on pleasantries. He didn't say anything to me. He just stood there and looked at me."

After expressing anger that she had checked out of the motel, Robinson insisted that Lisa and her daughter leave with him immediately. There was a heavy snowstorm when Lisa carried Tiffany to his car, which was parked down the street. She left her own damaged yellow Toyota Corolla and many of her belongings behind.

Like Paula Godfrey, Lisa Stasi was never seen again by her family.

Back at the motel, later the same day, Osborne produced four sheets of bank notepaper, which he asked Lisa to sign. He also asked for the addresses of her immediate family, saying that as she would be too busy to write letters when she got to Chicago. He would write them for her, just to let her relatives know her whereabouts. Perhaps she resisted, but we do know that she telephoned Betty.

"I took it for granted she was at her motel," Betty would tell investigators. "She was crying real hard, hysterical. She was telling me that 'they' said that they was going to take her baby from her, that she was an unfit mom. They wanted her to sign four sheets of blank paper. I said, 'Don't sign nothing, Lisa. Don't put your name in anything.'" According to Betty, the last words Lisa said were, "Here they come," before the phone was disconnected.

According to testimony given by J.R.'s wife, Nancy, years later, he had brought the baby home that night. She recalled that it was "snowing heavily" and that "the infant was not very clean and smelled badly. There was dirt under the child's fingernails. Apart from some spare diapers, the baby had only the clothes she was wearing and some baby food," Nancy recalled.

The next morning, the 10th, Betty Klinginsmith telephoned the Rodeway Inn, only to discover that Lisa and Tiffany had checked out and that the bill had been settled by a John Robinson, *not* John Osborne. She reported him to the Overland Park Police Department and the FBI.

That evening, J.R.'s brother Don and his wife Helen, who lived in metropolitan Chicago, received an unexpected telephone call from John Robinson. The childless couple had been trying to adopt a baby through traditional placement services for some years, and J.R. had previously told his brother that he had a contact with a Missouri attorney who handled private adoptions; that for an upfront consultancy fee of $2,000, he could act as a liaison for Don and Helen. The trusting couple soon handed over the cash, which J.R. pocketed.

That was back in 1983, and for the next two years Robinson put into place a plan to procure a child for his brother. If the scam was successful, he probably intended to expand it to "help" other childless families realize their dream of adoption. Several times in the following months, Robinson put Don and Helen on notice that an adoption was imminent, but a child never materialized.

John's crooked scheme required locating pregnant, single women, and he knew exactly where to find them. Putting on his civic philanthropist facade, he approached local pregnancy programs and social workers to alert them to the new program—Kansas City Outreach—that he and several fictitious leading businessmen from the East Coast had created to help single mothers.

Karen Gaddis was a social worker at the Truman Medical Center in the city of Independence, the county seat of Montgomery County. She had previously met Robinson when he had been seeking referrals in 1984. He was looking for young mothers, preferably white women, who had no close ties to family members. He even showed Gaddis an apartment, which he maintained on Troost Avenue, Overland Park. It was a place, he said, where the women would stay.

Gaddis knew Caucasian babies were valued on the adoption black market, and because Robinson couldn't provide her with any paperwork about the program, she didn't refer any women to him. "I think he thought we were a real fertile ground for young women that nobody would be looking for," Gaddis told NBC's *Dateline* when the Robinson story broke. Within days, however, Robinson was at Hope House, where he picked up Lisa Stasi.

Talking to his brother, John Robinson explained that a baby's mother [Lisa] had committed suicide at a woman's shelter and, for a further cash sum of $3,000, payable to an imaginary lawyer, and their signatures on an adoption certificate (which was bogus, of course), J.R. could hand the baby over to them.

On Thursday, January 10, 1985, Don and Helen Robinson flew down to visit Robinson at his Missouri home, where they handed over the $3,000 and were given extremely convincing adoption papers bearing the forged signatures of a notary, two lawyers, and a judge. They were delighted with their new child, whom they named Heather. By now, of course, Lisa had been murdered, and probably brutally raped, and it would be 15 years before Heather's true identity was revealed under the most shocking circumstances: The man she knew as "Uncle John" would stand trial, accused of killing her mother.

Several weeks after Lisa vanished, Betty received the first letter J.R. had typed. It was dated the day of Lisa's disappearance, and it immediately raised concerns because she knew that Lisa couldn't type:

> Betty:
> Thank you for all your help I really do appreciate it! I have decided to leave Kansas City and try and make a new life for myself and Tiffany. I wrote to Marty and told him to let the bank take the car back, the payments are so far behind that they either want the money or the car. I don't have the money to pay the bank all the back payments and the car needs a lot of work. When I wrote to Marty about the car I forgot to tell him about the lock box with all my papers in the trunk. Since the accident I couldn't get the trunk opened. Please tell him to force the trunk and get that box of papers out before the bank gets the car.
>
> Thanks for all your help, but I really need to get away and start a new life for me and Tiffany. She deserves a real mother who takes care of her who works. The people at Hope House and Outreach were really helpful, but I couldn't keep taking charity from them.
>
> I feel I have to get out on my own and prove that I can handle it myself.

Marty wanted me to go to Alabama to take care of Aunt Evelyn but I can't. She is so opinionated and hard to get along with right now. I just can't deal with her.

Marty and I fought about it and I know he will try and force me to go to Alabama. I am just not going there.

I will let you know from time to time how I am and what I am doing.

Tell Carl that I will write him and let him know where he can get in touch with me.

The second letter typed out by Robinson was mailed to Cathy Stackpole at Hope House:

Dear Cathy:
I want to thank you for all your help. I have decided to get away from this area and try to make a life for me and Tiffany. Marty my brother want me to take care of my aunt but I don't want to. He is trying to take over my life and I just am not going to let him. I borrowed some money from a friend and Tiffany and I are leaving Kansas City. The people you referred me to were really nice and helped me with everything. I am grateful for everyone's help.

I wrote to the outreach [sic] people, Carl's mother and my brother telling them all that I had made the decision to get a fresh start in life. If I stay here they will try and run my life more and more like they are trying to do. I finally realized that I have a baby to take care of and she is my first responsibility. I asked my brother to tell the bank to pick up the car because the tags have expired and I am so far behind with the payments that I could never get them up to date, and with no job the bank wants the car or the money.

> I will be fine. I know what I want and I am going to go after it. Again thanks for your help and Hope House and thanks for telling me about outreach [sic]. Everyone has been so helpful I owe you a great deal.

At the time that Lisa and Tiffany disappeared, Ann Smith, an employee of Birthright, had somewhat belatedly begun to check up on the details that Robinson had provided concerning Kansas City Outreach. They were false. Deeply concerned, she contacted two FBI agents, Thomas Lavin and Jeffery Dancer, who were assigned to investigate J.R., and they teamed up with his probation officer, Stephen Haymes.

During this period, information emerged that showed that J.R. was being investigated by Johnson County's district attorney. Under the glass was Equi-II, in connection with strong allegations that the company had defrauded its client, Back Care Systems. Not only that, but J.R. and fellow ex-convict Irvin Blattner (now deceased) were being investigated by the Secret Service for forgery involving a government check. None of this, however, was connected to the disappearance of Paula Godfrey, or Lisa Stasi and baby Tiffany, so the trail in this direction was in danger of going cold.

Although everything seemed to point to J.R. having abducted and murdered two women and a baby, despite their own strong suspicions the two FBI investigators and Haymes could do little. Nevertheless, Haymes decided to call Robinson in for a meeting, during which the plausible crook confirmed that he was involved in a group called Kansas City Outreach, but as might be expected, he declined to provide Haymes with a list of his colleagues.

In a second interview, Robinson admitted to Haymes that he knew Lisa Stasi and that he had put her up at the Rodeway Inn in Overland Park with her baby. He also said that she had come to his office on January 10, 1985, with a young man named Bill, and told him that she was going off to Colorado to start a new life.

In a third interview, in March 1985, Robinson told yet another story to Haymes. He claimed that Lisa and the baby had been found in the Kansas City area. Lisa had been babysitting for a young woman, and the woman had contacted his office to see if he had an address for Lisa so she could hire her again. Haymes pounced on this information and demanded the woman's name and address. J.R. stormed out of the interview, protesting that he was being harangued over the matter. However, a few days later, understanding that his parole could be revoked if he pissed Haymes off, he came up with the details.

The woman Robinson introduced to Haymes, a hooker called Theresa Williams, made a statement to Haymes claiming that she had indeed hired Lisa Stasi as a babysitter, but when FBI Agent Lavin questioned her more closely, she said that Robinson had made her go along with this false story because she owed him money and he had photographed her nude in order to promote her services as a prostitute.

With the FBI suspecting a violation of the federal Mann Act (also known colloquially as the "White Slave Act"), for possibly transporting Lisa and Tiffany Stasi across state lines, authorities in Missouri and Kansas started looking into J.R.'s activities on a local level connected to the missing Paula Godfrey.

Haymes, now suspecting that the embezzler had turned to abduction and murder, dug deeper and learned through the prostitute Williams that Robinson was heavily involved in the Kansas City underground sex industry and probably ran a string of hookers specializing in domination and submission sex practices.

With this new angle to pursue, the FBI arranged for a female agent to pose as a prostitute and approach J.R. on the pretext of looking for work.

According to author David McClintick, it was around this time that Robinson developed a taste for sadomasochistic sex, but he also saw its potential to make a lot of money, and very soon he was running a thriving business exploiting this lucrative sector of the sex market. He organized a string of prostitutes to service customers who enjoyed S&M. To look after his own carnal appetites, J.R. employed a male stripper nicknamed M&M to find suitable women for him.

The female FBI agent was wired to record any conversation and arranged to meet J.R. at a restaurant in Overland Park. During lunch, he explained to her that, working as a prostitute for him, she could earn up to $3,000 for a weekend, traveling to Denver or Dallas to service wealthy clients. She could also make $1,000 a night just working the Kansas City area. His clients, he said, were drawn mainly from the ranks of doctors, lawyers, and judges.

J.R. went on to explain that, as an S&M prostitute, the young woman would have to allow herself to be subjected to painful treatment, such as having her nipples manipulated with pliers. When they heard this part of the recording of the conversation, the FBI investigation team decided to end the undercover operation out of fear for their agent's safety, and it is doubtful that the female agent would have been enthusiastic enough to continue after hearing about that aspect of the job either.

J.R. had installed the attractive 21-year-old Theresa Williams in his Troost Avenue apartment in April 1985. She had been introduced to J.R. by M&M as a suitable candidate for prostitution, and having worked at various odd jobs around Kansas City, Theresa jumped at the chance. After photographing her nude and "test-driving" his new recruit in a motel room, J.R. initially offered her a position as his mistress. This involved her being given an apartment with all her expenses paid, and for her there was an added attraction: He would keep her well supplied with amphetamines and marijuana. She would also be expected to provide sexual services for others, for which she would receive prostitution fees. Theresa took the job, moved into the apartment, and became a candidate as J.R.'s next murder victim.

Haymes's suspicions that Robinson was running a string of streetwise hookers proved unfounded. In hindsight, although a cunning and devious individual, Robinson wasn't well enough connected to be able to pull off such an unpredictable enterprise. J.R. liked to be in control of his nefarious schemes. His preference was to be in charge, and a stable of prostitutes, all equally cunning and more streetwise than the portly "businessman," would have run rings around him. Nevertheless, life for Theresa was not to be a bed of roses.

To start with, J.R. began using her to discredit his ex-convict pal, Irvin Blattner, who was cooperating with the authorities over Back Care Systems and a postal scam. J.R. ordered Theresa to begin writing a diary, which he dictated, implicating Blattner in a number of other schemes. He also had her sign blank papers and a draft letter to his attorney, giving the lawyer the authority to recover the diary from a safety deposit box in the event she disappeared. Indeed, the last entry in the diary was meant to be the same day that Robinson and Theresa were leaving for the Bahamas—a trip police suspected he was never going to make with her.

Rewinding a little, one night toward the end of April, after being given $1,200 and a new outfit by J.R., Theresa was taken blindfolded in a limousine to a mansion. There she was introduced to a distinguished-looking man of about 60, who led her down to a basement, which was fitted out as a medieval torture chamber. Her host instructed her to remove all her clothes, and moments later she found herself being stretched on a rack. Theresa panicked and demanded to be allowed to leave. Blindfolded again, she was driven back to the Troost Avenue apartment. J.R. reacted angrily to this betrayal, and a few days later she had to refund him the $1,200.

On another occasion, J.R. took her to task for entertaining a boyfriend at the apartment. However, the worst was yet to come. In late May, he paid her a visit during which he did something that caused her more fear she had ever known in her life. She was asleep when he let himself into the apartment. He burst into the bedroom, dragged her out of bed by her hair, and spanked her until she began to scream. After throwing her onto the floor, J.R. drew a revolver, put it to her head, and pulled the trigger. Instead of an explosion, there was only a click—the chamber was empty. By now, Theresa was whimpering with fear, but she went rigid with terror as J.R. slid the revolver barrel slowly into her vagina. He left it there for several terrifying seconds before withdrawing it, replacing it in its holster and, without another word, storming out of the apartment.

About a week after the incident with the gun, FBI agents Lavin and Dancer called unannounced at Theresa's apartment. Having been told that they were investigating the disappearance of two women and a baby, and that J.R. was the prime suspect, Williams decided to reveal the truth. This, of course, involved telling them about the drugs that J.R. was supplying to her as well as the incident with the gun. When the feds learned that Theresa had been asked by J.R. to sign several blank sheets of notepaper, they felt they had reason to believe that her life was in danger and moved her to a secret location.

Together with Stephen Haymes, the FBI agents filed a report with the Missouri courts to the effect that Robinson had violated his probation conditions by carrying a firearm and supplying drugs to Theresa Williams. They asked a judge to revoke J.R.'s probation and put him where he belonged—behind bars.

In 1987 Robinson, started a prison term for his parole violation. He was held until the appeals court overturned the probation revocation order on a technicality: His attorney argued successfully that, because he had not been allowed to confront his accuser, Williams, his constitutional rights had been violated. However, his real-estate fraud case in Johnson County then ended with Robinson being sentenced to serve six to nineteen years. He would remain locked up until 1991.

The effect on J.R.'s family was what one would expect; they lost their expensive suburban home, and Nancy took a job managing a mobile home park to make ends meet.

Catherine Clampitt

Around the time that J.R. was about to enter the correctional system for the first time, police were searching for 27-year-old Catherine Clampitt. Born in Korea but adopted and raised by the Bales family in Texas, Catherine was a one-time drug user now seeking rehabilitation. J.R. hired her to work for him at Equi-II in early 1987, but the arrangement fell through. She vanished a few months later. Despite the fact that suspicion of murder once again fell on Robinson, no further action was taken against him.

Much later, in 2003, it emerged that Catherine had lived at several different locations in Cass County and had started visiting Robinson once or twice a week, usually receiving money in return for sexual favors. In May or June of 1987, she called Robinson and invited him to her apartment. There were two other people at the place when J.R. turned up—including a person identified only as "G.T." Clampitt. G.T. demanded money from J.R., who started arguing with the young woman. J.R. then grabbed a lead-filled baton known as a "tire thumper" and beat Catherine in the head. Robinson instructed "G.T." on how to dispose of the body, and the deed was done.

Strangely, like so many so-called "intelligent" serial murderers, such as John Wayne Gacy, J.R. took to the prison regime at the Hutchinson Correctional Facility like a duck takes to water.

Like Gacy and Arthur Shawcross, he was a model inmate, making such a good impression on the prison authorities that the parole board set him free in January 1991, after serving just four years.

However, J.R. still had to go to jail in Missouri for having violated the terms of his probation (resulting from the $40,000 fraud he had perpetrated more than a decade earlier). He was soon back behind bars, serving time at two facilities for a further two years.

It is interesting to read Stephen Haymes's assessment of Robinson in a memo that he wrote to a colleague in 1991:

> I believe him [Robinson] to be a con man out of control. He leaves in his wake many unanswered questions and missing persons . . . I have observed Robinson's sociopathic tendencies, habitual criminal behavior, inability to tell the truth and scheming to cover his own actions at the expense of others. I was not surprised to see he had a good institution adjustment [settled in well] in Kansas considering that he is personable and friendly to those around him.

Beverly Jean Bonner

While in jail at the Western Missouri Correctional Facility, the white-collar con man forged a friendship with the prison doctor, William Bonner. He also developed an extracurricular relationship with Bonner's vivacious 49-year-old wife, Beverly. She was the prison librarian, and J.R. very soon found that he had a job in the library.

For her part, Nancy Robinson had found the going tough without her husband's income. After selling the palatial home at Pleasant Valley Farms, she had taken a job to keep body and soul together, and she was fortunate in getting one that provided accommodation. She became the manager of a mobile-home development in Belton, it was to those modest quarters that J.R. went when he was released from prison early in 1993. The Robinsons' two older children had grown up and left home, and the twins were at college, so J.R. and Nancy had the place to themselves. They rented storage lockers nearby to house their surplus belongings.

Almost as soon as he'd set foot in the door, J.R. went about restoring the family fortunes. But there was never any real likelihood that he would stay on the straight and narrow for more than five minutes, so it wasn't long before he was back to his unctuous ways.

By now the completely besotted Beverly Jean Bonner had left her husband and begun divorce proceedings. She told him that she was moving abroad and would set up a post office box number where he could send her the alimony checks. A few months later, she moved to Kansas City, where she went to work with J.R., who appointed her a director of his company Hydro-Gro. Not long after this grand appointment, Beverley's alimony checks were finding their way into an Olathe post office box used by Robinson.

Sadly, Beverly Bonner was not seen nor heard from again after January 1994. Robinson placed her belongings into the storage locker in Belton, and later, when he was asked about Beverly by the storage facility staff, he said that the woman, whom he described as his sister, was in Australia, that she was enjoying herself so much "she probably would never come back."

No one could have ever guessed that Mrs. Bonner was actually rotting inside a steel barrel in locker E2; that next to her decomposing corpse were two other 55-gallon barrels containing the remains of one Sheila Dale Faith and her daughter, Debbie, whose government checks also continued to supplement Robinson's income.

Two of Beverly's brothers received several letters from her beginning in January 1994. The first one was handwritten. In it, the recently divorced Beverly wrote that she had taken a new job in the human resources department of a large international corporation and would be training in Chicago and then traveling to Europe. In subsequent letters, all typewritten, she said her new job was wonderful and she was working with her boss, Jim Redmond.

Sheila Dale and Debbie Faith

> Sheila was interested in BDSM [Bondage Domination Sadomasochism] and used the internet and personal ads to meet men. She would start to talk about BDSM, and I said, "I don't want to hear it. It's not my thing."
>
> —*Nancy Guerrero, close friend of Sheila Faith*

One of three sisters, Sheila Dale Faith, aged 45, was a widow. When her husband John died of cancer in 1993, she was left to raise their 15-year-old daughter Debbie alone. Mother and daughter had lived a lonely life in Fullerton, California, and Debbie, who suffered from spina bifida and cerebral palsy, spent her life in a wheelchair, having barely enough strength to manipulate the chair's joystick controller. Tired of California, they moved to Pueblo, Colorado, in their beat-up white van.

As with so many thousands of lonely adults, Sheila began trying to meet a man on the Internet, and she made a number of bad decisions before making the fatal choice of John E. Robinson. Sheila told family and friends that she had met her "dream man," John, who had promised to take her on a cruise. He portrayed himself as a wealthy man who would support her and Debbie, pay for therapy for the girl, and give Sheila a job.

One night in the summer of 1994, with no prior warning, "Dream Man" J.R. called at Sheila's home, and took her and Debbie away to live in the Kansas City area. As was the case with so many other women who were befriended by J.R., the two Faiths were never seen alive again. When they did eventually turn up, they were in barrels.

Both of Sheila's sisters received typewritten letters from Sheila and her daughter after their disappearance. "She always hand-wrote letters," said sister Kathy Norman, who received correspondence postmarked Canada and the Netherlands. "This isn't Sheila," said another sister, Michelle Fox. "It was a happy letter, and Sheila wasn't a happy person."

The fatal fiscal attraction for J.R. lay in his knowledge that Sheila had been receiving Social Security Disability benefits for herself and Debbie. Now these payments were being directed to a mail center in Olathe, where they were collected by Robinson. In the autumn of 1994, according to court documents, Robinson filed a medical report to the Social Security Administration.

J.R. was not a man to be diverted from his schemes by the mere technicality of morbid deceit, and in the report he claimed that Debbie was totally disabled and would require care for the rest of her life, which, under the circumstances, was not strictly true. She was already dead. The report, however, allegedly bore the signature of William Bonner, the doctor with whom J.R. had been friendly when he was in prison and who until recently had been Beverly Bonner's husband. When he was eventually questioned on the matter, Dr. Bonner categorically denied ever having met Sheila or Debbie Faith and had certainly *never* treated them. In any event, J.R. would continue to collect the Faiths' disability checks for almost six years. In July 2000, Cass County prosecutors alleged that, between 1994 and 1997, Robinson defrauded the U.S. Government of more than $29,000 in Social Security and disability payments by forging documents to suggest that Sheila and Debbie Faith were alive.

It was also later proven that J.R. received more than $14,000 in alimony checks that should have gone to Beverley Bonner. Colleen Davis, the owner of the mail center from which Robinson retrieved the checks, told police that she knew J.R. as James Turner.

If we are to give John any credit, and surely credit is due where deserved, we would have to say that at the very least, J.R. was going through a lifetime of psychopathologically determined trangressional retro-development with great consistency. In other words—words that John would understand—he was an out-of-control sado-sexual sociopath spiraling downhill fast. Indeed, at the time of writing, he still hasn't bottomed out, as the following extract from one of the nutball's diatribes to the author proves:

> You will have seen all the tripe published or on the internet. Eighty percent of which is grossly incorrect, exaggerated fiction with small tidbits of fact thrown in. For example the moniker given—internet slave master—hype provided by a prosecutor looking for votes and carried through to sell books and enhance TV ratings. According to reports I was an internet stalker who waited in "chat rooms" to locate victims. Great for publicity but factually incorrect and both the police and prosecutors knew it was a fabrication.

For the record, J.R.'s interest in sadomasochistic sex had continued to flourish, and he upped the ante by starting to place ads in the personal column of a Kansas City newspaper named *Pitch Weekly*. He met and had relationships with a number of women before he fell in with Chloe Elizabeth, who described herself as a businesswoman from Topeka, Kansas. She claimed that J.R. sent her a wealth of publicity material selected to show him in a good light. He included newspaper clippings describing his appearance before the Queen when he was a Boy Scout, his hydroponics brochure, details of his phony Man of the Year award, and a Kansas University brochure containing pictures of two of his children. It was altogether an odd portfolio for someone wishing to engage in a BDSM encounter—the term widely used to describe relationships involving bondage and sadomasochism. Unsurprisingly, J.R. failed to mention his lengthy and distinguished criminal record.

In later years, Chloe Elizabeth described an event that took place during the afternoon of Wednesday, October 25, 1995:

"I was to meet him at the door of my house wearing only a sheer robe, black-mesh thong panties, a matching demi-cup bra, stockings, and black high heels. My eyes were to be made up dark and lips red. I was to kneel before him," she recounted.

The red-blooded male reader would find nothing at all wrong with J.R.'s request at this point—indeed, there might be thousands of men who would applaud John for his imagination—but things later turned sour, for upon his arrival, J.R. took a leather-studded collar from his pocket, placed it around Chloe's neck, and attached a long leash to the collar. After a drink and some small talk, he made her remove all her clothes except for her stockings and then took from another pocket a "Contract for Slavery" in which she consented to let him use her as a sexual toy in any way he saw fit.

"I read the contract and signed it," said Chloe Elizabeth. "He asked if I was sure. I said 'Yes, very sure.'"

With her signature on the dotted line, he tied her to the bed, whipped her and carried out a variety of visionary acts on her breasts with ropes and nipple clamps. J.R. was in his element. Sweating profusely, he concluded their first date by making her perform oral sex on him. Chloe Elizabeth, it seems, was delighted with her "slave master," and he was pretty much delighted with her.

"That was the first date," she later told Robinson's trial judge, who had been jolted from his slumbers by gasps from the stunned jury. "It was sensational!" she added. "He had the ability to command, control, to corral someone as strong and aggressive and spirited as I am."

In any event, before the perspiring and head-to-toe-trembling J.R. left the house that evening, he told his new slave that she had been stupid for allowing him to do everything he had done to her. "I could have killed you," he said with a smirk on his face.

For J.R., this master-slave contract with the amply proportioned Chloe Elizabeth had to be about as good as it could get, but she was not as naïve as he may have thought. Without his knowledge, she had taken the precaution of having a male friend stationed in another room of her house, listening vigilantly, upturned tumbler to the wall, for any sound of dangerously excessive behavior.

The relationship between J.R. and Chloe Elizabeth then blossomed, and they began meeting at least twice a week before it waned as she started to find out that Robinson was not all he claimed to be.

It is not unusual in BDSM relationships for the dominant partner to take control of the submissive partner's assets, as in financial affairs—an arrangement that is sometimes included in the contract drawn up between slave and master. In Chloe Elizabeth's case, she was required to sign over power of attorney to J.R. In return for sex, he promised to get her a job in the entertainment industry, for which he needed publicity photographs and her Social Security number. Like a good submissive, she *should* have followed his orders explicitly. She didn't—and refused. The penny had dropped, as she now suspected that he was after her money.

If J.R. had imagined that Chloe Elizabeth's submissiveness extended beyond her sexual inclinations, he was badly mistaken. She was an intelligent and successful businesswoman, not an ill-educated teenage mother desperate for help and support. Moreover, their relationship was now moving in the wrong direction as she found out more and more about him, and she started to voice her concerns to J.R.. Realizing that he was coming unstuck, he told her that he was going to Australia and would be away for some time—perhaps a *very* long time. However, she soon discovered that he had not even left Kansas. When she telephoned his office, the phone was answered but remained utterly silent. About an hour afterward, her own phone rang and she found herself being berated by a furious J.R. He accused her of checking up on him and warned her in very unpleasant tones against that sort of behavior.

The final straw for Chloe Elizabeth was when she found out about J.R.'s criminal record, and in February 1996, she ended their relationship.

Another woman [her name omitted for legal reasons] who entered into a master-slave contract with Robinson and struck a deal for financial support didn't learn until years later how close she had also come to ending up in a barrel alongside Sheila and Debbie Faith and Beverly Bonner.

J.R. told this woman that he was divorcing his wife and that's why he could never stay the night. He showered this "Ms. X" with gifts and clothes, but she soon noticed that most of the clothes he presented to her appeared worn. When she asked about this, Robinson said they were left behind at his office by former employees. Given that most of the clothes were raunchy undergarments leaves us begging the question, what on earth was going through "Ms. X"'s mind in accepting them?

This notwithstanding, the relationship was going fine until one day Robinson told her to get ready to travel with him. He was going to take her to London on an extended business trip. He told her that she should leave her job and advise friends that she would be gone for some time. She gave up her apartment, and Robinson moved her into a local motel. Like those before her, she was told she would be so busy that she should take the time to write letters to her family straight away—there would be no time while traveling. Robinson said that he would take care of her passport application, as he had friends in the U.S. State Department.

The woman thought it was rather strange when the day came for the pair to leave and J.R. turned up at the motel with his truck and a trailer loaded with clothing. What further concerned her was that he said that he was going to spend the night in the motel with her.

Nevertheless, excited at the thought of the trip, the woman awoke the next morning at 5 a.m. and roused Robinson. "He was like a man possessed," she said later. "He jumped out of bed yelling at me and barely stopped berating me as he showered and dressed." Still angry, J.R. said that he was going to check her out of the motel and that he had errands to run. He told her that he would meet her at a nearby restaurant, but he never turned up. Confused and very disappointed, she tried to call him. He refused to take her calls. She persisted. When she finally connected with J.R., he said that he was unable to trust her and that the relationship was over. For some reason, he had gotten cold feet. But it wasn't until Robinson was arrested for murder that the woman realized how close she had come to being killed that day. It is thought that J.R. brought his trailer as a means of removing her corpse from the motel and, by rising before he did, she thwarted his plans. The motel being busy with guests, he would have preferred a quick and silent kill while the woman slumbered.

In pursuit of his sexual preferences, J.R. had by this time left the personal ads behind him and enthusiastically embraced the Internet. That same year, the Robinsons left the mobile home park and went to live on the Kansas side of the state line, near Olathe. The upmarket mobile-home development they moved to was called Santa Barbara Estates, where again Nancy worked as property manager.

Their new address was an immaculate gray-and-white mobile home at 36 Monterey Lane, and they certainly didn't opt for inconspicuous anonymity. They erected a statue of St. Francis of Assisi in the yard in front of their home, hung wind chimes over their front door, and at Christmas, earned quite a reputation for their spectacular display of decorations.

As well as their home, which came as part of the perks of Nancy's job on the Santa Barbara Estates, J.R. and his wife somehow managed to lease farmland near the small town of La Cygne, south of Olathe. They had about 16 acres that also contained a fishing pond to which J.R. invited his few friends from time to time. The couple improved the place by putting a mobile home there and erecting a shed on the site.

And it was at 36 Monterey Lane, using five computers and the handle "Slavemaster"—while at once trying to set up a legit wheeling-and-dealing website business—he spent a lot of time browsing BDSM websites. Ultimately, it would be two of his Internet contacts who would be instrumental in bringing his world crashing around his ears, but in 1996 that crash was still years away.

Izabela Lewicka

In 1997, Robinson encountered a young Polish-born undergraduate on the Internet. Her name was Izabela Lewicka, and the perky girl was studying fine arts at Purdue University in West Lafayette, Indiana.

Izabela's parents became very concerned when, in the spring of 1997, she told them she was moving to Kansas, having been offered an internship. She wasn't forthcoming with the details, doing nothing to allay her parents' misgivings other than leave an e-mail and a contact address on Metcalf Avenue in Overland Park.

Her father, Andrew Lewicki [Lewicki's last name is spelled differently from the women in his family because the suffixes of Polish last names depend on gender] and his wife Danuta attempted to talk Izabela, who had just finished her freshman year, out of leaving home.

"She was past eighteen," explained Danuta. "She's protected by law. We could not stop her." So, in June, Izabela packed up her 1987 Pontiac Bonneville with books, clothes, and several of her paintings, then left Purdue for Kansas City. Her parents would never see her again.

In August, when it was time for school to start, and after receiving no reply to their letters, the Lewickis grew extremely anxious about their daughter, so they drove to Kansas to find out what was the matter. They arrived to find that the address on Metcalf Avenue was simply a mailbox; their daughter didn't live there. When they asked the manager of the place for Izabela's forwarding address, he refused to divulge the information. Despite their anxiety, Izabela's parents did not bother to contact the police but returned to Indiana. Shortly afterward, Andrew received an e-mail from his daughter: "What the hell do you want? I will not tolerate your harassment." The e-mail said to contact her in the future at another address: izabela@usa.net. When he later testified at Robinson's trial, Andrew said, "We exchanged e-mail messages every couple of weeks. In most cases, it was her response to my e-mail messages."

Izabela was, in fact, still alive at that time and living a life far removed from the one she had known in Indiana. And she had good reason to keep it a secret from her parents, for her new friend, J.R., had provided her with an apartment in south Kansas City, where they enjoyed a BDSM relationship. They even had a "slave contract," one that contained more than 100 clauses governing their conduct—she as the slave, he as the master.

In return for her submission, J.R maintained Izabela financially, paying all her bills. When she wasn't engaged in sexual activity with him, Izabela enjoyed the life of a lady of leisure. Her main interest was reading gothic and vampire novels bought from a specialty bookstore that she visited frequently in Overland Park. But she didn't abandon her studies completely, for in the autumn of 1998, using the name Lewicka-Robinson, she enrolled at Johnson County Community College. Her adoption of J.R.'s name lends weight to reports that concluded the young woman believed they were going to marry—though he was 58 and she was only 18.

Around Thanksgiving, 1997, Andrew e-mailed his daughter in Polish. "I write in Polish because I'm not 100 percent positive that your letters are coming from you," he said. "As you know anyone could create an e-mail account and sign it as you. If you would telephone, I would feel much, much better." Izabela purportedly replied, insisting that all further contact be in English.

"I have told you I'm happy," she wrote. "I'm well. I have a wonderful job and a wonderful man in my life who loves me. I want to be left alone. I don't know how I can make it any clearer."

At J.R.'s subsequent trial for Izabela's murder, a friend of the dead girl testified that Izabela had confided in her that she was going to do secretarial work for an international publishing agent named "John," who was also going to train her to be an S&M dominatrix. Jennifer Hayes also told the court that Izabela was going to begin her sex education as a slave.

In January 1999, J.R. moved Izabela into another apartment in Olathe. This was closer to his own home, which may account for his sometimes describing her as a graphic designer employed by his new internet company, Specialty Publications. On occasion, however, he is known to have referred to her as his adopted daughter, while at other times he described her as his niece.

Then, in August 1999, Izabela Lewicka disappeared and was never heard from again. Police believe that she was killed and disposed of around that time. However, her parents continued to receive e-mails purportedly from their daughter up until

Robinson's arrest. In the final months, John said that she was always traveling in some exotic land. One of her last e-mails in the spring of 2000 said that she had just returned from China.

Suzette Trouten

We all finally find what we want and need and I found mine.

—*Suzette Trouten*
last e-mail to her friend

The "Slavemaster" soon returned to the world of sadomasochistic chat rooms. He made contact with Suzette Trouten, a bored 27-year-old licensed nurse from Newport, Michigan, who lived a double life: nurse by day, submissive slave by night. A substantially built young woman with a mass of curly brown hair, Suzette, whose non-sexual interests were collecting teapots and doting on her two Pekingese dogs, pursued a highly active BDSM lifestyle, carrying on relationships with as many as four dominants at once.

Suzette had pierced not only her nipples and navel but also five places in and around her genitalia, all to accommodate rings and other devices used in BDSM rituals. A photograph of Suzette, with nails driven through her breasts, had been circulated on the internet, specifically at www.alt.com, and would have acted like a magnet to J.R. Quite understandably, a relationship soon developed. In fact, J.R. was so enamored of his new, submissive friend that he concocted a very attractive job offer to entice her to fly down from Michigan for an interview. He paid for her flight, and when she arrived in Kansas City there was a limousine waiting at the airport to meet her.

The job, J.R. told her, involved being a companion and nurse to his very rich, elderly father, who traveled a lot but needed constant care. He went on to say that his father did most of his traveling on a yacht and that her duties would involve her sailing with them between California and Hawaii. For this, she would be paid a salary of $60,000 and be provided with an apartment and a car. J.R neglected to mention that the only way to have contact with his father would be through the use of an Ouija board or a medium, as the old man had been dead for some ten years, and that any spare money he had left in his pocket while working as a machinist for Western Electric had been spent on booze. But as we have already established, J.R. was not a man to let such trivial details inhibit his grand design, so he gave Suzette to understand that the interview had gone well and the job was hers. She returned to Michigan and began putting her affairs in order before relocating to Kansas.

While she was getting ready to move, Suzette spoke to her mother, Carolyn, with whom she was very close, telling her all about her new job. In fact she also gave her mother J.R.'s telephone numbers—providing police with a lead to follow when she later disappeared in March. She also discussed the job offer with Lore Remington, an eastern Canadian friend. The two women had met in a chat room and shared an interest in BDSM. Later Suzette introduced Lore to J.R. on the Internet, and they too developed a long-distance, dominant-submissive cybersex relationship.

In February 2000, Suzette rented a truck, loaded it with her belongings, and headed off to her new life in Kansas City. She took with her clothes, books, her collection of teapots, and the two Pekingese, along with her array of BDSM accessories including whips, paddles, handcuffs, various lengths of chains, numerous items made from rubber, and just about anything else that a self-respecting, bona-fide BDSM enthusiast might care to invent.

Lenexa is a busy suburb of Kansas City, lying west of Overland Park and north of Olathe, and it was there that Robinson took Suzette when she arrived on Monday, February 14, 2000. He had reserved accommodation for her, specifically Room 216 at the Guesthouse Suites, an extended-stay hotel, and he had generously arranged for her dogs, Peka and Harry, to be boarded at the kennels of Ridgeview Animal Hospital in Olathe. "They will be allowed to go with you on the yacht," he explained, but the Guesthouse Suites didn't allow dogs. This was patently untrue, because Guesthouse Suites did, and still *does*, permit pets.

Almost immediately after Suzette had settled in, J.R. told her to get herself a passport, as they would be leaving in two weeks. He also produced a "master-slave" contract covering their BDSM activities, which she duly signed. Then, ominously, he got her to attach her signature to 30 sheets of blank paper and to address more than 40 envelopes to relatives and some of her friends. Just as he had done with other women, he told Suzette that he would take care of her correspondence while they were traveling, as she would be too busy to do so herself.

Suzette was the youngest of a family of five children, and according to her mother, Carolyn, "She was a kind of mama's girl." While she was in Kansas, she phoned her mother every day, keeping her informed of how things were going, and although Mom had at first worried that she would be homesick, she seemed to be in good spirits and was certainly happy with her employer, John Robinson. Evidently, he was happy with her too.

On March 1, Carolyn spoke to her daughter, who was looking forward to her impending yacht cruise with her wealthy boss and his father, and Suzette promised to phone Carolyn regularly. But she didn't, and after not having spoken with her daughter for some time, Carolyn made a few discreet inquiries, then called the police.

Detective David Brown began an immediate and thorough investigation of the man he saw as the prime suspect, John Robinson. He obtained J.R.'s criminal records, then contacted the Overland Park Police. The rap sheet acquainted him with the reports of other missing women, and soon he saw the potential connection. After he had spoken to two other detectives and Stephen Haymes, Robinson's probation officer in Missouri, it became clear that he could possibly be investigating a serial killer, and a somewhat clumsy one at that.

Detective Brown instructed the Trouten family and a few other acquaintances of J.R. to tape their telephone conversations with J.R. and to pass to the police copies of all e-mail from him.

For several weeks after March 1, Robinson spent time contacting Suzette's submissive friends and some of her relatives by e-mail, pretending to be her. Most weren't fooled by the subterfuge. He soon dropped the act and set his sights on Suzette's Canadian friend, Lore.

Lore and another Canadian woman began their own amateur investigation of the man they believed was named J.R. Turner, and Robinson moved quickly after Lore told him she was interested in finding a dominant master for a friend.

The e-mail and chat sessions turned to telephone calls, which were picked up by the police wiretaps now in place. The Lenexa Police Department contacted Lore and told her they were investigating Robinson. They did not explain the extent of the probe but asked her to continue the relationship.

"The police didn't tell me to get John Robinson to lure me to Kansas City," Lore said later at Robinson's trial. "I was willing to help."

Robinson made vague offers to Lore about meeting in her person. "He offered nothing other than I would be financially taken care of and never have to work," she said.

At the time that Suzette had been preparing to move to Kansas, the sexually insatiable J.R., using the name James Turner, had established two more BDSM friendships on the internet. The first woman, Vicki, was a psychologist from Texas who had placed an ad on a BDSM site. She had recently lost her job, and when J.R. became aware of this he promised to help her find work in the Kansas City area.

Vicki arrived in Lenexa on April 6 and, while staying at the Guesthouse Suites, spent five days getting to know J.R. During this time she signed a slave contract in which she consented to "give my body to him in any way he sees fit." They also discussed her working for Hydro-Gro before he told her to return home and prepare to move to Kansas City.

Vicki, who suffered from depression and a lack of meaningful companionship, was eager to change her life, and she fell for Robinson's lies hook, line, and sinker. She returned to Kansas City for another long weekend in late April, and it was then that she found that J.R. was eager to pursue more severe and violent forms of bondage sex than she wanted, but as she believed he was going to find work for her, she consented to his demands, allowing him to brutalize her far beyond the limits she had intended.

Vicki later testified that he took photographs of her bound and nude, and he hit her hard across the face. "I had never been slapped that hard by anybody before," she later told the court. She also stressed that the photographs were taken against her wishes and despite her protests.

Fortunately for Vicki, the promised move to Kansas never took place, and she demanded the return of her sex toys, worth more than $500. J.R. refused. Moreover, he threatened to publicly reveal the slave contract and the explicit, compromising photographs.

Vicki's response was to report the matter to the police, and she was astonished to learn that all her phone conversations with J.R. had been tape-recorded from the outset.

A woman named Jeanne, the second of the two women, turned out to be the last one to fall afoul of the "Slavemaster." She was an accountant, and after some weeks of preamble on the internet, agreed to become Robinson's sex slave. In mid-May, she journeyed to Kansas for a few days with J.R. and was installed in an apartment at the Guesthouse Suites, where by now Robinson was regarded as an excellent customer.

Later, Jeanne recalled that on Friday, May 19, she received a phone call from Robinson telling her that he would be coming around to see her. During the call he instructed her that when he arrived she was to be kneeling in the corner of the room completely naked with her hair tied back.

Submissive Jeanne was ready, as instructed, when J.R. arrived. Yet she wasn't prepared for what would actually happen. He walked into the room, grabbed her by her hair and flogged her brutally across her breasts and back. Like Vicki before her, Jeanne was discovering that J.R. was interested in a much rougher relationship than she had anticipated. She, too, didn't like being photographed during sex, but he insisted on doing so; he seemed excited by recording the marks his beatings made on her body. However, Jeanne's genuine distaste for that level of treatment must have spoiled his enjoyment, because he told her he didn't like her attitude and wanted to end their relationship. Her body burning and bruised from the flogging, Jeanne became hysterical to the extent that after J.R. had left she got dressed and made her way in tears to the reception desk. There she asked for the registration card and discovered that her host's name was not James Turner but John Robinson. Worried and distraught, she called the Lenexa police, who, on hearing that J.R. was involved, gave her complaint the utmost priority.

The detective who arrived at the hotel in response to Jeanne's call was David Brown, who had been investigating Robinson for more than two months since the disappearance of Suzette Trouten. Convinced that J.R. was a killer, Brown was not going to risk leaving another woman in the position of becoming a potential victim. When he heard Jeanne's tearful story, he got her to collect her belongings together and moved her to another hotel.

The next day, Jeanne gave a full statement to Detective Brown. She explained how she had met "James Turner" via the Internet and how she had been invited to Kansas to embark on a master-and-slave relationship. She told him that Robinson had beaten her with a violence far beyond her desires, explaining that she didn't go in for pain and punishment or marks on her skin. "I'm a submissive, not a masochist," she said.

The statements made by Vicki and Jeanne gave police the means to justify arresting the man who had been the subject of their investigation into the unexplained disappearances of several women.

For decades, J.R. had been setting traps for other people, baiting them, killing eight of his victims in the process, but the traps he set for his prey ultimately became his own. On Friday, June 2, 2000, it snapped shut when nine police cars drove to Santa Barbara Estates in Olathe, where officers surrounded 36 Monterey Avenue and pounded on his door.

Detectives arrested John E. Robinson and charged him with aggravated sexual battery and felony theft, although by the end of the following few days he would willingly have settled for such simple charges. Visibly shocked, J.R. was handcuffed and driven away to the red brick edifice that is the Johnson County Jail in Olathe, where he was detained on a $5 million bond. At the same time, police and detectives from a number of agencies, including the FBI, spilled from eight other vehicles and began to execute a search warrant on the Robinson home.

> Man is the only kind of varmint sets his own trap, baits it, then steps in it.
> —John Steinbeck

Inside, besides seizing all five of J.R.'s computers and fax machines, police found a blank sheet of paper that had been signed some 15 years earlier in January 1985 by Lisa Stasi. There were also receipts from the Rodeway Inn, Overland Park, which showed that J.R. had checked Lisa out on January 10 of that year, the day after she had last been seen alive by the inn's manager and her mother-in-law. However, those first scraps of evidence were only the tip of a gigantic iceberg of evidence; far more would come to light over the next few days, and it would horrify those who found it.

The police investigation had been thorough and involved all of the property owned or rented by Robinson. Consequently, a second search warrant had been obtained for that morning, and as J.R. was being driven to jail, detectives were busy searching his storage locker in Olathe. There, they unearthed a cornucopia of items connecting him to two of the missing women, Izabela Lewicka and Suzette Trouten. They found Trouten's birth certificate, her Social Security card, several sheets of blank notepaper signed, "Love ya, Suzette," and a slave contract signed by her. Beside Suzette's things, they located Izabela's driver's license, several photographs of her, nude and in bondage, a slave contract and several BDSM sex implements. They also found a stun gun and a pillowcase.

The following day, Saturday, June 3, another search warrant was served. This time the police descended on the small farm that Robinson owned near La Cygne. They found two 55-gallon metal barrels near a shed and opened one. Inside was the body of a naked woman, head down and immersed in the fluid that had been produced by decomposition of the corpse.

After prying the lid off the first barrel, crime scene investigator Harold Hughes turned his attention to the second barrel and opened the lid of that one. Inside he found a pillowcase, which he removed to reveal another body. Again, it was that of a woman, but this one was clothed. Like the first body, it was immersed in the fluid resulting from its own decomposition. Hughes completed the procedures of photographing and fingerprinting the barrels before resealing them and marking them "Unknown 1" and "Unknown 2."

Later that day, Stephen Haymes, Robinson's former probation officer, was told of the discovery of the bodies. After so many years of suspicion, his judgment of J.R. was vindicated. He later told writer David McClintick, "It confirmed what I had always believed, but the move from theory to reality was chilling."

At the time Haymes was learning of J.R.'s arrest, the District Attorney for Johnson County, Paul Morrison, was contacting his counterpart in Cass County, across the state line in Missouri, to negotiate the issuance of yet another search warrant. Detectives had discovered that Robinson maintained a locker at the Stor-Mor-For-Less depot in Raymore, a Missouri suburb of Kansas City. Morrison, an influential figure, was given total cooperation in cutting through the red tape inevitable in jurisdictional issues negotiated between two states. As a result of this discussion, he and a group of detectives from Johnson County arrived at the office of Cass County's Deputy Prosecutor Mark Tracy early the next morning. They carried with them the longest affidavit in support of a search warrant that Tracy had ever seen. It asserted that Robinson was believed to have killed several women and that it was suspected that evidence connected with the murders was

We started removing boxes from the front [of Locker E2]. After less than ten minutes there was a very foul odor that, with my past experience, I associated with a dead body.

—Douglas Borcherding
Overland Police
Department officer

hidden in the storage locker in Raymore. He had paid to rent his locker with a company check to conceal his identity.

At 8 a.m. on Monday morning, Tracy served the search warrant at the storage depot, and the Johnson County detectives were led to Robinson's locker—effectively a small garage with a brown lift-up shutter door. Inside was a lot of clutter, and the task force spent more than half an hour sifting through it before they saw, hidden at the back, three barrels. Wafting from the barrels came the nauseating, unmistakable stench of decomposing flesh.

As it was virtually certain that the barrels contained dead bodies, Tracy summoned his boss, Chris Koster, and the state of Missouri assumed immediate control of the crime scene. A new team of police investigators arrived, and the locker was emptied of all its contents except the three barrels. These were found to be standing on piles of cat litter, obviously a futile attempt by J.R. to reduce the smell that was emanating from them.

The first barrel, a black one with the words "rendered pork fat" on the label, was opened by senior criminalist Kevin Winer. The contents revealed a body wrapped in blue-gray duct tape and a light brown sheet. There were a pair of glasses and a shoe. When the crime scene technician had removed the sheet, he took hold of the shoe, only to find that the foot was still attached to a leg. On the assumption that the storage depot wasn't the best place to investigate the barrels and their contents, it was decided to reseal them and take them to the medical examiner's office in Kansas City. This was not as simple as it seemed. There was a very real fear that the bottoms of the barrels were corroded and might give way, so a police officer was sent to a nearby Wal-Mart to buy three children's plastic wading pools, and these were slipped underneath the barrels before they were loaded onto a truck.

Back at the medical examiner's office, the barrels were opened, and as expected, each contained the severely decomposed body of a female. Dr.. Thomas Young determined that the females had been beaten to death with an instrument, probably a hammer, and had been dead for some six years. Sheila Faith's also had a fracture on her right forearm that was consistent with a defensive injury.

The first body was fully clothed. The second was wearing only a T-shirt, and in its mouth was a denture, which was broken in two. Body three, that of a teenager, was wearing green trousers and a silver-gray beret. Identification was not immediately possible and was going to take some days.

I was represented by court-appointed attorneys who did *no investigation*, hired no experts, tested nothing, and admitted in open court a day prior to my trial they had not read the discovery.

—John E. Robinson
letter to the author dated
January 24, 2008.

Over in Kansas, in Topeka, the two bodies found on the Robinson farm were identified by a forensic odontologist as those of Izabela Lewicka and Suzette Trouten.

A few days later, with the help of another forensic odontologist, two of the bodies that had been found at the storage depot were identified. One was Beverly Bonner; the other was Sheila Faith. Debbie, who suffered from spina bifida and cerebral palsy, was identified as the third body by means of a spinal X-ray.

The case against Robinson was beginning to assume a structure, although there remained the problem of jurisdiction in relation to which state, Kansas or Missouri, would be responsible for each murder. Eventually, it was resolved that Robinson would be tried first in Kansas, and the date was set for January 14, 2002, before being postponed until September of the same year.

> I resent the fact that people are now claiming that Mr. Robinson, either directly or indirectly, is a serial killer. As each day has passed, the surreal events have built into a narrative that is almost beyond comprehension. While we do not discount the information that has, and continues to, come to light, we do not know the person whom we have read and heard about on TV. The John Robinson I know has always been a loving and caring father.
>
> —*Byron Cerrillo*
> *Public Defender for Robinson at his trial*

Suggesting that five decomposing bodies found in barrels could *never* indicate that his client was a serial killer, Byron Cerrillo seemed to have watched too many episodes of *The Practice*, a TV legal drama created by David E. Kelly based on the partners and associates at a Boston law firm. Nevertheless, with elements of kinky sex and infidelity, the trial was a sordid affair.

Carolyn Trouten was forced to come to terms with her daughter's bizarre sex life on the stand and, on October 14, 2002, jurors were subjected to a 40-minute videotape of Trouten and Robinson engaging in sadomasochistic sex. Early in the video, Trouten sat on the bed, looked into the camera and said to Robinson, "This is what you wanted me to tell you . . . I'm your slave . . . everything is yours." Robinson replied: "The most important thing in life is that you *are* my slave."

All in all, the jurors were confronted with solid evidence that could only point to J.R.'s guilt. In counterargument, the defense team could only say that there was no physical evidence, except a few fingerprints, to link Robinson with anything connected to the bodies.

Indeed, although J.R. grumbles and complains about the negligence of his trial attorneys, he was as guilty as sin. The court heard from Don Robinson, who testified about how Tiffany was delivered to him by his brother J.R., as well as from the notary public, the judge, and two lawyers, all of whom said their signatures on the adoption papers had been forged.

DNA tests showed that Robinson's saliva was on the seals of letters sent to Carolyn Trouten. A criminalist gave evidence that Izabela Lewicka's blood was found in Robinson's trailer in La Cygne and on a roll of duct tape of the same type used to bind some of the bodies.

Suzette Trouten's hair was also found in J.R's trailer, and maids at the motel where she had been staying testified that the amount of blood on the bed sheets in her room was much more than they had ever encountered when cleaning before.

Even Suzette's prized Pekingese became evidence when a veterinarian testified that Robinson had dropped the two dogs off for boarding. The animals were later abandoned in the mobile home park where J.R. lived. (Dog lovers will be delighted to learn that Peka and Harry were later adopted from the Humane Society.)

The pillowcase found in a barrel also formed a solid link between Izabela Lewicka and Robinson. Her mother had given her daughter some distinctive bed linen with a pattern identical in every single respect to the pillowcase that ended up in the barrel containing Izabela's body. A former lover of Robinson recalled that J.R. had given her similar sheets, but she didn't recall there being any pillowcases.

Nancy Robinson talked of her husband's philandering and how several times she wanted to divorce him but reconsidered because of the children. At the penalty phase of the trial, J.R's family asked the jury to spare his life, but when the jury had reached a decision about his punishment, the Robinson family was nowhere to be seen.

Nancy divorced her husband on February 25, 2005, and wants nothing more to do with him. In a letter to the author on January 10, 2008, J.R. writes:

> My family worked for two years to put together a team which included every possible requirement from database setup to forensic testing, most volunteers. Unfortunately, the actual cost budget put together was $2.5 million dollars, an impossible amount.

In reality, Robinson's family did zilch.

In January 2003, Judge John Anderson III sentenced Robinson to death twice and handed down a life sentence for the killing of Lisa Stasi.

With John Robinson sentenced to death row in Kansas, the state of Missouri was still prosecuting the three murders that had been committed within their jurisdiction. For his part, J.R. was more worried about being extradited to stand trial in Missouri, because that state was much more aggressive in using capital punishment than Kansas. In point of fact, Kansas had not executed anyone since the reinstatement of the death penalty in 1976.

Despite Robinson's argument that his attorneys were all but useless, they negotiated tirelessly with Chris Koster, the Missouri prosecutor, who stood firm against their offers and tried to get Robinson to lead investigators to the bodies of Lisa Stasi, Paula Godfrey, and Catherine Clampitt.

Because he either could not or would not reveal where he had dumped the bodies, Robinson demurred until Koster and his team became convinced the women's remains would never be found. Only then did Koster, with the permission of the victims' families, agree to accept guilty pleas in return for life sentences without parole. J.R. would never be executed in Missouri.

In mid-October 2003, J.R., looking much older than his 59 years, stood before a Missouri judge and, in a carefully scripted plea, acknowledged that the prosecutor had enough evidence to convict him of capital murder for the deaths of Godfrey, Clampitt, Bonner, and the Faiths. He demanded the unusual plea agreement because an admission of guilt in Missouri might have been used against him in Kansas—Kansas prosecutor Paul Morrison said he wasn't convinced the murders actually occurred in Koster's jurisdiction—and nothing he said in Cass County, Missouri, resembled anything like a confession of guilt.

> This was classic John Robinson. The guy was a gamesman to the end.
>
> —DA Paul Morrison to the *Kansas City Star*

Once again, J.R. gave no statement or even a hint of what prompted his homicidal acts. As the victims' next-of-kin shared their feelings of anger and pain before his sentencing to life in prison in Missouri—should he ever complete his other sentences—he ignored them and stared straight ahead, oblivious to the hurt he had caused. His mind unable to empathize with them, Robinson appeared bored with the entire process. In this, the final time he was ever likely to appear in public, it was clear that the depth of their emotions was something he had never experienced and cared not a bit about.

And, there is some good news, amazingly enough, after such a tragic account.

On July 6, 2000, authorities located Lisa Stasi's daughter, Tiffany, alive and living with Robinson's older brother, Don, in Hammond, Indiana. Unaware that the adoption was not legal, or that the girl's mother had been murdered by Robinson, whom the child knew as "Uncle John," Don and his wife raised the little girl in a loving and normal fashion. At the time of writing, Tiffany is 26. She has been made aware of the true identity and fate of her mother and has since met her biological father.

The deal this author offered J.R. was that he could write what he wanted to say in this chapter without edit. Indeed, my brief was that he could have his *own* book if he agreed. This was his chance, perhaps his one and only chance, to come clean, to atone for his dreadful crimes—and more importantly, to put the minds of his victims' loved ones to rest and to give them closure.

I also offered J.R. the opportunity to be interviewed by one of the UK's leading television producers of documentaries, on camera, to say what he needed to say, to clear the slate as he saw fit.

I have tried this approach more than 15 times over the years, and succeeded with 13 of America's most notorious serial murderers. I have cleared up a number of homicide cases and other serious related offenses as a result. My books *Talking with Serial Killers I* and *II* testify to this success, as did my TV documentary series, *The Serial Killers*, which is still being screened several decades after the series first appeared on TV.

My offer to J.R., however, included a proviso: that I would not change a word that he sent to me, *providing* that he told the truth and was up-front. He broke this agreement from the outset, so it now falls upon me to provide a summary of Mr. John E. Robinson; to provide a psychological profile, if you will, in the absence of any worthwhile input from J.R. Let's visit the dysfunctional mind of John Robinson.

J.R. has always imagined that he is more intelligent than anyone around him. It is an ego thing—a state of mind not uncommon among the more learned and intelligent of the serial murderer breed. But whereas a sane, intelligent person might learn from previous errors of judgment, alas, the true sociopath does not.

J.R. *is* a true sociopath. He understands the difference between right and wrong, yet he carried on committing antisocial offenses, regardless of the pain and suffering he caused. Sociopaths—once labeled psychopaths—just don't feel remorse for their actions. They simply don't care.

Like so many sado-sexual serial killers, John trolled for his victims. In a few instances he selected vulnerable women from places where women felt safe—in one case at least, a hostel for women in danger.

John conned them.

John abducted, used, and horrifically sexually abused them.

John bludgeoned these terrified women to death before disposing of them as so much garbage, most of them in barrels, to decompose and rot in their own bodily fluids.

That's how this lowlife disposed of his victims. Some of the deceased have never been found, while other intended victims escaped by the skin of their teeth. If the truth were known, if law enforcement had not been on their toes when J.R. first appeared on their radar as a potential homicidal maniac, many more women would have been murdered.

J.R. however, was also the first serial killer in criminal history to use the Internet, hanging out in S&M chat rooms like a deadly spider waiting to entrap his intended prey.

But where did all this start?

Unlike the majority of those who graduate into the serial taking of human life, John did not suffer from an abusive childhood. His folks were decent and hard-working, and followed the strong Catholic faith. There is no evidence whatsoever that he was inclined toward criminal activity during his teens. Then, one day in his twenties, he embarked on a series of frauds, becoming a plausible liar and a serial swindler who embezzled his employers and friends, even his own brother, out of considerable sums of money. He had suddenly metamorphosed into a real life Dr. Jekyll and Mr. Hyde, and it was all about money, lots of it too!

Simply put, John mutated. However, unlike a sudden change in a single gene, the whole genetic package of his makeup underwent a complete deviation into evil personified. The motive for his first murder was not sexual deviancy. J.R. needed cash, even if it meant deceiving his own brother, Don, over the adoption of baby Tiffany. Here was a quick way to earn

$5,000, and the disposal of the baby's mother, Lisa, was merely a side issue. But there can be no doubt that having this young, attractive mother begging him for mercy turned him on. I think that the very act of control over Lisa gave him sexual pleasure. This control freak was then psychologically pressed to commit the most violent sexual acts on any woman who fell into his clutches. And, as most psychiatrists and psychologists might agree, once the pleasure/reward switch for certain actions has been flicked on in the human brain, it is almost impossible to switch off. This state of mind is called "addiction." Mesh sexual addiction into a sociopathic mind, and disaster is as sure to follow as night does day.

Whatever the case, to satisfy his perverted cravings, J.R. soon graduated into trolling for sex by exploiting women who were lonely and dissatisfied with the dreariness of their day-to-day existence. He could smell them a mile off and was able to hone in on them with unerring accuracy.

> Your unwarranted accusation of attempted manipulation and flimflam pretty much says it all.
>
> —*John Robinson in a letter to the author, March 4, 2008*

Here was John Robinson, "Mr. Flimflam Man," who portrayed himself as a respectable businessman. A high achiever, the well-dressed, immaculately turned out "Man of the Year," who used blatantly false credentials that had fooled even the distinguished former physician to President Harry S. Truman. What chance did vulnerable women have when confronted with the philanthropic generosity and charms of a man like John E. Robinson, a pillar of the community? The answer is, *none*!

So, where do we go from here, bearing in mind that John is now locked up and will remain so until he dies?

One might have thought that this man could one day tell us the truth of what happened—the *total* truth, without flimflam—and how he became one of the most heinous serial killers in recent history. God only knows how J.R. must feel about having deceived his loving wife of so many years. Regarding his doting children, is there any sorrow and regret? No!

Does this man feel any remorse for his homicidal activities? I think not, and it is at this point that we return to his correspondence with the author.

"Certified" radiographer; CEO of various companies and one of America's pioneers in hydroponics; Man of the Year; wannabe St. Jude; philanthropist to the mentally disabled and young, homeless, disenfranchised women, John is certainly qualified to run a successful business—at least, this is what he would wish us to believe.

Of *course* J.R. *is* innocent of the crimes of which he has been found guilty by a jury—at least this is what he wishes us to now believe. Of *course*, he is even innocent of the murders he has more recently pled guilty to.

His family supports him in proving his innocence—at least this is what John claims in his letters. And, let us not forget that he demands $400,000 to help him prove his innocence, and to further prove that he was inadequately represented at his trial, and that the prosecutor is a crook.

Indeed, so plausible is John Robinson, it should be obvious to anyone reading this chapter that the man *is* a fucking saint; he should be released from prison immediately and showered with apologies for having been detained for so long. The American justice system should, without further hesitation, offer him substantial compensation for his troubles—well, that's the least society could do for such a decent, homespun guy!

"Don't blow smoke!" J.R. demands in one of his letters to this author. "I don't have time for meaningless delays. I don't have the time or the funds to play games," he says, while at once stating that it will take at least a year before he could even discuss his childhood, and that is after his attorney—no name or address given in his letters—receives funds to the not insubstantial tune of almost half-million bucks.[23]

While demanding that the author and a TV production company dig deep to follow his every whim, he goes on to say—and bear in mind, he has *already* pled guilty to each murder:

> Next we will proceed to the expert phase. First to examine and evaluate documents, photos and testing. Then to complete the necessary testing that has never been done. Each step of the way, we will evaluate and adjust our investigation or approach as required. The proposed budget is fairly simple at this point but may have to be adjusted depending on need:
>
> Database: $100,000
> Investigator: $150,000
> Travel: $20,000
> Experts: $60,000

23 This author has not had so much as a sniff from any attorney allegedly representing John Robinson. What this author has had are a number of letters and e-mails from a bunch of brain-dead morons who think that J.R. is the Second Coming.

Attorney: $50,000
Communication, copies, supplies: $10,000
Equipment: $8,000
Misc.: $2,000

Total: $400,000.

My attorney would control all information and distribution of funds. Nothing will begin until there is a firm written agreement in place!

My first letter was clear about the possibilities available to you. Yet you responded with a request for information about my formative years, assuming it would be no threat to my present or future legal status. Unfortunately, that is not the case. When I win a new trial, it will be necessary to prepare a "mitigation case" containing the very information you now seek. My attorneys did not investigate or provide any mitigation evidence at my first trial.

And hurrying on, he adds:

I did offer you a smidgen of palpable researchable material right there in England. In November of 1957 I was a 13-year-old Boy Scout who traveled to London to appear in the Command Performance for the Queen. No one has as of yet recovered the newspaper articles of that trip. As you see, everything is tied together.

Sadly for J.R. this "smidgen of palpable research material" which he offered as an "exclusive" for the author has already been plastered all over the Internet, and the newspaper articles are freely available on the worldwide web, too.

John goes on to say: "I offered you the opportunity to do a real life true crime book and documentary. One that would expose blatant police and prosecutorial misconduct, fairly present the real evidence including complete details of the lives of the victims, and perhaps unveil the real killer. You could, of course, simply go for titillating, sensationalized products based on the fiction already out there. That decision, of course, is yours."

The titillating and sensationalized products John refers to *are the official trial records*.

John E. Robinson is very much like John Wayne Gacy—another businessman/sado-sexual serial killer who also had all the apparent trappings of integrity. Both men used their human hunting skills to find and entrap their prey. However, whereas bisexual Gacy tortured and murdered young men, in many instances male prostitutes, J.R. actively searched for victims in the S&M Internet chat rooms.

I would use the analogy of J.R. being very similar to an insect that fools others into approaching it by using a flashing code. This predator and human parasite, Robinson, sent out attractive signals, like promises of money and sexual satisfaction, that were intended to lure the vulnerable toward him. The intended prey approaches the flashing predator and is summarily eaten. So it was with the prey of John Edward Robinson.

John is a determined man if anything, and he says that for the past five years he has been "tireless [in his] attempts to locate individuals, companies, or organizations willing to assist in the completion of the necessary investigation, testing, etc., required to fully disclose the real story." Blah, blah, blah.

J.R. adds:

> Determined to either prove my innocence or die trying, I began writing letters to anyone and everyone I could think

> of for both the UK portion of my case as well as those who might possibly help on this side of the pond. I wrote to Alana Hayling—head of producing documentaries at the BBC in March 2007—and received not even a courtesy reply. I recently wrote to Mr. Felix Dennis, owner of *Maxim* magazine who lives in Stratford-Upon-Avon and have no word yet.
>
> My basic offer has been very simple. If they would provide funding for the investigation and testing, along with some equipment necessary, I would give them access to the results, no matter the outcome as long as everyone agreed that nothing would be made public until my attorney authorized release.

No doubt that the BBC and *Maxim* were bowled over by the generosity and business opportunity offered them by J.R., and the reason they haven't replied? Because they haven't, as yet, recovered their composure, perhaps. Nevertheless, moving up a gear, J.R. gets into full swing:

> The cost of putting all discovery information onto a searchable interactive database, investigating, testing, travel, and equipment will be about $400K and will require at least twelve months to complete. The investigator will need some specialized equipment—video and digital recorders capable of two concurrent recordings. All funds would be disbursed by an attorney. I would receive nothing but an allocation to cover supplies and postage.

Now completely carried away, J.R. almost bursts into song:

> We are starting from scratch with a thorough methodical investigation of everything. Every document, every photo, every video, every witness, testing every item and utilizing

acknowledged experts to evaluate to calculate every person or object.

Ah, yes, John, that sounds fine, but what about the five decomposing bodies found in barrels on your property and in your unit at the storage depot . . . ?

To facilitate this investigation, we have obtained every page of material connected to my case, some 300,000 more or less. Here is how we anticipate proceedings:

A) A database will be designed with unlimited search capabilities. All documents will be scanned, cross-referenced with new documents added as developed.

B) A full-time investigator will be hired under the supervision of my attorney. He/she will complete the legwork required to secure records and documents previously ignored, and conduct video interviews with all witnesses.

John, please stop right there . . .

You, your publisher and your media firm could end up getting two for one. I will tell you that my attorney has been contacted by other publishers and media companies as the result of the letters from me . . .

J.R. . . . please hold on here . . .

. . . and she has passed along that information and [is] presently checking out the veracity of those individuals and firms . . .

John, what about the fact that at least eight of the women you met ended up beaten to death . . . ?

. . . Don't blow smoke.

. . . John, please . . .

. . . I may be able to up the ante for you. For several years I have been in contact with a person who befriended Dennis Rader, the confessed B.T.K. serial killer of ten. This person visited him in jail and corresponded with him regularly. This individual claims to have details and information never before revealed and has been working on a book. This person has the information, wants to do a book but has no industry name. The two of you should be able to do a great "insider" True-Crime book and a documentary about B.T.K. You and your publisher could end up getting two for the price of one. I will await word from you . . .

. . . for God's sake J.R., shut the *fuck up*!

. . . I was embezzled out of over two hundred thousand pounds over a three-year period. To that end I have received preliminary word that a nonprofit organization—Reprieve—operated by an attorney Clive Stafford-Smith OBE has agreed to help. My attorney has replied to a letter I received from them, by e-mail, and [like the BBC and *Maxim*] we are still awaiting a reply . . . Finally I must tell you that I am working with a group of college students to publish a book of my poetry and short stories. An attempt to raise the money for the required investigation. No credit would be given—no author named. The book will, if published, simply be written by "A Condemned on Kansas Death Row." I will receive nothing. Arrangements are still in the embryonic stage . . . .if you, your publisher . . . are interested . . . you need to put your heads together and let me know . . . It will take me a little time to make arrangements with the attorney . . .

. . . John . . . the five bodies in barrels . . . ?

> For the record, I will explain exactly how the Kansas Department of Corrections mail system works. When a letter is received, it is automatically date-stamped on the outside of the envelope. Then the letter is opened by the censors, date- and time-stamped, read, and all the letters to the inmates in segregation copied . . .
>
> . . . John please account for the five bodies . . .
>
> . . . Outgoing letters go to the mailroom unsealed. Letters to companies and individuals not relayed (family) are copied, the letter is sealed, and the notice stamp placed on the outside of the envelope . . .

And so he goes on, and on, and on for ten pages of mind-numbingly excruciating drivel.

If John Robinson wasn't such a deadly serious man, one could read his letters and have a rib-tickling good laugh. It *is* the funniest stuff I have read for years—I mean carpet-rolling, hyperventilating, rib-aching bouts of laughter, full of zip, pizzazz. Packed full of his usual *joie de vivre,* his unadorned prose, and the gamut of all those other great American qualities we have come to expect from such a sassy serial killer as J.R.

***

But has J.R. actually learned a single thing from his past mistakes? Laci [name changed to protect her true identity], wrote to John Robinson in August 2008. This is his unedited reply, and the grammatical errors are his:

> Laci, I received your letter. First of all let me explain that I have some simple rules for anyone that I write.
>
> You must realize that all kinds of people write. It usually happens when some story is run on TV. All claim to want

to "be my friend" when actually all they want is to receive a letter from a death row inmate. My attorney even located a blog that tells people how to write me to receive a response. If that was your goal, here you are . . .

I laughed when you said you were into true crime, if you have read either of the books written about me, you just read a media created fairytale. 85% of the material is false, but people like to read crap so that's what they write. The DA who prosecuted me had his wife, who owns a media company; create quite an evil persona of me.

Okay the rules—first, if you really want to communicate with me you *must* send me a photocopy of your driver's license and a photo ID that shows who you are, your birth date, address. Second, don't ask me about my case. I have maintained my innocence from the beginning. My case is on appeal and I don't need to discuss it. Third, if I detect any phony b.s I won't [sic] respond again. Fourth, you must guarantee me that anything we write will remain completely confidential!

If you write to me here is a way to do it. On the front of each page write a very normal letter. If you want to write other information about your experiences fantasies, etc, write them on the back of the page like a separate letter.

Your list of lifestyle interests looks like you copied it from the alt.com website questionnaire [the website where he found Suzette Trouten].

If you are seeking, tell me but understand I am very demanding! I am enclosing information that tells you what can and cannot be sent in . . . actually it's a list of don'ts. Look good at the information about photo's "sexually obscene material or nudity" Yes I want you to send pictures but they have to get past the censors so use your head. I'm also enclosing you information about how you can help out financially. I live in solitary confinement, I don't work (they won't allow it) and I have very limited funds. If you want to help out with postage and supplies you need to follow the directions.

You say you have two degrees, in what, from where and when?

How involved do you want to get? Are you interested in helping if I need typing complete, computer searches, light investigation? Tell me about your computer literacy, etc. I will give you the opportunity to tell me all about yourself and I want you to be very frank about what you're looking for! I need someone who will be committed to helping me. If I'm ever going to prove my innocence I need a person on the outside I can really trust.

So, there you have it. The beginning, where we go from here is up to you! You know all about me, I need to learn everything about you . . . I mean everything!!!

What kind of animals do you have? How long a sub in the lifestyle? Are you willing to take this to whatever level?

There may come a time when I need to ask a favor, are you willing to help?

Ok, you got my last stamp.

Thanks for the letter and the picture. I hope it's just the first . . . Oh, last rule—if I were going to do that you have to commit to write at least once a week! J.R.

P.S. If you have experience in setting up websites or blogs, let me know!!!

Clearly J.R. Robinson hasn't learned a thing.

***

Other Ulysses Press Books

Cannibal Serial Killers: Profiles of Depraved Flesh-Eating Murderers

Christopher Berry-Dee with Victoria Redstall, $14.95

Delving deep into the twisted actions of Hannibal Lecter–type murderers, *Cannibal Serial Killers* profiles the depraved individuals who prolong their horrific crimes beyond the thrill of the chase to a perverse ritualized finale.

Online Killers: Portraits of Murderers, Cannibals and Sex Predators Who Stalked the Web for Their Victims

Christopher Berry-Dee and Steven Morris, $14.95

It starts as a harmless online date but can quickly turn to kidnap, torture, and death. More than just tales of sinister criminals, this collection of true horror store chronicles the stories of men, women, and children whose Internet adventures led them into disastrous circumstances.

Serial Killers: Up Close and Personal: Inside the World of Torturers, Psychopaths, and Mass Murderers

Christopher Berry-Dee, $15.95

The headline-grabbing crime. The grizzly facts in the coroner's report. The shocking revelations from the trial. Going deep into the bowels of the world's toughest prisons to face these monsters and hear their stories, this book provides all these details plus one more: the murderer's first-person perspective.

How to Make a Serial Killer: The Twisted Development of Innocent Children into the World's Most Sadistic Murderers

Christopher Berry-Dee and Steven Morris, $13.95

They were born into this world as innocent children. They ended up as merciless killing machines. This book leads the reader on an insightful, scary, and often disturbing investigation into what made these infamous murderers go bad.

Serial Killers and Mass Murderers: Profiles of the World's Most Barbaric Criminals

Nigel Cawthorne, $14.95

In one chilling chapter after another, this book profiles a terrifying succession of homicidal maniacs. It takes readers inside the minds of the people who committed the world's most notorious and horrendous crimes.

Serial Killer Timelines: Illustrated Day-by-Day Accounts of the World's Most Gruesome Murders

Dr. Chris McNab, $16.95

By examining the depraved, deceptive, very deliberate actions of famed serial killers as a series of specific events, this fully illustrated book offers a unique perspective on the working of the criminal mind and breaks down step by step how they did it, how they got away with it for so long, and how they finally got caught.

ABOUT THE AUTHOR

Christopher Berry-Dee is an investigative criminologist who has published several papers and books, including *Online Killers*, *Serial Killers: Up Close and Personal*, and *How to Make a Serial Killer*. He is the director of The Criminology Research Institute and owner of *The New Criminologist*, the world's most respected professional journal on all matters criminology. He consults with law enforcement worldwide, lectures on serial murder, and is responsible for solving a number of U.S. murder cases. Chris has homes in the UK and Samara, Russia.